WARTS and ALL

Ken Chant

A Memoir

Edited by
Alison Chant and
Sharon Chant Jones

Copyright © 2025 KEN CHANT

ISBN 978-1-7641318-0-3

Published by

Ken Chant Ministries

website kenchantministries.au

email kenchantministries@outlook.com

All rights in this book are reserved worldwide. No part of this book may be reproduced in any manner whatsoever without written permission of the Editor except for brief quotations embodied in critical articles or reviews.

Books by Ken Chant

ANGELOLOGY
A study of the splendours of the heavenly realm.

ATTRIBUTES OF SPLENDOUR
Reflections on the nature, being, and glory of God.

AUTHORITY AND AUTHENTICITY OF THE BIBLE
An exploration on the authenticity and authority of Scripture.

BETTER THAN REVIVAL
A pragmatic look at Christian ministry and the idea of Revival.

BUILDING THE CHURCH GOD WANTS
Not goal setting or programmes, nor statistics, but faithfulness in ministry.

CHRISTIAN LIFE
A positive and creative approach to Christian life.

CHRISTIAN REVIVAL CRUSADE
A short history of the CRC movement from its beginnings (previously entitled, *Born in Oz*.)

CLOTHED WITH POWER
A Pentecostal theology of Holy Spirit baptism.

CROSS AND THE CROWN
The passion and resurrection of Christ taken from the viewpoint of Jesus's earthly journey.

DEMONOLOGY
Understanding and overcoming our dark enemy.

DISCOVERY
Learning and living the will of God.

DYNAMIC CHRISTIAN FOUNDATIONS
Eight foundational Christian truths explored.

EMMANUEL ONE
A focus on Jesus as the Son of Man.

EMMANUEL TWO
A focus on Jesus as part of the Trinity.

EQUIPPED TO SERVE
Understanding, receiving, and using the charismata to serve others.

FAITH DYNAMICS
The limitless power of faith in God.

GREAT WORDS OF THE GOSPEL
Explores major themes in the Bible including salvation, holiness, and predestination.

HEALING IN THE NEW TESTAMENT
The healing covenant as presented by Scripture but from a current perspective.

HEALING IN THE OLD TESTAMENT
The healing covenant as presented by Scripture in the Old Testament.

HIGHLY EXALTED
The ascension and heavenly ministry of Christ.

MOUNTAIN MOVERS
The secrets of mountain moving prayer.

PENTECOSTAL PULPIT
The art of preaching in the power of the Holy Spirit.

ROYAL PRIESTHOOD
The High Priesthood of Jesus and the priesthood of all believers.

SITTING ON TOP OF THE WORLD
Guidelines for successful living (Ken's first book).

SONGS TO LIVE BY
Studies taken from Psalms and Christian worship.

STRONG REASONS
The Bible, science, and the proofs of God.

THIS WE BELIEVE
Outlines the beliefs of the Christian Revival Crusade, including some now outdated views.

THRONE RIGHTS
Our position and spiritual authority in Christ.

TREASURES FROM PAUL – A Series
These books are not a systematic theology of each book but a selection of treasured ideas from Paul.
Book 1 – Ephesians
Book 2 – Philippians
Book 3 – Colossians
Book 4 – Corinthians I
Book 5 – Corinthians II
Book 6 – Galatians
Book 7 – Thessalonians

UNDERSTANDING YOUR BIBLE
Studies in biblical hermeneutics.

WHEN THE TRUMPET SOUNDS
Studies in the return of Christ.

WARTS AND ALL
A personal memoir drawn from the life of Ken Chant.*

WORLD'S GREATEST STORY
Covers the dramatic first millennium of church history.

*__Editor's Note:__ Several of the stories in this memoir have been slightly modified to protect the families who may still be living. There are also a few additions by the Editors which provide clarification, or an added scene to the events of his life that Ken could no longer recall in detail. These were contributed at Ken's discretion. Almost every word in this book was dictated over the course of 6 months whilst Ken was confined to his armchair. The authenticity of the work can be seen in the distinctive writing style of Ken himself.

2024 TRUTH

Before Charles the First was executed with the connivance of Oliver Cromwell in 1649, the king called upon the renowned British artist, Sir Peter Lely, to paint his likeness. Lely created a superb picture which showed the king in splendid majesty. Later, after the monarch's death and Cromwell had become the Lord Protector of the United Kingdom, Lely was introduced to Cromwell who commissioned the artist to paint him. But Cromwell added, "I would desire you use all your skill to paint your picture truly like me … but remark all these roughness, pimples, warts, and everything as you see me." From that directive has emerged a popular saying - *warts and all*. The phrase has in it the sense of 'the truth, the whole truth, and nothing but the truth.'

This small book you are holding makes no pretence of being a total biography of my 91 years of life and ministry. It is a series of anecdotes in which I have tried to recount some of my many adventures and failures. Mostly the stories are positive, and I hope you will find many of them humorous, but since I did not want to leave anyone with the impression that I had been faultless, or some kind of improbable saint, I have also included a number of anecdotes that show me in a less than flattering character.

The book is sequential, beginning with the year 1937, that is four years after my birth in 1933. But the sequence includes only those years where something significant has happened, including the humorous, the life changing, and the catastrophic. So, it comes to you with a prayer that this biographically based book will be a lively source of instruction, amusement and inspiration.

Since I am now too old to see a computer screen clearly, my sincere thanks goes to my wife Alison, and my daughter Sharon, who were my amanuenses, an invaluable resource in producing this documentary evidence of my life.

In the grace of Christ,

K. D. Chant

July 1st 2024

1907 PARENTS

My father was born in 1907 and died in 2002 aged 94 (an age I hope to reach). He met my mother in 1932, and they were married six months before I was born. In other words, they were very naughty, and I was already three months along before they were married. I only discovered this fact after my father's death when I examined his wedding certificate. It came as a shock, and then indignation that I had lived 69 years in ignorance of this fact, and then amusement that God had used 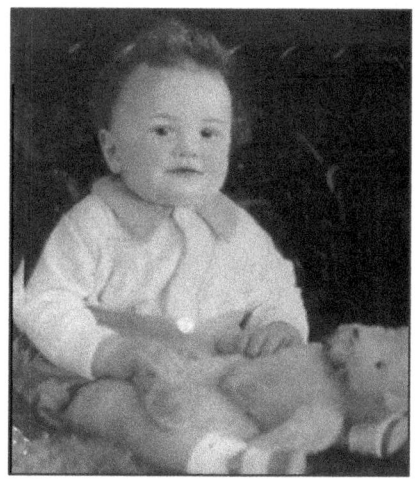 my life for his glory despite what would have been considered in the 30's a nefarious beginning. For several weeks my father's ashes sat on the shelf in my office, and I had great satisfaction berating him for his many weaknesses. He was an argumentative man, and we enjoyed many ferocious debates throughout his life. Now, unable to verbally respond, I could yet hear his authoritative voice. I still won each round.

For reasons I never could discover my parents' marriage brought my father's university education to an end, although the reasons were probably fiscal. As a consequence, my mother's several sisters all disliked my father, and their marriage was not a particularly happy one. This was probably because my father partly blamed my mother for the cessation of his degree level studies. However, they seldom quarrelled when I or my siblings could hear them. But we did observe their discontent often enough to know that they were not deeply in love with each other. Nonetheless, I mostly have happy memories of my childhood.

My father and his eleven siblings were all born into a farming family at a property called *German Creek* some twenty miles out from Mt Gambier (a country town some 500kms southeast of Adelaide, the capital city of South Australia). The land was dark, rich volcanic soil, and while at one point it extended to several thousand acres, when my grandfather died it was split between 12 children so none of them received more than a few hundred acres. Among them was my father, except that he contracted poliomyelitis when he was still an infant, which left him partly crippled in one leg and rendered him unfit for work on the farm. Accordingly, out of all his siblings he was the only one who was sent to Adelaide to get a university degree. That was when he met my mother, which was disastrous for his degree, but a miracle for me. And although he did not complete his degree, he was still able to work as a teacher and eventually worked his way up to headmaster. So, I hope you can see where I'm heading here. So many things had to come together for me to be born in Adelaide. Indeed, without that concatenation of events, I wouldn't have been born at all.

Unless God chose someone else to accomplish his will, several churches I have founded would not exist; the hundreds of souls who have committed their lives to Christ would not have heard the salvation message from my ministry; many miracles of healing would not have occurred when I laid hands on believers in Jesus' name; and perhaps most significantly the books I have written would not have been published. In turn, those books led to the creation of Vision Colleges which is currently a worldwide ministry with hundreds of students.

Surely, in all these things, from my father developing polio and choosing to go to university, the guiding hand of God can be clearly seen. At least, I have no doubt even if God had to overlook my parents' yielding to passion, he has constantly kept his hand upon me all the ninety-one years of my life.

In him we were also chosen, having been predestined according to the plan of him who works out everything in conformity with the purpose of his will. (Ephesians 1:11)

1937 SCREAMS

The air was torn apart with a terrible scream. The voice was mine. I was sitting naked in a tin bath in my mother's kitchen. It was winter and my mother and a few of her friends, were gathered around the kitchen table gossiping and sharing a morning tea. The room was a favoured spot for family activities during the cold winter months. The room was kept cosily warm by the wood and coke (coal) burning stove. My mother had placed me in the bath just in front of the stove not realising there was a kettle on the hotplate with its nozzle pointing outwards. It boiled and the scalding water cascaded all over my back. My cries of agony instantly halted the session, and my mother leaped to my assistance.

What did my mother do? I can't remember, but I presume she plucked me out of the bath, rushed me over to the nearby sink, doused me with cold water (while I suppose I kept shrieking) and then covered my back with the Calamine Lotion that was commonly used in those days for burns, scratches, rashes and bites. It was sufficient to alleviate long term scarring.

It is my earliest memory. I was four years old. My sister Coralie would have been three and my brother Barry not yet born.

Did this traumatic happening affect me in any way? I don't know. However, it may have had something to do with the impediment I developed in my speech which greatly troubled me in my younger years. I would begin to say a word and my tongue would freeze leaving me gaping like a codfish out of water, unable to complete the sentence. What embarrassing moments I endured on those occasions. At school, I was terrified the teacher would ask me a question and I would freeze in the attempt to answer. At home too, especially when people who were not part of my immediate family were present. Such times of shame continued throughout my childhood and into my adolescence. It may have been that this childhood trauma had a significant effect on my language development, however, two of my grandsons also have a speech impediment. So, it may have happened anyway.

I tried various expedients as I was growing up to overcome this issue, especially during my adolescent years. Among the helpers I turned to were singing coaches (because most people who stutter can sing without hesitation), elocution teachers, speech therapists, and the like. They all helped. But the impediment largely remained unimpeded. I will come back to this when I tell the exciting story of my call to ministry.

One good thing resulted from the peculiarities of my impediment, I became, as my wife Alison describes it, a walking dictionary of synonyms and antonyms, which enabled me to very quickly replace the word I couldn't say with another which I could then speak without hesitation. Hence, by the time I was into my mid-adolescence very few people recognized that I even had a speech impediment. Nonetheless it was still there. I could always feel it hovering somewhere in the back of my mind ready to swoop like a vulture and take over my tongue. I never could tell when, or even if this would happen on any given occasion. I eventually spoke regularly on a nation-wide radio broadcast and every time I approached the microphone with much trepidation, hoping I would conclude the broadcast without embarrassment. These were scary moments but on the whole by the stratagem of replacing the word I could not speak with one that flowed easily, I managed to avoid disaster.

Matters were even worse on the many occasions when I had to appear on live television. How hard that was! But by the grace of God and by using my already tried and true methods very few, if any viewers, would have realised that speech problems troubled me. A shrewder person might have chosen the expedient way of not exposing himself to public ridicule by appearing live on radio and television. But that would, I think, have been a poor-spirited choice when the opportunity was there.

Is there something to learn from these events?

Several things come to mind -

- With God's help the human spirit can overcome any problem or difficulty.
- Have the courage of your convictions and pursue your goals whatever the barriers may be.
- There is no problem for which the wisdom of God is inadequate. Find out what the Lord is saying and do it.

Lastly, back to me screaming in the bathtub. Good things and bad things happen to the good and the evil alike. We could blame God for allowing an innocent and helpless four-year-old to be so terribly burnt, but my mother should have been more vigilant and in this case learned a valuable lesson.

Our part in every situation is to trust his providence, echoing the words of Scripture -

Trust in the Lord with all your heart and do not lean on your own understanding. In all your ways acknowledge him and he will make straight your paths. Proverbs 3:5-6

He causes the rain to fall on both the just and on the unjust. Matthew 5:45

Shall not the Lord of all the earth do what is right. Genesis 18:25b

1938 NEMESIS

It hung there like some sort of hellish nemesis, menacing with the promise of a barrage of shrieks and of loud cries of pain. What was it? It was the thick leather razor strap that my father had placed on a hook screwed into our bathroom windowsill. Dad used it for two purposes. One was to hone the sharpness of his cut-throat razor, and the other was to discipline his errant children.

How long did it hang there? I don't know. Presumably Dad stopped using it when he discarded the cut-throat and began using the safety razor instead. How many times did he use it on me? Perhaps only once or twice a year, perhaps more often. His practice was to send the errant child into the bathroom for half an hour or more to gaze with horror upon the implement of torture before he would finally arrive and administer a dozen or so blows with the strap on that child's leg. The snap and crack of the strap was accompanied by the loudest frantic shrieks I could summon. I reckoned if I could howl loudly and piteously enough it would calm my father's wrath and persuade him to stop flailing that strap.

When I was a child, I used to be furious with him because of what seemed to me to be wanton cruelty. Later I came to realise three things:

First - He acted on what he thought the Bible taught, summed up in the English proverb, *spare the rod and spoil the child.*

Second - He only used such corporal punishment when the offence was serious enough to arouse him to burning anger.

Third - He did not make us sit trembling in the bathroom out of a malevolent desire to make our suffering more intense but rather because he wanted to allow enough time for his anger to dissipate. In other words, he was motivated by love rather than by any kind of harsh vindictiveness.

This raises an interesting question. Does the Bible truly demand that we use a cane or a whip to discipline a child? Within the context of the Old Testament, the culture and customs of the time demanded the use of corporal punishment. But already when we turn to the New Testament, we find no mention of rods or whips but instead Paul's kinder instruction to father's not to provoke their children to anger (Ephesians 6:4). I choose to see in that at least a suggestion that some other way than inflicting pain should be found to punish a naughty child. I endorse the modern rejection of applying the Old Testament Hebrew injunctions.

Some may point to the austere laws of the Romans which permitted a father to kill their child if they displeased him, but the limitless barbarity of the ancient Romans surely should not be cited as an example as to how Christians should behave. Personally, I find the sight of an adult striking a helpless child repulsive. So, I warmly endorse the shift in society to ban the use of a cane or a strap at home, in schools, and other institutions. Our laws allow a little more flexibility for parents with defiant toddlers but generally there are many ways to discipline children rather than resort to physical violence; whilst also remembering it is imperative that we teach them right from wrong.

Fathers do not exasperate your children; instead, bring them up in the training and instruction of the Lord. Ephesians 5:4

1943 CHILDHOOD

My mother died when I was 15 and she was 40. She expressed excellent love toward us children, and I remember walking to Sunday School where sometimes mother played piano. She took us on many excursions - by train to the Botanical Gardens in Adelaide, or to Semaphore and Henley Beach; and by tram to Morialta Conservation Park with its hiking trails and waterfalls. To board the train, we had to walk to Woodville Station and from there we travelled to either the City of Adelaide, with its museums and botanical gardens, or to one of the beautiful Adelaide beaches. The tram ride was a shorter journey, just around the corner from our house, and onto the main Woodville Road where there was a convenient tram stop.

We carried a beach rug, towels, and a basket of cheese and tomato, or vegemite sandwiches; grapes, mandarins, apricots, whatever was in season; and sweet cordial flavoured water. When we arrived at our destination mother would turn us loose and not give us a thought until we turned up hungry and thirsty. She read a book or knitted or dozed. Our Dad, a schoolteacher, was working during the holidays at a munitions factory, making shells for the war effort, so he could not join us on these trips.

Mum cooked homemade biscuits and cakes. She was an average cook, but we didn't care. We had different dishes each night of the week. On Friday nights there were pancakes with butter and sugar, or occasionally cream; though as this was too expensive to buy, we used cream from the top of the milk. The milk was delivered by the milkman, ladled into our empty milk can which sat on the front step every morning. We usually ordered four pints of milk each day.

Breakfast was always hot milk on Weet Bix with sugar, and we were never short of this staple as it was fairly cheap; and then we had porridge in winter. Dad had cornflakes, but this was too expensive for us kids. Dad was only earning three quid (pound) a week as a schoolteacher, and that was a low wage even then. Everyone had to help with the war effort, and we had ration books so that the food available was divided equally between families. Much of the produce from the farms went to Britain by boat as the British needed the food (their farmers were fighting in the war).

Most mums stayed at home in those days, and the family had to survive on the father's income. We weren't poor, but far from rich. We always had toys for birthdays and Christmas, though often not the ones we wanted. I remember feeling very resentful against Father Christmas because one of my friends received a battery-operated child-sized car and I received a pedal car. I had to pedal like blazes to keep up with him! We had two or three scooters over the years, and I had a perpetual sore on my ankle from banging on the brake attached to the rear wheel. Today's scooters have handbrakes. Although we couldn't afford luxuries, I never felt shortchanged as a child, as my sister Coralie (a year younger than myself) and I received tuppence or sixpence a week for the lolly shop, or to go to the Saturday afternoon flicks (cinema). Barry was five years younger, so he missed out.

At this age (around eight) you were old enough to walk anywhere without any risk of getting lost on the way home. No one worried in those days as we were well trained to be turned loose on day excursions. We just roamed at will, learning independence and resilience to solve any problem we faced. Adelaide was a big country town after all, hardly a major city in 1940. Taking the tram from Woodville, we would visit the city which held the main shopping area for Adelaide - Rundle Street, the

Beehive Corner, Myers, John Martins, and many other shops. It was an adventure in those days. (This was normal for most older children until the kidnapping of the Beaumont children in 1966.)

Grandfather James, my father's father, lived at German Creek, located outside of Mt Gambier where my father grew up. We sometimes travelled there during the Christmas Holidays as a family, but travel was a luxury in those days, so you didn't travel unless you had to. Visiting family wasn't a good enough reason when each penny was used for living. Coming home we had a seven-hour train ride to Adelaide from Mt Gambier and then another train to Woodville. A journey would take all day as the trains did 20 miles an hour at best. We only had very slow antique steam trains, not modern diesels. My father's mother, Grandma Chant, would visit us maybe two or three times a year. She would stay for about a week and bring a round of cheese from a Mt Gambier cheese factory where one of my cousins worked. I developed a great appetite for a 'bitey' cheddar cheese.

We looked forward to her visits because she would bring us pennies she had saved. The lolly shop was a place you could buy liquorice straps as long as your arm! We used to enjoy any kind of chewy lolly, including jellybeans or a jelly babies, where you could buy so many for a penny. Freddo frogs cost a thrippence (three penny coin), and that we could only rarely afford. I think I was an adult before I could finally buy a chocolate milkshake which became my favourite treat, after I tried them all. We could only afford a suburban movie theatre which was a temporary affair set up in the local town hall. The only city picture theatre had cushioned fold down seats, where you would have to stand for the national anthem before the film began and sing, God Save the King (George VI), as this was before the time of Queen Elizabeth.

Leslie Street where I lived was a dead-end street, so it was safe to play on as it ended in paddocks (it's now a throughway). There was a gorgeous fig tree that we climbed a lot and raided in season when the figs were ripe. My father put a gate in our back fence so we could get through easily to play in the empty block next to our home. We gradually opened up the boxthorn bushes and created a fort. (These boxthorn bushes were imported from South Africa and were prolific, overcoming native vegetation, until the government was able to eliminate them). People would walk past our fort and never know we were there. We thought this was a great joke! Coralie and I, and later Barry, enjoyed this game immensely.

Across the road from our house was the local high school, which was out of bounds, but our quiet street had many neighbour's kids my age playing various ball games like hopscotch, hopping games, and French cricket with a bucket or a rubbish tin, although occasionally we had proper stumps. We played chasing games, skipping games, and running games with no adults supervising. If we couldn't sort out a disagreement, we would go off in a huff taking our equipment with us, until the lure of the game drew us back. We had ping pong bats, tennis racquets and whatever we could scrounge up, we were never lacking in equipment to play with. It might not have been in great shape, but it kept us amused for hours.

This freedom to play together would be deemed too unsafe these days. And we have lost something in today's world as most kids don't want to play as we used to do, preferring competitive sport games or indoor activities with streaming services, iPads/tablets, and video games.

There are three things my soul delights in, and which are delightful to God and to all people: concord between brothers, friendship between neighbours, and a wife and husband who live happily together. Sirach 25:1 Apocrypha Jerusalem Bible

1941 LACERATED

Bang! The loud crash of one car smashing into another was followed by the sickening sound of splintering glass as my head was driven through the windscreen of my father's car. I bounced back and recoiled onto my seat. My face was laid open with an awful gash from the very corner of my left eye, over my nose, and right down to the bottom of my right cheek. It was a terrible, profusely bleeding wound for an eight-year-old boy.

There was no law mandating seatbelts in 1941. And despite my age I was allowed to be in the passenger front seat with my siblings in the back seat. My father was driving us down the Port Road to view the *Queen Elizabeth*, which up to that time was the largest ship ever to visit Adelaide's outer harbour.

I have no memory of what happened just after the accident, except that I ended up in the Royal Adelaide Children's Hospital with my face cleaned up, my blood-stained clothing changed, and sporting a long row of surgical stitches closing the wound. However, it was a jagged laceration and impossible for surgeons at that time to pull the edges together neatly. Perhaps modern methodologies might have left me with a scarcely visible injury but at this time I was left with a rather ugly and protuberant scar across my nose and right cheek.

That disfigurement was no bother to me while I was still a young child but after I reached adolescence it became a torment. I felt no pretty girl would look at me twice. By the time I was 16 and twice the size I had been in 1941, the scar had in fact become much smaller in relation to the rest of my features. It was far from being gross in the eyes of others than it seemed to my own eyes. In any case, when I met Alison at age nineteen, she failed to notice the scar until I pointed it out to her and told her how it had happened. I accepted her evaluation and from that day on scarcely ever noticed it and certainly stopped worrying about it.

Around 18 months later, shortly before Alison and I were married, she too gained a large and ugly scar. Her throat was opened for thyroid surgery, and she was as much embarrassed about this lurid mark around her neck as I had been about the vivid scar across my nose. She too wondered if I might stop loving her but of course I took no more notice of her scar than she had of mine. Indeed, love which can be squashed by a mere superficial blemish is not love but only a callow infatuation. True love reaches far deeper than a person's skin. It entwines itself around the essence of the other's personality. Love, in its deepest meaning, is rooted in a person's inner qualities and innate character. Or as Shakespeare put it –

> Let me not to the marriage of true minds,
> Admit impediments. Love is not love,
> Which alters when it alteration finds;
> Or bends, with the remover to remove;
> Ah no! it is an ever-fixed mark,
> That looks on tempests,
> and is never shaken.
> *Sonnet 116, lines 1-6*

Or even better as the Lord God said to Israel –

I have loved you with an everlasting love: I have drawn you with unfailing kindness. Jeremiah 31:3 and *The Lord is gracious and compassionate, slow to anger and rich in love.* Psalm 145:8

And Jesus to his disciples –

Surely, I am with you always, to the very end of the age. Matthew 28:20

Of course, if love is not reciprocated or if one partner wilfully abandons, or foully deceives the other, the story must have a different outcome. We learn this from God's relationship with Israel. Although God could not abandon the Israelites, nor could his love diminish, Nonetheless he was frequently obliged to 'divorce' them; that is, to punish them severely in various terrible ways. Yet always he left the door open for his people to repent and to come back to him with contrition, casting themselves upon his mercy, which was always given to them extravagantly. So, too, we should behave toward one another. In one place Jesus makes an arresting demand -

So, watch yourselves. If your brother or sister sins against you, rebuke them; and if they repent, forgive them. Even if they sin against you seven times in a day, and seven times come back to you saying "I repent" you must forgive them. Luke 17:3-4

Imagine someone comes up to me early one morning and knocks me down. At once he apologises and says he has no idea why he did it and begs my forgiveness.

I would forgive him.

But then an hour later he does the same thing again, and every hour on the hour until he has knocked me down seven times and repented seven times. Will I still be so forgiving? I would like to think I would be, but instead, I think I would be furious and deeply resentful of the injuries and insults he had heaped on me. Or perhaps I would think of a strategy to put myself into a different position, so it didn't happen again.

Yet that remorseless saying of Jesus remains; you must forgive from the heart any offence your brother or sister has caused you. Forgiveness sets you free. Holding onto unforgiveness puts you in an emotional prison, tied to that event.

Bear with each other and forgive one another if any of you has a grievance against someone. Forgive as the Lord forgave you. Colossians 3:13

1942 DROWNING

The rip tide had me in its relentless grip and was forcibly carrying me out to sea to a certain death by drowning. Suddenly, seemingly out of nowhere, a strong man appeared who swam with me back to the shore and deposited me safely on the beach.

It was school holiday time, and my mother had brought me and my siblings by train to a town, possibly Port Elliot, at least an hour south of the Adelaide Railway Station. I'm unsure of the name of the town knowing only that we spent a week there in a rented holiday home. I have happy memories of clambering among the rocky pools hunting for starfish, crabs, anemones, and whatever else was interesting. On the morning of my rip tide experience my mother was sitting on the beach under a large umbrella keeping an eye on us children. I assume Coralie and Barry were playing in the sand while I went for a swim. This quickly yielded to terror when I realised the rip was carrying me irresistibly out to sea.

As soon as the stranger had got me safely ashore, I ran to my mother to tell her about how close to death I had come. Both of us wanted to thank him for his kind rescue but when we looked around there was no sign of him. This was surprising. The morning was still young and the long white beach nearly deserted. He certainly did not have sufficient time to walk out of our sight. He just disappeared. At once I concluded that he had been an angel sent by God, which I still firmly believe.

The moral? As the Psalmist said, *Our times are in your hands*! (Psalm 31:15) Would it be reasonable for me to doubt that, as the popular saying has it, "My time had not yet come." There are many mysteries when it comes to the length of our life on earth but as you will see from later anecdotes, this miracle of divine rescue was only one of many (some of them far more dramatic) for which I praise God most heartily.

Never doubt it: the Lord loves you, cares for you, and will keep you all the days of your life, so long as you are committed to doing, being, and becoming all that he asks of you. In the end, for a Christian, there is no other valid definition of success except this: find the will of God and do it.

The angel of the Lord encamps around those who fear him, and he delivers them. Psalm 34:7

May he give you the desire of your heart and make all your plans succeed. Psalm 20:4

1942 FIRE

I was terrified! Flames were dancing all around me and I had no idea what to do. I ran home as quickly as I could and took refuge inside our house. In the meantime, the fire I had kindled in the grassy paddock that lay behind several of the houses in our street was burning brightly. It threatened to consume every house. But one neighbour alerted another, including my parents, and they were soon standing at their back fences with hoses pouring water onto the flames. What a relief! They managed to extinguish the burning grass and none of the properties suffered any harm. No-one ever discovered that I was the one who had purloined a box of matches and played in the grass with them. So, I was the one who had accidently caused the blaze! I confess it now, hoping that the law will have no interest in juvenile misbehaviour which occurred so long ago!

I was a mischievous and deeply curious boy. Those qualities led me twice more into a childhood scrape. I saw an open window in the Woodville High School which occupied, with its playing fields, the entirety of the land on the other side of our street. The open window led into the art room. Intrigued I climbed in and discovered to my excitement many tubes of brightly coloured paint. I didn't have any of my own and my parents could not afford to buy them for me. Quickly, I stuffed them into my pockets and then fled home. I saw them, liked them, and stole them. But I was too scared to use them! The end result, the paints hardened in the tubes and became worthless. On another occasion I was in a local grocery store and saw a small can of tinned cream. I filched it and carried it home. I had great difficulty getting the can open, and in the process largely spoiled its contents. But I managed to save enough of the cream to make me feel quite ill!

Those two disappointments were enough to teach me that crime does not pay, and I resolved never ever to steal anything again. I can truthfully say that since then, except for the rare speeding ticket, I have never done anything unlawful. In the meantime, I comforted myself with the fact that my mother each week purchased a significant quantity of groceries from that same grocer, which would have abundantly compensated him for the loss of the can of cream. The cans must have been a wartime commodity since I don't think they are sold today.

The torments of conscience those thefts caused me, along with their disappointing outcomes, fully persuaded me to remain a scrupulously law-abiding citizen. I daresay the devil was deeply chagrined at having to release his grip on such a budding young criminal.

In any case, my deep conversion to Christ when I was sixteen settled the matter beyond doubt. I was from that time on fully committed to a life of righteousness and honest dealings with everyone I met.

Recompense to no man evil for evil. Provide things honest in the sight of all men. Romans 12:17

For we are taking pains to do what is right, not only in the eyes of the Lord but also in the eyes of men. 2 Corinthians 8:21

1943 MUSIC

One of the most disheartening aspects of life appears when you come to the realisation that you are good enough to know you're not good enough. That is the story of my life. A good enough preacher to know that I will never preach to thousands. A good enough musician to know that I will never headline a concert. Clever enough to know that I will never be a true expert in any field. A good enough writer to recognise that I am a better editor than a creator of original works. And in music, a good enough composer to know that I will never produce works that will endure for centuries. True, several of my songs have been printed in various collections and have been sung around the world but their popularity will not be lasting.

Nonetheless music has been and remains one of the most precious gifts in my life. My tastes are eclectic. While from childhood I have mostly preferred the classics, in the end I enjoy listening to all kinds of exceptional music: jazz, sacred songs, oratorios, motets, cantatas, anthems, choruses, hymns, and the like, which are popular in many churches worldwide. I have enjoyed listening to the classical music of other nations - Indian, Japanese, Chinese, Greek, Hungarian, and many other kinds. Until more recently my advancing years have obliged me to abandon my library and to satisfy any musical inclination through YouTube videos. My compact disc (CD) and digital musical library contained superb examples of the kinds of music I have listed but I have no access now being confined to my armchair.

Let me stress however that I am talking about only the best creative music in composition and performance in all genres. Of course, there is a huge quantity of second and third rate music descending to even worse cacophonies.

This love of fine music in many categories must have been born in me. At any rate, one of my earliest memories is taking a tram from our home in Woodville to downtown Adelaide where for some two years I attended the Adelaide College of Music. This school taught students how to play a variety of instruments which in my case included the banjo mandolin. Banjo mandolins are constructed like a regular banjo but have only four strings which, depending on the quality of the instrument, give it a rather metallic sound. The tuning of a banjo mandolin is the same as a classical violin (G-D-A-E).

It was not practical for either of my parents to accompany me to these weekly lessons, so I travelled alone which was unusual for such a young child of ten years but in that era was reasonably safe. The College also presented a concert once a year in the old Tivoli Theatre in downtown Adelaide. Each concert included a bracket of banjo mandolin pieces, and I was one of the players. Thus, the love of good music was deeply instilled in me. From there I went on to teach myself to play several instruments, most notably the Hawaiian steel guitar. I purchased several of these culminating in a lovely pedal steel guitar with six strings, four pedals, and two knee levers. Every time I touched a pedal or knee lever the tuning of the instrument was changed so that it was initially fiendishly difficult to play any songs. I eventually became good enough to play it at church thus adding an unusual element to our church music.

I also taught myself to play a 120 bass piano accordion, a ukelele, a Spanish guitar, a vibraharp (a two-rank metal keyed electric xylophone with a spinning wheel which gave a vibrato effect), electric organ, and of course, the piano. Of all these instruments I achieved sufficient competence to be able to play for church services, prayer meetings, and the like.

You may be startled to learn that I taught myself to play the piano by purchasing a book of boogie woogie pieces and thumping away at them until the rhythms flowed easily out of my fingers. Remember, however, that my banjo mandolin lessons six years earlier had taught me the rudiments of music which I had refined over the intervening years. (My daughter has happy memories of watching me play with great expertise a boogie woogie piece at church state camps and conferences to the delight of the audience who had not known that this was one of my hidden skills.)

I loved boogie woogie and still do but soon realised it had little use in everyday church life. To compensate for this deficiency, I purchased a book on harmony and set myself to master the circle of fifths which embraced all the possible chords on a normal piano and practised them hour after hour. Once I had learned the structure of each chord and how they related to each other there was no hymn or gospel song that I could not play. I have often felt sad for people who cannot play an instrument. Although even the most crow-like among us can croak out a song of some sort. Everyone should have an opportunity to be enriched by learning to play some type of instrument.

Music is an ineffable gift from God! How wonderfully it soothes the sad heart! How divinely it brightens the darkest hours of life! What delights and comfort it brings into the most wretched of hours! Praise to the Lord for the exquisite songs of Zion that bring all the sweet comforts of heaven to this often gloomy vale we call earth.

My advice? If you have not already done so, make some effort to learn to perform on an instrument of your choice. Even the humble recorder can bring joyful satisfaction and merry pleasure even to an amateur performer and, in the hands of a virtuoso, can produce astounding music. You might even find in yourself an ability to compose, whether lyrics or melodies or both. I have written 50-60 songs, sometimes words without music, sometimes music without words, sometimes both. Two of my most popular compositions, *Be Glad Ye Sons of Zion* and *Fill My Eyes O My God,* have been sung by hundreds, if not thousands of believers, which gives me great satisfaction.

Let me close this story with these exhortations:

Praise the Lord. Praise him in his sanctuary; praise him in his mighty heavens. Praise him for his acts of power; praise him for his surpassing greatness. Praise him with the sounding of the trumpet, praise him with the harp and lyre, praise him with timbrel and dancing, praise him with the strings and pipe, praise him with the clash of cymbals, praise him with resounding cymbals. Let everything that has breath praise the Lord. Psalm 150

Let the message of Christ dwell among you richly as you teach and admonish one another with all wisdom through psalms, hymns, and songs from the Spirit, singing to God with gratitude in your hearts. And whatever you do, whether in word or deed, do it all in the name of the Lord Jesus, giving thanks to God the Father through him. Colossians 3:16-17

1943 MECCANO

On my seventieth birthday Alison asked me what I would like as a present. As I was feeling nostalgic for my long-ago childhood when one of my preferred games was the setting up of Meccano models, I asked her to buy me a set of Meccano pieces to make a model of some kind. We travelled into

Sydney to the Queen Victoria building which housed a very large hobby shop and found many Meccano models to choose from.

Well, that was the beginning of a hobby that grew into a monster, taking up far too much space in my office and overflowing into Alison's office as well. Later, when she complained, that her bookshelves were filling up I had to rearrange my shelves to accommodate any new models I created. I joined the Meccano club and began collecting old Meccano sets. I liked making Meccano models because this gave me a complete mental rest from the intricacies of theology, as I usually spent up to ten hours each day writing textbooks for our Vision College Correspondence Course.

The problem was that after spending hours, sometimes days, making a model, I could not bear to dismantle it again. Finally, in my eighty-fifth year, after fifteen years of making models, I could no longer see well enough to put the tiny nuts and bolts together, so had to resign from model making. Two of my largest models were a model of the Eiffel Tower I built for Sharon for her fiftieth birthday that stands 4 feet tall; and my last model, a magnificent crane made up of 1,228 pieces, which we have kept and photographed for this book.

One good thing about my Meccano modelling career was that the grandchildren and then greatgrandchildren had a great time with the movable models. The swings, the Ferris wheel, various cars, trucks and motorbikes. Some of these could be fitted with an engine driven by batteries, others were push-along models.

We bought some small, knitted dolls which fitted into the seats of the swings, the Ferris wheel, and the trucks, and this gave the grandchildren much satisfaction as they used these objects in imaginative play.

We still have many of the models, but we have removed the batteries to preserve the engines. Our son, Eric and his wife Belinda, have shown some interest in taking over the Meccano but no one else seems to be enthusiastic about this beloved toy of my childhood. The grandchildren and great grandchildren are into Lego these days.

Command those who are rich in this present world not to be arrogant nor to put their hope in wealth, which is so uncertain, but to put their hope in God, who richly provides us with everything for our enjoyment. 1 Timothy 6:17

1944 PATRIOTIC

The Second World War was fought from 1939-1945. I was seven when it began and twelve when it finished. I was very patriotic during the war years and spent time collecting newspapers for the war effort, along with many other boys who also collected.

I was inspired to contribute by raising money for the School's Patriotic Fund. As well as collecting newspapers, I also collected cotton waste from the Actil Cotton factory near our home in Woodville. The manager agreed to my collecting cotton waste if I both gathered it from the yard and carried it away myself. I borrowed a horse cart and pushed and pulled it. I was the horse!

Most days after school, I would push the cart to the factory and collect the left-over waste and then push it back to school. It wasn't heavy, just awkward. It often had other stuff in it that I had to discard first but I managed to move it back and forth on my own. I'm not sure how many carts full I was able to gather and wheel to school, but it was sufficient to earn me a large cluster of blue and silver medals and then when I had reached that limit, red and gold medals. Each cluster consisted of a larger round medal (probably about two centimetres across) under which a number of straight bars were secured by small rings. These were issued by the School Patriotic Fund (SPF) to children who had made a diligent effort to contribute to the war effort.

Because of this hard work I won many wonderful medals which unfortunately were stolen during our robbery in the USA. They were in the form of little silver aeroplanes, and I had at least seven or eight of them linked together. I remember two gold medals also as well as the aeroplanes. Sharon researched the medals for me, and we now have a letter from the SPF outlining their purpose and accomplishments of the recipients.

And whatever you do, in word or deed, do everything in the name of the Lord Jesus, giving thanks to God the Father through him. Colossians 3:17

1944 COMMANDER

Commander Harvey visited our local primary school several times. He was a grizzled and bearded sea captain who all his life had been the master of windjammers carrying cargo all over the world and known seas at their most serene beauty and also their most savage ferocity. He had often been becalmed or enjoyed balmy seas and moderate breezes. At other times he had been battered by ferocious seas that threatened to pull his ship forever under the green depths. Along with the psalmist, Commander Harvey had seen the wonders of the Lord in the majesty of the deep. (Psalm 107:24)

When I first met the swarthy captain, he had retired from the sea and purchased a very colourful gypsy caravan which he adorned with a brass ship's bell, a cutlass, and other mementoes of his ocean voyages. The van was pulled by a huge draught horse that looked as ancient as its owner. The Commander would drive this caravan up to a public school when the children were coming out of an afternoon, then he would loudly clang his bell to attract attention. Immediately he would begin to preach to the gathered children who stood there listening, astonished by the spectacle. This was no saccharine sermon! The Captain preached with the thunder of the roaring ocean, surging storms, howling winds, and shrieking and storm-tossed seas echoing in his voice. He preached the fear of God as the beginning of wisdom.

I heard him several times and on one occasion received from him a copy of the *Gospel of St John*, which I took home and read. On the last page there was an invitation to accept Christ as Saviour and a form to fill in to declare that you had repented of your sins and affirmed Jesus Christ as your personal Lord and Saviour. I was eleven or thereabouts. On one occasion after a particularly fiery message, I remember walking home from school with a vision of a burning hell opening up before me. I can still see that vision in my mind's eye eighty years later. Perhaps, surprisingly, I do not remember feeling terrified, only convinced that I needed a Saviour.

Some went out on the sea in ships; they were merchants on the mighty waters. They saw the works of the Lord, his wonderful deeds in the deep. For he spoke and stirred up a tempest that lifted high the waves. They mounted up to the heavens and went down to the depths; in their peril their courage melted away. They reeled and staggered like drunkards; they were at their wits' end. Then they cried out to the Lord in their trouble, and he brought them out of their distress. He stilled the storm to a whisper; the waves of the sea were hushed. They were glad when it grew calm, and he guided them to their desired haven. Psalm 107:23-30

1945 BOMBS

It was deep, dark, and damp, and we children were forbidden to play in it. What was it? An air-raid shelter dug into our backyard by my father. It was big enough to accommodate our family of five, deep enough for us children to stand up in, and protected from falling bombs by a corrugated iron roof covered with heaped up dirt. Such shelters were commonly built throughout suburbia in Adelaide and indeed around the nation. During the Second World War they were deemed sufficient protection from all but a direct hit from a bomb or a shell. Our shelter was equipped with several oil lamps along with a considerable amount of reading material which was renewed from time to time. We never had to use the shelter as a protective measure, but we did have fun playing in it after the war was over. I presume that my father finally filled it in after removing everything from it.

Along with all the homes and buildings in Australia we had to make sure no light could escape from any window. Wardens (one of whom was my father) patrolled the streets to ensure that no chinks of light were escaping from any house. The war seemed far distant to us children and we treated the various survival exercises we had to practice at home and at school as delightful games. We thought the same about the plastic identity discs we had to wear around our necks. They contained our name, address, and blood type in case of injury.

The story about the air-raid shelter and its heap of books and other reading matter highlights how important books were in our family. I was an avid reader and devoured everything I could get my hands on suitable for my age group from as far back as I can remember. The first book that made an impact on me was a large picture book of pirates which I read so often it fell into tatters but some of the pictures, eighty-five years after I first saw them, are still vivid in my mind. Gradually my reading tastes were extended until by the time I was eleven or twelve I had read through all ten volumes of Arthur Mee's, *The Children's Encyclopedia.*

From the several thousand pages of those wonderful books I developed a vast curiosity about almost everything along with a love for poetry, history, and other literary forms. I used to try to wheedle my mother into believing I was too sick to go to school and instead would curl up in bed with one or two books of Mee's Volumes, along with other books that were part of my parent's small library scattered on the bed around me. My enjoyment of reading has never abated and still embraces a wide array of titles, themes, and subjects (although now that my eyes are failing, I am forced to listen to audiobooks).

Of course, prime among my reading since my adolescent years has been the Bible, which I have read right through many times, and in any of thirty or more different translations at least once, and in some translations several times. Currently my favourite version is the English Standard Version which was published in 2001. It uses contemporary English with some paraphrasing, but not to a great extent, and is a sound and reliable translation. I do not mean other translations don't have value. Some, like the Revised English Bible, are pleasurably easier to read but probably contain too much paraphrasing to be reliable as a study version. And I listen to David Suchet's wonderful recitation of the NIV Bible, which expressively brings Scripture to life.

I will add one more thing - there is no substitute for reading your Bible every day. It is the bread of life for the believer. Christians who are weak in the Word will simply be weak. You will be no stronger in your Christian life than you are in the Word of God.

Oh, the depth of the riches of the wisdom and knowledge of God! How unsearchable his judgments, and his paths beyond tracing out! Who has known the mind of the Lord? Or who has been his counsellor? Who has ever given to God, that God should repay them? For from him and through him and for him are all things. To him be the glory forever! Amen. Romans 11:33-36

Do not conform to the pattern of this world but be transformed by the renewing of your mind. Then you will be able to test and approve what God's will is – his good, pleasing and perfect will. Romans 12:2

1948 FARMING

I was very unhappy. My mother had recently died of ovarian cancer in my fifteenth year soon after giving birth to our little sister, Christine, who had only lived for a few hours. I was working in a dull job as a bank clerk, so I decided to search for a new environment. I wrote to my father's brother, my Uncle Bob, who I knew owned a prosperous mixed farm some twenty miles out of Mt Gambier in the South-East corner of South Australia. Mostly it was a dairy farm, milking some eighty cows, morning and evening. But the farm also contained several different crops, each about forty acres, plus at least 200 sheep. I was familiar with the countryside. On several occasions during the long summer school holidays my mother had taken the train from Adelaide to Mt Gambier to spend a few weeks at the old farm owned by my paternal grandparents at *German Creek.*

Conditions there were primitive, although exciting for city born and bred children. That old weatherboard farmhouse has long since been demolished but at the time we children thought it was marvellous. There was no electricity, not even a motor driven generator; there was no running water, only what we could pump up from a deep well just outside the back door of the house; the only lights were candles or kerosene lamps. The most thrilling of all for us were the pump-up kerosene lamps which gained their luminosity from a brilliant incandescent ball of woven cotton or asbestos surrounded by gorgeous stained-glass shades. The glowing light of the white-hot mantles added a kind of ethereal brilliance to the led-lined stained glass.

My grandparents owned and travelled occasionally by horse and buggy, which fascinated us children. The only ploughs on the farm as far as I can remember were pulled by huge draft horses with great shaggy feet and enormous collars into which they would lean with superb strength. I think that on at least one occasion we children broke every imaginable safety rule by riding on the plough as the massive horses pulled it through the rich black volcanic soil.

I remember the floors of the old home rocking when we children ran over them. I remember the large cluster of pine trees which had begun life at least a century earlier. Most of all, I remember a huge barn packed with an enthralling collection of ancient farm equipment - horse riggings, old carts, a small mountain of hay bales, and indeed all the clutter of goods collected and stored there from the year 1865 after John Chant arrived from England. We spent hours in that old barn, many times terrified by encountering a huge rat, sometimes several of them! At once we would summon the farm dogs whose frenzied barking would frighten the rats away more quickly than they could scare us out of the barn.

Back to Uncle Bob whose farm was a few miles away from the German Creek property. He wrote back to me to say he would be willing to employ me as a farm labourer. I replied with a letter whose contents I have quite forgotten except for the use of the tautology, "Advent of my arrival." I still writhe with embarrassment when I remember it. Advent? Yes! Arrival? Yes! But both together? That was a solecism scarcely to be forgiven!

Sometime prior to my departure to the farm I had begun to court a young lady my own age whose name was Maureen. She came with me to the Adelaide Railway Station where I was due to board the Mt Gambier train. There, rather absurdly, I proposed to her, and she accepted. I promised to place a notice in the Adelaide Advertiser and then Maureen was obliged to leave the train as it was about to depart. The advert duly appeared, and my father was told about it by one of my mother's sisters who you may remember disliked him intensely. He wrote me a scorching letter reminding me that I was well under the age of consent, which was then twenty-one, and told me that he would be inserting another notice in the Advertiser cancelling my notice.

What an affront! Adolescent indignation rose in me like a hurricane. To his angry missive I replied with equal fury, with a total lack of respect for my revered and loved father. I still cringe at the memory. My next few letters to Dad were saturated with love and laughter which ended in our complete reconciliation and renewal of a healthy father-son relationship. Why did I behave so irresponsibly? I don't really know except that it was probably linked with the too early and too awful death of my mother.

Anyway, the train chuffed its way out of Adelaide and some ten hours later deposited me at the Mt. Gambier station where, I presume, Uncle Bob met me and drove me out to the farm some twenty miles distant. Twice during the year or two I worked for Bob my life was imperilled. Only to be rescued by Bob's help. He had amazingly quick reflexes and was quite strong.

First - I was ploughing a field using a nine-farrow disk plough drawn by a powerful Marshall Diesel tractor. What a remarkable machine! Possessing only one large cylinder and a heavy weight flywheel. We started the engine by inserting a cartridge into the cylinder head and then hitting the firing pin with a hammer. With a loud bang and a roar, the piston and flywheel would start moving and accelerate rapidly so that its 140 horse-power energy was swiftly available. Almost nothing could stop that tractor, its force was so colossal, but on this day while I was driving the tractor merrily across a paddock striving to keep a straight furrow, the plough struck a large and deeply buried stump. Not even the Marshall was strong enough to pull the tractor over or through that stump, so tractor and plough came to a sudden halt, except that the huge piston kept roaring backwards and forwards in its lateral cylinder and so the whole tractor began to rotate upward on its rear wheels. I can remember sitting there transfixed with fright by the sight of the machine rising before my eyes threatening to crush me instantly to death. And indeed, I would have died if Bob had not been close enough to see my peril. Like a flash he covered the ground and reached the tractor in time to thrust his hand on the clutch pedal and exert all his strength to push it down hard. Quickly the tractor began to subside while Bob urged me without delay to disengage the gears which of course I did. Rather shakily I managed to redirect the plough around the stump and continued to plough the remainder of the field. What happened to the stump? I'm unsure but I presume my uncle found a way to dig it out.

Second - There was a time when Bob and I, perhaps foolishly, were erecting a metal windmill standing about thirty feet high and with a wheel diameter of around ten feet. We had assembled the windmill on the ground and then had to raise and secure it to its foundations. Half-way up, inevitably, the wind caught the large wheel and plucked the whole thing out of our hands knocking me to the ground where I lay gasping for air as the windmill began to fall on me. I was a dead man! Except that Bob with astonishing agility, speed, and strength leaped to the side of the falling windmill and gave it an immense push so that it fell, instead of straight on to me, safely alongside me. Both of us shared the folly of trying to lift that heavy piece of machinery on a windy day.

I have deep cause to be grateful to my uncle. Without wanting to diminish his promptitude and skill or my gratitude to him, I can't help but give thanks to God for events which could have cut off my life before reaching my seventeenth year.

A shadow was cast over my time at the farm. Bob had been a Japanese prisoner during the Second World War, forced to work on the Burma Siam railway for long hours on scant rations. This suddenly exacted its toll. Bob became very ill and had to sit in a dark room all day every day for several months. Consequently, I had to take over the running of the farm, being helped as much as she could by Bob's wife, my Aunt Christine. Happily, the owners of neighbouring farms frequently offered me advice and assistance, so I was able to manage tolerably well. I continued milking the eighty cows, morning and evening, which led to a contretemps with Christine. The milking task occupied four hours at each end of the day, which obliged me to arise at four am in the morning. It seemed I had hardly gone to bed exhausted at night when it was time to wake in the morning. It was hardly worthwhile to get undressed as it felt like it was only a few moments later to be obliged to get dressed again. So, I took to collapsing into bed at night fully clothed. I became quite rank. Christine demanded that I shower more often and so, no matter how exhausted I was after finishing the milking at eight pm and eating an enormous dinner, I washed and changed into my pyjamas like a good boy. A sweet harmony was restored, and I continued caring for the farm. Bob eventually emerged from the dark room so that we were all able to resume our normal and proper positions.

Two or three other tasks I had to do on the farm were arduous but also interesting. One was using the major milking machines to strip those eighty cows of their milk morning and evening. (I had a favourite cow, Sooky, who was always very affectionate in the cowshed. She used to come up to me and rub her head on my shoulder. I used to call Alison, Sooky, but when she discovered Sooky was a cow, she objected!) Sometimes we would separate the milk into cream and skim milk. The decision on whether or not to do this depended on current market prices for which Bob had an extraordinary instinct on whether or not there were lambs or calves in the flocks who could be fed with skim milk. Another was building new fences which required erecting a massive corner post at each end of the fence, then every few metres along its length drilling holes to contain the slighter fence posts and finally threading fencing wire through four or five holes in each post and firmly stretching it. There was science, skill, and perhaps even art, in achieving a line of fence that was quite straight and with all the wires properly taut.

Sometimes when a proposed crop was ready to be sown Bob would attach a trailer to the tractor piled high with bags of superphosphate each weighing 185 pounds (84 kilos). This powdered chemical fertilisers the soil. Using that rig my uncle would drive up and down the previously harrowed field while I stood on the trailer hefting bags of super down to the hopper at the end of the trailer. The hopper contained a belt driven spinner which spread the superphosphate evenly over the surface of the paddock. I was in those days muscular and very strong, with a vast reserve of energy. I could maintain this onerous task for a full working day. The main trick was to keep pace with the tractor so that every meter of the paddock was covered evenly.

Then one morning I was tightening the girth on a muster horse I was about to ride when a terrible pain seized my abdomen forcing me to cry out in anguish. Bob was nearby and he at once saw that I was seriously ill, so he bundled me into the farm utility and set off to drive me along the twenty miles of the rough dirt road that led from his farm to Mt Gambier. I writhed in the seat beside him at each bump and jolt but there was nothing for it but to endure the unendurable! We arrived at the hospital where the doctors quickly diagnosed a case of a seriously enlarged appendix and recommended immediate surgery. Acting in the name of my father, Bob gave his approval and within minutes the ghastly experience of being put to sleep with ether (or was it chloroform), a frenzy of nightmare images tumbling through my rapidly stupefying mind.

My main memories of that first week in the Mt Gambier hospital include

- the embarrassment of being washed all over by nurses who were often only a couple of years older than myself; and
- I had a particular petite nurse who nonetheless stomped across the wobbly floorboards of the ancient hospital like an elephant, so that whatever cannula or needles were stuck into me shook and trembled in response. The pain was not great, but it was annoying enough to make me tremble with some trepidation whenever she approached my bed. I've no doubt she was a sweet young thing but obviously she had no awareness of how heavily she walked.

By the end of the week, I was preparing to go back to Adelaide when I was again twisted with agony. The medical staff rushed me into surgery where the surgeon discovered I had a strangulated bowel, that is, during the appendectomy a week earlier some fat from my abdomen had come loose and wrapped itself around my bowel preventing it from working. That second piece of surgery was deemed successful and a week later my father was able to drive to Mt Gambier and take me back to Adelaide where I spent the next several weeks convalescing.

Mostly, I spent that time in bed reading a wide variety of books. Perhaps ten weeks later when I was expected to discard my invalid status and get back to normal life a savage pain once again gripped my abdomen. My brother Barry discovered me writhing on my bed and groaning. He at once told our father and Dad took me to the main hospital in Adelaide. The doctors were sceptical and told Dad that it was only a pretence, and the pain was only in my imagination. Thank God he refused to believe them and insisted they keep me in hospital under observation. The next morning Dad rang to see how I was and they told him they had to operate at midnight to save my life from another strangulated bowel. Dad was pleased to be vindicated but sad that I had to go through yet another operation. After this surgery it took a long time for me to recuperate.

Although appendicitis is not considered a genetic condition (passed down from parent to child) it is interesting to note that my father had appendicitis at 82; my son, Eric, at 15; and my grandson, Kristian, at 12. Due to modern medicine, it was caught early, and they survived. So far, this propensity has not passed on to any of my other grandchildren or great grandchildren.

So, my career on the farm came to an inglorious end. Yet, while I enjoyed working on the farm, which included a spell of working in a pine forest, and another of working on the roads, I was glad to get back to my familiar environment in the city. There were, however, three aspects of farm life I did not enjoy -

First - My uncle was a keen fisherman, revelling particularly in wading out to sea at night near Carpenter Rocks on the coast of South Australia, and in each sweep netting several potato bags full of a variety of fish that are common to the Carpenter Rocks coast. These bags of course had to be carried back to the farm where the fish had to be scaled and gutted by the menial labourer, whose name you can guess. And then we ate fish morning, noon, and night, after giving away as much as we could, until the fridge was empty. I don't know how long my uncle's fishing lasted but this I can say, after the first two or three expeditions I vowed if I never saw another fish until the day I died, I would be delighted.

Perhaps an even worse aspect of my fishing duties as the employee of Bob Chant, was a requirement to act as a mule and carry in a pack on my back a heavy twelve-volt car battery. This was used to light a lamp so my uncle could see to spear flounder. Each evening would begin with the battery scarcely pulling on me at all, but after several hours of splashing through the shallows, following my uncle as he speared flounder after flounder, filling another potato sack which I also had to carry, both loads grew heavier and heavier. And I knew that as soon as we got back these fish would have to be scaled, gutted, and cleaned!

Second - To provide winter forage for the farm animals Uncle Bob gathered several hundred bales of oat hay, lucerne hay, and probably several other grasses as well. He achieved this goal by using a rather old-fashioned hay baler driven by a thick belt attached to a nearby tractor. The baler stood in the middle of the paddock while other workmen carried the mown hay to the baler and piled it up on either side. A farmhand stood alongside each pile and forked it into the barrels of the baler. There a large piston would begin to push it through the baling chute pressing it into oblong bales which each weighed about fifty pounds. Two other men had to squat on each side of the chute and as each new bale appeared we would insert a small board either end and then two pieces of heavy wire which we pulled out along the length of the bale and inserted through the slots at the other end. My partner on the other side would have to catch the ends of the wires and twist them tightly together so they would not tumble apart when they fell out of the far end of the chute.

The work was not laborious, but it was certainly filthy. By the end of the day, we were covered from head to toe in hay dust, bits of straw, chaff, and other refuse from the paddock. I might also add that the fields were infested with snakes, most of them deadly poisonous, and who were occasionally tossed into the baler, against which rude treatment they protested with hissing fury. But venomous snakes were so prevalent that we treated them with disdain and tossed them as far away from the baler as we could. And so, after a day spent squatting alongside that blighted baler, I would go back to the farmhouse aching from head to foot, itching and scratching, almost unrecognisable under the camouflage of the detritus of the hay.

Third - Perhaps an even worse bone-bending and back-breaking task was helping to gather the forty acres of potatoes my uncle had planted earlier in the year. The potatoes, of course, had been planted in straight furrows, forty acres of them, so that when they were full grown a small potato harrow could be driven down each row turning up the potatoes into open view. Several helpers, mostly family members, plus a couple of other employees (myself included), had to walk behind the harrow, potato sacks in hand, picking up the grown vegetable, dusting off each piece, and putting it into a sack which we dragged behind us. This too, was a tedious and wearisome task and left one feeling that every bone in the back had been hit several times with a hammer. The only good thing to say about those forty acres of spuds was that, apart from the excellent income my uncle gained from them year by year, were the very tasty fresh potatoes served at the farm-house meals.

I have reason to thank God for that time on the farm. My strength was mightily increased by the strenuous activity which is probably one of the main reasons why I did not die under the surgeon's knife in any of the three abdominal operations.

The Bible is full of agricultural allusions and illustrations which my toils on the farm made vividly real and provided also much anecdotal material to use in my later teaching and preaching ministry. And I was able to learn afresh what Scripture means when it talks about the wonders of creation, the beauty of the natural world, and the enthralling mysteries that every new day reveals. Driving a horse and cart through vast pine forests, herding sheep and cattle on horseback, dealing intimately with animals in the milk shed cattle corrals, and even several household dogs and cats, were all exhilarating and taught me many things about myself, and about nature, and best of all about God.

When I consider your heavens, the work of your fingers, the moon and the stars, which you have set in place, what is mankind that you are mindful of them, human beings that you care for them? You have made them a little lower than the angels and crowned them with glory and honour. You made them rulers over the works of your hands; you put everything under their feet: all flocks and herds, and the animals of the wild, the birds in the sky, and the fish in the sea, all that swim the paths of the seas. Lord our Lord, how majestic is your name in all the earth!
Psalms 8:3-9

1948 SNAKES

A spectacular sight - snakes! Sparkling in all the colours of the rainbow in their new skins as they sunbaked on the rocks. They were scattered across the paddock that I was driving past in my horse and cart.

They looked so magnificent that I stopped the cart and throwing the reins over the fence to hold the horse I jumped into the paddock and began to wander among the rocks. But as I was admiring and wondering about all the radiance shimmering from the new skins on that early summer day, it suddenly dawned on me that nearly all those sleepy serpents were amongst some of the most deadly creatures in the world. A number of them were Tiger Snakes whose venom is 40 times stronger than the Eastern Diamondback Rattle Snakes in North America. Others were the equally or more venomous Copperheads. The venom of all three species of Copperheads is neurotoxic (damaging the nerves). Some were gorgeous Carpet Pythons and there were lethal Eastern Brown Snakes, rated as the second most venomous of all snakes in the world, next only to the Inland Taipan, also a native of Australia.

I came to a sudden halt, turned slowly around and tiptoed out of that cluster of death and over the fence again to the safety of my cart. That was 74 years ago but the image of that serpent infested paddock is still vivid in my mind and has always remained as a glorious example of the creator's extravagant artistic and creative ability. What a contrast! Such an awful threat to my life on one hand and yet on the other such a dazzling and beautiful sight. It is a metaphor for the whole of creation which seems to abound equally in life and death, sickness and health, war and peace.

Whoever dwells in the shelter of the Most High will rest in the shadow of the Almighty. I will say of the Lord, "He is my refuge and my fortress, my God in whom I trust." Surely, he will save you from the fowler's snare and from the deadly pestilence. Psalm 91: 1-5

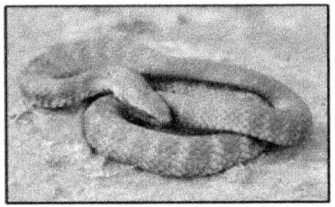

1949 CLARE

The stars blazed in the country night sky, but I had little interest in allowing them to speak to me. Instead, I had buried myself between the huge roots of an enormous gum tree trying to breakthrough to God. The more earnestly I prayed the more impenetrable the heavens became. I nearly despaired of ever catching the Lord's attention but decided to press on with a passionate prayer.

Why was I there? What was this all about? I was attending a Baptist Youth Camp in Clare South Australia, 130 kms north of Adelaide. It was Easter Saturday evening in 1949. Several hundred young people were at the camp church service that night and heard the preacher (of whom I can only recall that he was a Methodist evangelist) challenge us all to get serious about our commitment to serve Christ. Then he did something unusual, instead of a normal altar call to go to the platform and seal that commitment he bade everyone who wanted to respond to his call to go instead out into the night and find a secret place to pray until we knew our surrender to Christ was complete.

I was among those who responded. After searching around the showground for some minutes I discovered an ancient gum tree and the hollow place between its roots. I began to pray ever more fervently for the Lord to show me his purpose. The more I prayed the darker it got. It seemed like the blazing glory of the starry night sky had vanished and all I could see was blackness. I prayed harder still, and it got still darker. I felt like Jacob wrestling with God. (Genesis 32: 22-32) It would have been easy to shrug, give up, and go back into the camp buildings to share a late supper with most of the other young people. But somehow I knew that I had to continue, so with even more passion I pleaded with the Lord to shine his own radiance upon me and disclose his will. How long was I there? I don't know. But it was long enough for the Lord finally to respond. As I looked up into what was for me the pitch-black sky, I saw a tiny crack appear in the heavens through which a radiant light was glowing.

Despair melted away and with increasing fervour I pressed on, doubting no longer that the Lord would speak to me. And he did. Not with an audible voice but nonetheless with an impact on my spirit that left me in no doubt that I was called to serve him in the preaching of the gospel for the rest of my life. That was not so easy to do as you might think, for I had a firm ambition to go into business, make a million dollars before I was forty, purchase a yacht, and spend the rest of my life sailing the seven seas. But as surely as if he were standing right there beside me, I heard the Lord say, "Chant, that may be your ambition, but it is not mine!" I felt there was no other choice left to me except to capitulate and commit myself to discovering (what I have elsewhere said further in this book) that for a Christian there is no possible definition of true success except to discover what God wants you to do and do it. I have never resiled or moved from that belief.

So, that night was the true beginning of my Christian pilgrimage from earth to heaven. And this I knew beyond doubt I was truly born again and called by God into full time ministry in the church.

After giving my life to God I began to offer myself for ministry in the Baptist church. I became a youth leader, state secretary of the Home Missions department, and secretary of the Christian Endeavour department. I attended a weekly prayer meeting in the board room of the Baptist headquarters in Flinders Street where I can remember praying with the other members most fervently for nation-wide revival which (some 70 years later) still hasn't happened! (See my books, *This We Believe* and *Born in Oz,* about the Christian Revival Crusade for further details on this topic.)

Eventually I came to realise that spontaneous outpourings of the Spirit depend upon several different factors coming together - political, social, and cultural. In other words, the circumstances have to be dire enough for the mass of people to realise that the only answer can be found in divine intervention. Revivals never break out in times of peace and prosperity. In those times the best key to solving national problems is to plant a multitude of lively churches. If there is a church in revival in every suburb and town in the nation there will be a nation in revival as well.

Later, I discovered an amazing coincidence. On that same day, Easter Saturday 1949, the girl who would later become my wife, was also resolving to devote her life to Christ and the service of the church. She sealed this at the same time by having hands laid on her and receiving Holy Spirit baptism along with the sign of glossolalia – but three years were to pass by before we even met.

Teach me to do your will, for you are my God; may your Spirit lead me on level ground. Psalm 143:10

1949 SURPRISES

The American love song, *Two lovely blue eyes*, reached the top of the hit parade in the late 19th century but was soon superseded a few years later by a British parody recorded and released to an unsuspecting public in 1913. It was written and performed by the Music Hall comedian Charles Coborn. The opening lines of the chorus where:

> Two lovely black eyes,
> Oh! what a surprise,
> Only for telling a man he was wrong,
> Two lovely black eyes.

At the end of their quarrel those unwary sods were surprised by two blazing black eyes. This was certainly equalled by the astonishment lighting the eyes of a lady, a dear friend of the family named Grace, who came to me and asked what I wanted for my rapidly approaching 16th birthday. She was not a wealthy woman, but I knew she could readily afford the book I wanted, although she had no idea what that price would be.

I told her I wanted a *Thompson Chain Reference Bible*. She was twice startled. Once, by being astonished that a 16-year-old youth would request a Bible as a gift, and twice by the fact that the book would cost more than she anticipated. You can imagine her double surprise that a red-blooded Aussie male desired such a gift and that it was going to cost her at least ten pounds which in those days was about equal to one week's wage for an average worker.

She gulped and her countenance blanched! But she bravely and lovingly kept to her promise, opened her purse and handed me the ten pounds in cash. With great delight I went to the Baptist book shop and purchased my beautiful, leather bound, gilt edged, rice paper Bible which I carefully wrapped and put aside until the actual day of my birthday. On that day, after opening the gift, I proudly displayed it to Grace and listened for her admiring comments and declarations about what a wise young man I was.

I waited in vain! No doubt Grace did have some nice things to say, but they were much inferior to the superlative comments for which I was hoping. Grace has long since departed this life and I will never know what her real reaction was. But this I can tell you, that gilt garnished Bible became, over the next few years, an amazingly precious possession. I devoured every one of its Study Guides, its finely drawn maps, various Histories, Graphs, and other Guides. Indeed, I soon exhausted them and began to build on them.

I found a shop in downtown Adelaide that sold the finest and strongest rice papers. I was able to trim them to the correct size and with a thin strip of adhesive, glue them into the appropriate positions in that book. I developed outline studies on a large array of biblical dogmas, doctrines, and theological constructs, and over a period of several years the thickness of that Bible was doubled from its original size. My added studies included - justification by faith alone, sanctification, holiness (what it did and did not mean), baptism, Christian life, the return of Christ, and a variety of other subjects and topics, so that by the time I was 20 years of age, just over 70 years ago, I already had a thorough grip of a wide variety of sound doctrine. The truth I learned from that Thompson Bible and the truths I inserted into its pages became the irrefragable foundation of my life and ministry across the nearly eight decades since.

Moral? Learn this! Just as you cannot get anything more, or better, from a slice of bread than what you are prepared to put on it, neither can you get anything more out of Scripture than the quality of the diligence and toil you put into studying it. Make yourself rich in the Word of God and you will be rich indeed.

My son, if you accept my words and store up my commands within you, turning your ear to wisdom and applying your heart to understanding – indeed if you call out for insight and cry aloud for understanding, and if you look for it as for silver and search for it as for hidden treasure, then you will understand the fear of the Lord and find the knowledge of God. For the Lord gives wisdom; from his mouth come knowledge and understanding. Proverbs 2:1-6

1950 MILITARY

I groaned! There were hundreds of potatoes, and I had to peel them all knowing that when I had emptied the chute another avalanche of potatoes would arrive!

I was eighteen and had been drafted by the government for compulsory army training in the national service. The first three months were spent in Caloote in the Adelaide Hills which were to be followed by some two years of weekly parades at the army barracks in Keswick, and an annual two-week camp.

I was a terrible soldier. I loathed the regimentation of the army and performed every task listlessly and without interest which led to me being punished with many potato peelings. I had no special pride in my uniform and as a result on several occasions wore it incorrectly and had to march around the parade ground, sometimes accompanied by the jeers of other watching troops. My platoon was part of a thousand strong regiment of young men, some eager and some like myself reluctant.

The authorities, in their wisdom, had decided to erect true country showers on one edge of the campground. These were protected on the camp side only by a long canvas wall. The other side of the shower recess was open to the view of anyone who travelled down the road which ran along the perimeter fence. The showers were simply shower heads attached to a cold-water hose which I think we had to operate by turning the tap, or perhaps the showers were operated by a drawstring. In any case the water was very cold!

As we hastily tried to wash ourselves word got around the countryside that a large group of naked men could be seen showering and shivering at a certain time each morning, so it was not long before cars of laughing maidens were travelling down the road as we modestly turned our buttocks toward them! I presume the camp authorities quickly closed off the roadside of those showers but my memory of those mocking young ladies was so stark that my recollection of what followed has been obliterated.

You would have read in my 1949 story that I had become a deeply committed Christian at a Youth Camp at Clare. Now in Caloote, that zeal was still burning brightly, so as soon as I had arrived at the thirty-man hut that was to be my abode, I pulled out my large Thompson Bible and planted it beside my bed. I also found as many other ways as I could to demonstrate my Christian commitment. In the meantime, a report had begun to circulate among the scores of barracks that housed the regiment. It was rumoured that a number of professing Christians had been stripped naked by their platoon mates and bootblacked from head to toe. Alarm stirred inside me. If a similar attempt was made on me, should I meekly submit to it or furiously reject it?

My conscience was still undecided until one evening while I was preparing for bed four men approached me with bootblacking in their hands and I knew that my turn had come. I had an innate hatred of being manhandled, especially for no useful purpose, by a bunch of hooligans. Wrath arose in me. I grabbed the nearest weapon which was an empty glass soft drink bottle and threatened them: "I know one or two of you must succeed but even so one or two of you will be savagely wounded."

They looked at me. They imagined the first blow, which would have smashed the bottle, and then no doubt they imagined the second blow and the ghastly wound that might result from the jagged glass. They looked at the bottle. They looked at me. They saw the blazing anger in my eyes and backed away. It was the last time in my military career that anyone threatened me with physical violence. My fellow platoon members began to esteem me highly for thwarting those bullies rather than supinely submitting to their foul intentions. A very positive result from that encounter was the growing number of soldiers who sidled up to me and privately asked for my advice on a wide range of problems, including spiritual troubles.

At the time I measured more than six feet in height, and after working on my uncle's dairy farm for some two years I was all muscle. Indeed, on that farm I several times had to spend the whole day on a trailer my uncle was pulling with his tractor while I picked up and tossed into a spreader-hopper on the rear of the trailer a 187 pound (85 kilograms) bag of super phosphate. The first few bags were no trouble, but I can't deny that at the end of the day, with the trailer covered with empty sacks, I was somewhat weary. (You may be wondering how my experiences with appendicitis affected my brawn and my strength. Of course, they did have some effect but by the time of my draft to enter the army I had recovered much of my muscle tone.)

I keep remembering examples of what a poor soldier I was. There was a time when the army officers set up a long row of straw-filled replicas of enemy soldiers. New recruits were told to fix bayonets to our 303 Enfield Rifles, relics of the first World War, and to run as fast as we could down the paddock screaming hatred and abuse against the enemy and to thrust our bayonet deeply into the effigy we were charging. I refused to do it. Instead, I trotted quietly across the grass, tickled the effigy I was aiming for without penetrating its canvas skin and walked casually around it without affecting any damage at all upon it. In the meantime, my sergeant was screaming foul abuse at me which I chose to ignore. No doubt some penalty was imposed upon me for such a serious infraction, but I can't remember what it was. Perhaps it was just too awful! Probably more potato duty!!

Ordinary army life was so intolerable to me that I resolved to find ways to rid myself of it. I enrolled in a training course on camp hygiene and topped the state of South Australia in my final exam on that subject. I became an expert in setting up a urinal, digging drainage trenches, and in fashioning rubbish bins out of forty-gallon fuel tanks. This served to separate me from more of the humdrum aspects of military discipline. I also applied for admission to an elite signal corps to which I was entitled to belong because of several years' experience of making and operating various kinds of crystal sets, radios, and audio equipment in my teens. I was accepted and at once entered a comparative paradise.

We were barely a score of men under a lieutenant who lived in a separated, rather haphazard group of tents, pitched under shady trees in one corner of the camp site. We never had to participate in the endless marches and drills that the infantry men had to endure. On the contrary, we spent our time careering around the country laying down signal wires for sundry army installations, establishing communications systems, and making sure that all the field telephones were functioning correctly. Sometimes we would pass by a local pub and of course we would have to stop and refresh ourselves! Some in our company were old enough to order a beer, but we younger recruits had to be content with a soft drink. So, my last few weeks at Caloote were spent quite pleasurably.

Nonetheless, it was at Caloote where I first unconsciously broke a temperance pledge. I had made this vow some years before at primary school at the urging of a passionate Temperance Crusader who, I think, was called Mrs Meithke. It happened like this.

I became a perjurer when, one Sunday morning at Caloote, I heard that a church service would be conducted so I resolved to attend. Apart from the captain, who was also the camp chaplain, I was the only congregant. I was enjoying the service until it came time for the eucharist. The chaplain brought me a small biscuit, the symbol of the broken body of Christ, which I ate most earnestly. He then proffered me a silver goblet which in true Baptist fashion I took out of his hand and downed the entire contents while the Anglican chaplain stood there spluttering with indignation. Innocently I asked him what kind of grape juice was that as I had never tasted its like. Still deeply exasperated, and somewhat hoarse, the chaplain croaked, "Young man that was not grape juice that was Penfolds Royal Reserve Port Wine and you were supposed to do no more than take one small sip!"

So, there it is! I had to go to church to break my solemn pledge! And having broken it once there seemed to be no point in trying to renew it. However, across the 72 years since then, I have remained only a temperate drinker, finding pleasure in a variety of wines and spirits without ever getting even mildly tipsy.

When that camp ended and we returned home, we were obliged for the next two years of our national service to attend a weekly parade which I presume was held at Keswick. Except that in that first year I decided that the army and I should part ways. I had become a Conscientious Objector! I packed up my uniform, my rifle, and whatever else the army had issued me, caught the tram to Keswick Barracks, walked up to the Quarter Master's desk, dumped everything there and told him, "This is everything the army issued me, and I am done with military service. I decline to wear this uniform ever again or to attend any more parades."

He looked at me rather shocked and said, "You can't do this!"

"I have done it," I said with spurious interest, and turning on my heels, I left the barracks never to return.

In the meantime, I had secured a job with the Department of Works working on the Woomera Rocket Range. I was greeted by two members of the military police and driven up to my new office in an army jeep. They asked if I was willing to resume my military training which of course I declined. So, they drove off saying they would have to report the matter further and the penalty for refusing National Service was two years hard labour breaking rocks in the Adelaide Yatala Prison. I shrugged and said, "I won't be changing my mind," and bade them farewell.

During my time at Woomera one of my tasks was to drive along with the paymaster to pay all the workers. To do this I was required to carry a gun in case we were robbed. It wasn't until later that I realised how incongruous this was considering my stance as a conscientious objector!

Did I learn anything from all this? Presumably those events reinforced in me the need to be true to myself no matter what the cost. The boot-blacking incident at Camp Caloote with its godly outcome confirmed to me how right Jesus was when he fashioned a whip and violently drove the moneychangers out of the temple (John 2:13-17). My reluctance to thrust a bayonet into a straw dummy showed I was already on the way to becoming a conscientious objector.

Indeed, the overall biblical testimony on warfare, on the definition of justice and related matters, is rather ambiguous. People have markedly different opinions on which theology is better. God does not seem to have any problem with war according to the Old Testament, however, the New Testament promotes peace whenever possible. After my marriage and the birth of our son Dale, I realised I would fight to protect my family against any violence, so my views concerning conscientious objection changed dramatically.

In the Garden of Gethsemane Jesus said to his disciple, "Put your sword back in its place, for all who draw the sword will die by the sword." (Matthew 26:52) Violence is not the answer to life's conflicts but sometimes it is necessary. Before Jesus was arrested, he told his disciples to bring a sword with them for protection. (Luke 22:36) And Paul affirms that the magistrate bears the sword by the will of God, which means that in the apostle's eyes magistrates had a right under God to execute a death penalty. (Romans 13:4)

In the end I was not sentenced to hard labour. In point of fact, I did not hear from the military police again. My belief is that my Captain, of whom I shared a good relationship, must have spoken up on my behalf, or else delayed any proceedings until my service time was completed, which was not long. And as I later became a pastor (who were exempt from duty) it was resolved. My heavenly Father once more had looked out for my interests.

For the Word of God is living and powerful, and sharper than any two-edged sword, piercing even to the division of soul and spirit, and of joints and marrow, and is a discerner of the thoughts and intents of the heart. Hebrews 4:12

For though we live in the world, we do not wage war as the world does. The weapons we fight with are not the weapons of the world. On the contrary, they have divine power to demolish strongholds. 2 Corinthians 10:3-4

1952 PENTECOST

I was on the floor pleading with God to give me his heavenly gift. Then, as I had been taught in my Baptist church I stood on my feet, endeavouring to believe I had been given the fullness of the Holy Spirit, and went on my way. Across the previous weeks I had spent many hours in the same futile exercise with the same dry result. Nothing changed.

My quest had begun with the realisation that there was a huge discrepancy between my Christian life and the dynamic and rewarding life of the early Christians. This gulf was plainly the result of Holy Spirit Baptism. In other words, they had received 'the promise of the Father' whereas I had not. My regular boast was that where the Bible spoke, I would speak; but where the Bible was silent, I too would be silent. The early church after the first Day of Pentecost had enjoyed a powerful experience about which I knew almost nothing, I felt that I had no choice but to pursue it for myself. Hence, those many hours pursuant to Baptist belief when I prayed, often on my face on the floor, for my own personal baptism in the Holy Spirit.

In the meantime, I became acquainted with a Methodist brother and sister. Methodists, of course, practise the sprinkling of infants rather than baptism in water of true believers only. I resolved to challenge them on this but to my astonishment the couple told me they had already been baptised by full immersion. Startled, I demanded, "What church?" fully expecting them to name a Baptist church. Once again, they startled me by answering, "The National Revival Crusade, Adelaide." I demanded to know what kind of church it was and where it was located. I had never heard about this Pentecostal church which held its meetings in the Old King's Ballroom in downtown Adelaide. In fact, the term 'Pentecostal' baffled me. I had no idea what they were talking about, so they told me, and went on to share their marvellous experience of Holy Spirit baptism with the accompanying sign of glossolalia or 'speaking in other tongues'. (Acts 2:1-4)

How amazing! How astonishing! However, I told them that I would research the matter and when I had collected enough evidence that showed they were wrong (which I knew that they had to be) I would come back and share it with them. Since my personal resources were limited, I caught the tram on several occasions to the Adelaide Public Library and scoured every book I could find on Pentecostal churches and dogma. The end result? I was so irritated by the paltry arguments the authors were able to raise against the Pentecostal position that I became convinced of the opposite. So, over several more visits to the library, I repeated my search, this time looking for evidence supporting the Pentecostal position - namely that Holy Spirit baptism is a dynamic experience discrete from, and usually subsequent to, the new birth accompanied by glossolalia.

I went back to my Methodist friends, admitted my folly, and asked them how I should go about receiving the promise of the Father. They directed me to a Monday night prayer meeting, in those days held every week at Vic and Ciceley Schroeder's home in Prospect, Adelaide. The very next Monday saw me at that prayer meeting earnestly pleading for and expecting a powerful outpouring of the Holy Spirit and to speak in other tongues. And suddenly it happened! The Holy Spirit fell upon me and for the next three hours I rapturously enjoyed that river of living water flowing from my inmost being. (John 7:37-38)

I was in an ecstasy of worship pouring out my joy to the Lord in English but mostly in other tongues. Poor Vic and Cicely, although the other attendees had all gone home, they had to wait until my exuberance was exhausted, and I came off my knees and stood up. Still trembling, still prone to burst out in glossolalia, still alive in the Spirit, I allowed them to usher me out of their home and I returned to my own home in Woodville. Seventy-eight years later I still find deep refreshing, holy pleasure, and unalloyed joy, from the regular use of glossolalia.

For anyone who speaks in a tongue does not speak to people but to God. Indeed, no one understands them; they utter mysteries by the Spirit. But the one who prophesies speaks to people for their strengthening, encouraging and comfort. Anyone who speaks in a tongue edifies themselves, but the one who prophesies edifies the church. 1 Corinthians 14:2-4

1953 MOTORBIKE

In my 20th year I bought a BSA 250. An upgrade from my push bike but I didn't keep it long as I had a few bad moments when I could have been killed.

One day I was riding my bike along the Port Road toward Woodville when a large timber truck piled high with enormous tree trunks stopped suddenly in front of me and I braked as hard as I could. By the grace of God, I stopped! My head could feel the cool wood resting against my forehead. It is moments like these when you realise you were just a few seconds from the hand of death!

I sold the bike determined not to let anything come between me and the destiny God had determined for my life. I travelled to Melbourne by train for pastoral ministry in the Melbourne Christian Revival Crusade under Pastor Lloyd Longfield. I was ordained there and after Alison and I were married we went to our first church in Ballarat, Victoria. (See Ordained)

Years later my brother Barry had a terrible accident on his motorbike on that same road. It nearly killed him, but God was good and spared his life, but that is a story for him to tell. And years after that incident my son, Eric, also came close to entering the pearly gates when his motorbike slipped on the freeway and he went sliding down the road only to discover that God also had his hand outstretched to prevent death.

Be strong and courageous. Do not fear or be in dread of them, for it is the Lord your God who goes with you. He will not leave you or forsake you. Deuteronomy 31:6

The fear of the Lord is the beginning of wisdom, and knowledge of the Holy One is understanding. For through wisdom your days will be many, and years will be added to your life. Proverbs 9:10-11

1953 PROMOTIONS

An elder from the local Finsbury Park Baptist Church in Adelaide came up to the young man and with all solemnity said, "You will be Australia's next Elijah!" The ramifications, of course, were astonishing. If that young man was truly going to be a harbinger of the return of Christ, then his status in Christian history would be beyond measure. (Matthew 11:14) It meant that his place in church history would have no equal. It meant that as he developed and grew in ministry and spiritual power then the revelation of Elijah would become clearer and clearer and the return of Christ as King of kings and Lord of lords nearer and nearer. (Malachi 4:5-6)

No-one could ever say why a sobered minded and God-fearing Baptist elder would ever make such a shattering statement. Least of all to that young man! Happily, that young man was able to throw it aside with a chuckle, never for a moment taking it seriously. Quite the contrary, he deemed it a piece of ecclesiastical folly and dismissed the assertion from his mind. Who was that young man? Me! Imagine what enormous harm would have been done to my ministry if I had taken the matter seriously.

But then I received another remarkable promotion. I joined the Pentecostals (the Adelaide Christian Revival Crusade Assembly) where I received an astonishing promotion to twice the status of Elijah. An elder there told me that I was destined to be Australia's Elisha, an Old Testament prophet who had performed twice as many miracles as Elijah had done. Once again, who can imagine what harm that oracle might have done to me personally if I had taken it seriously. I am, of course, too whimsical in my temperament to be even mildly tempted to embrace such a surge of spiritual power.

Again, if that were not enough, I was rushed into an even more soaring ambition when an elder at that church told me my real destiny was to be Australia's next Billy Graham. Now that was a temptation! My reason was momentarily suspended, and I wondered how seriously I should take it. Billy Graham was in Australia ministering in a number of cities with great crusades, the largest being in excess of 140,000 people who attended his final rally in the Melbourne Cricket Grounds. And on many other occasions he had gathered audiences of over 100,000 people in the largest arenas in the land. Such phenomenal success garnered incredible media interest to the point where the *Australian Women's Weekly*, which then had the greatest penetration into the media market of any publication worldwide, called him the 'Debonair Divine' (*Australian Women's Weekly*, Edition February 25, 1959).

I learned my lesson about Billy Graham in a special ministerial meeting which attracted an audience of some 2,000 clergymen, civic leaders, and media representatives from around the country. I was seated in the larger congregational area in the second, or third row. Dr Graham spoke for about an hour, but I will come back to that in a moment. First let me say this -

Billy was renowned in his crusade meetings for holding up his Bible and quoting from this text with, "The Bible says!" which he declaimed with masterful authority. Of course, everyone supposed that he was actually reading from the Bible. So, imagine my surprise and amusement when after the meeting I walked up to the pulpit which was vacant at the time and glanced at his Bible. There I discovered that the book had been hollowed out and in its place a ring back notebook had been inserted. In reality this eminent preacher was quoting all the Biblical references which had been typed up with his preaching notes so that he was actually reading from his notes, instead of the Bible, both in Biblical references and in his sermon outline. This enabled great accuracy in his delivery.

This brings me back to the earlier declamation by the Pentecostal elder that I would be the next Billy Graham. I realised that this style of preaching from notes, greatly minimised the possibility of Dr Graham making any serious error in either Scripture or fact. It also explained why, and how, Dr Graham was able to confront every challenge that was thrust at him by a vicious media, challenging the viability or even the truth of many things that he was saying. Everything he said had a biblical basis.

After he had delivered his message to the press, clergy, and political figures, he opened the whole meeting to questions. The ravaging Melbourne press tried every way they could to tear him to pieces, calling into question his statements of facts, his claims of authenticity, and his spiritual right to make any sort of pronouncement. Dr Graham handled all their attacks with perfect aplomb and integrity. I realised then that I could never maintain his poise and dignity in the face of so many challenges.

At the time, I watched in a kind of horrified dismay as the media hounds snapped and snarled, barked and bit, at this evangelist. But he remained unruffled, undisturbed, and in perfect command of the situation, every riposte expertly wielded. It could easily have become a verbal riot but instead the situation remained tolerably intelligent. I at once renounced all ambition to be a nationally famous evangelist and became convinced to serve God and the church at a much lesser level.

So, what should I think of those rather foolish men who made such startling proclamations over my life, and who now have all of them already received the highest promotion they will ever enjoy by passing from earth to glory. Their shattering oracles, with no doubt excellent intentions, and who obviously saw my potential as a young man devoted to God, were indeed false. Nevertheless, I believe I have achieved what God had destined for my life.

Humble yourselves, therefore, under God's mighty hand, that he may lift you up in due time. Cast all your anxiety upon him for he cares for you. 1 Peter 5:6-7

In him we were also chosen, having been predestined according to him who works out everything in conformity with the purpose of his will, in order that we, who were the first to put our hope in Christ, might be for the praise of his glory. Ephesians 1:11-12

1954 LOVE

It was the most magical voice I had ever heard! At once I said to myself, "That is the girl I am going to marry." Yet I had not so much as seen her. It was a Monday night, and I was again attending the prayer meeting at Vic and Cicely's home. We were all praying aloud one by one, bringing various

petitions to the Lord. I was kneeling in front of an armchair with my head buried in a cushion and the last thing on my mind was a girlfriend and marriage. But no sooner did that lovely voice impassion my heart than all holy thoughts were driven out of my mind. I continued kneeling, apparently in prayer, but in a fever of impatience waiting for those loud warriors to desist their efforts so that at long last I could stand up and match a form and face to that extraordinary voice. I soon learned that her name was Alison, and one look was enough to lead me to her further acquaintance. The result?

After nine months of delightful courtship, we became engaged. Being poverty stricken the only engagement ring I could afford was one that belonged to my late father. My mother had died several years before but now Dad had met and begun to court a younger woman. The courtship had even progressed to the point where he persuaded her to marry him and bought her an expensive diamond engagement ring. But for some reason that engagement never occurred and when my father learned, despite my poverty I wanted to give Alison a truly sparkling and apparently costly ring, he offered to sell me his. Alison tells me that Dad charged me sixty pounds to be paid back in instalments. Finding this agreeable, I accepted Dad's terms and proudly presented the shimmering, alluring diamond to a delighted Alison. Then we experienced a further nine months as an engaged couple leading up to our marriage in the Goodwood Baptist Church in Adelaide, on March the 6th 1954.

We celebrated our 70th year of marriage this year (2024). Across those seven decades we have enjoyed a splendidly happy marriage, with few disagreements, many wonderful delights, and adventures in ministry, all filled with God's love and grace. I have often been asked, "Why has your marriage been so happy?" And without hesitation I would begin to rattle off several vital keys including:

First - Before we were ever engaged, we promised each other in the words of Scripture to never let the sun go down on our wrath. (Ephesians 4:26) I cannot deny that this promise caused a handful of very long days, where the sun had long gone down before we found a way to reconcile ourselves to each other and with God. But it did mean that every new day we awoke still amicably in love with each other, in a joyfully peaceful relationship, ready to begin each new day hand in hand with God.

Second - We determined not to become engaged until we knew each other as well as it is possible for any two persons to know each other before a physical union in marriage. So, we spent many hours, often of a summer's evening at the end of the Semaphore Jetty, exchanging views on everything we could think of - raising children, ministry and church commitments, finances, divorce, a call to overseas missions, household management (which in the main required me to attend to the outside of the house and the yard while Alison looked after the inside of the house, any children we might have, and the meals, as in those days very few women worked outside of the home), politics, social and educational levels (three of our parents were teachers, and both our fathers supported the Australian Football League and voted for the Labor party, although in later years both of us voted for other candidates, thus voiding our choices!); and I suppose many other pertinent issues that were important to us. Only after we discovered a high degree of unanimity in these matters did I "pop the question", and Alison replied with a firm, "Yes!"

Third - We agreed that patience with each other and unwavering tolerance were essential components of a happy marriage, in which purpose we were sometimes more and sometimes less successful. But mostly across the seventy years of our marriage we have managed to treat each other with courtesy and respect.

Fourth - We also agreed that the proverb, 'Manners maketh man' (from the 14th century), should be one of the rules that governed our life together. When I was still a young man, I heard about the shopper who held open the door of the department store for a lady. She mocked him saying, "I'm no lady, you don't need to hold open a door for me." And he replied, "Madam, you may not be a lady, but I am a gentleman, and I will hold the door for you!"

In my teen years I read through the apocryphal book, *The Wisdom of Jesus Ben Sirach,* which contains many passages on good manners. I thought it remarkable that two hundred years before Christ was born, the old Rabbi fully understood that good manners offend no one, but bad manners are repulsive to many. Thus, Sirach wrote -

> Do not reach for everything you see or jostle your fellow guest at the dish; judge his feeling by your own and always behave

considerately. Eat what is set before you like a gentleman; do not munch and make yourself objectionable. Be the first to stop for good manners' sake and do not be insatiable, or you will give offence. *Sirach 31:14-17*

If they choose you to preside at a feast, do not put on airs; behave to them as one of themselves. Look after the others before you sit down; do not take your place until you have discharged all your duties. Let their enjoyment be your pleasure, and you will win the prize for good manners. *Sirach 32:1-2*

Sirach's book, for several hundred years, was treated as Scripture by almost the entire church. There are some twenty quotations from it, or allusions to it, in the sayings of Jesus and in the New Testament letters. So well regarded was it that it came to be known as *Ecclesiasticus,* which means, the book of the church. Probably wisely the church fathers around the 5th century decided that *Ecclesiasticus* should no longer be part of the New Testament canon. Their decision was based on the fact that the book was never actually sanctioned by an apostle, nor had it the endorsement of a prophet. Also, it did contain ideas such as raw chauvinism, that is, it gave women a low status in family and in civic life.

I suppose there is no better gift that any young couple can give themselves than to follow the guideline below. It does indeed provide a framework in which a deeply happy marriage may flourish across a union lasting many decades.

The apostle Peter enjoins courtesy as a true Christian virtue.

Finally, all of you, be like-minded, be sympathetic, love one another, be compassionate and humble. Do not repay evil with evil or insult with insult. On the contrary, repay evil with blessing, because to this you were called so that you may inherit a blessing. 1 Peter 3:8-9

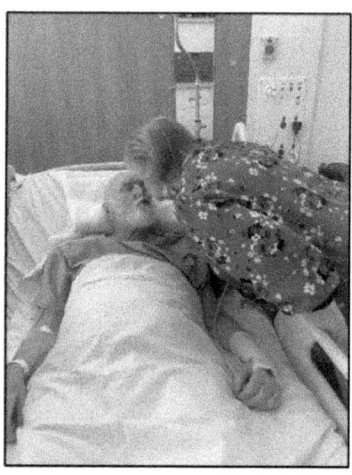

1954 WEDDING

I left Melbourne three days before our wedding (conducted in our hometown of Adelaide) as Leo and Belle Harris (founders of the CRC movement), who were in Ballarat at the time, offered to drive me to Adelaide for the wedding. Somehow I got to Ballarat, probably by train from Melbourne, and they picked me up. Somewhere on the road Leo's car broke down and we had to wait for two of the elders to come from the Adelaide church to pick us up and drive us back for the wedding. Those happenings delayed us for three days so that I did not arrive in  Adelaide until the Friday night before the wedding on March 6th. Alison had not seen me for two months, so she was anxious for us to meet as soon as I arrived. This was frowned on by the family as it was supposed to be bad luck to see your fiancé the night before the wedding. What rot! But I was exhausted anyway from the trip so she gave in.

When Alison first stepped into the vestry and the wedding march began to play, she saw me standing at the altar with the wedding party and stopped for a moment or two. After a separation of eight weeks and her not being able to see me until that moment she felt she was looking at a stranger. However, she summoned all her courage and as the *Wedding March* began, she quashed her nervousness and began to walk down the aisle toward me, accompanied by her father James McIntyre.

Belle made the service particularly memorable for us by fulfilling our request to sing a love-filled rendering of four verses of the *Consecration Hymn* by Frances Ridley Havergal –

Take my life and let it be
Consecrated Lord to thee!
Take my moments and my days,
Let them flow in ceaseless praise.

Take my hands and let them move
At the impulse of thy love;
Take my feet, and let them be
Swift and beautiful for thee.

Take my will and make it Thine,
It shall be no longer mine.
Take my heart it is Thine own;
It shall be Thy royal throne.

Take my love; my Lord, I pour
At Thy feet its treasure store;
Take myself, and I will be
Ever, only, all for Thee.

Alison and I like to think of ourselves as both thoroughly modern yet quite traditional. Pastor Leo used the usual wedding vows based on the old Anglican Prayer Book, where the couple vow lifelong fidelity along with other important promises. Now, here we are 70 years later still happily married and very content with our life together.

Let me tell you a story. A young couple was being counselled by an ancient Chinese philosopher. They asked him about the key to building a successful marriage. He spoke not a word. Instead, he took up a blank parchment and began to fill the page with Chinese characters. When he was done, still without saying a word, he handed the sheet to the couple. They took it and with eager curiosity began to read what the sage had written. To their surprise the parchment contained only one word, repeated over, and over again. What was that word? Simply: *Patience*.

To patience, I would add tolerance, and a willingness to forgive any presumed offence. An earlier anecdote has already told how Alison and

I have applied these rules by solemnly promising each other to heed Paul's injunction -

Do not let the sun go down while you are still angry. Ephesians 4:26

Gracious words are a honeycomb, sweet to the soul and healing to the bones. Proverbs 16:24

Be completely humble and gentle; be patient, bearing with one another. Make every effort to keep the unity of the Spirit through the bond of peace. Ephesians 4:2-3

1954 HONEYMOON

Neither the Chant nor the McIntyre families were wealthy, so we couldn't afford a lavish wedding breakfast. Alison's mother, helped by a number of family friends and church members, prepared a rich and overflowing feast that was spread on trestles in the decorated backyard of her house. I still have visions of that vast array of delicious delicacies but at the time I was too excited to do more than nibble a few crumbs. Later I learned that Alison had been the same, so that a few hours later, on the Overland express from Adelaide to Melbourne, we became quite hungry. The basket of food that had been especially prepared for us had been left behind!

The train only travelled so far as Bordertown when it broke down and we had to wait for a replacement train, which was an old red rattler set of carriages pulled by a diesel locomotive. This carried us, not to Melbourne, but to Geelong! From there we took a regular suburban train to Melbourne and then on to Moorabbin where we had a small apartment.

By this time it was 2pm and we had been starving for more than 24 hours. (There was no food available on trains or at stations in those days.) A memorable beginning to our marriage!

Our first quarrel took place that first week in Moorabbin. We were unpacking our clothing and Alison demanded all the drawers in the only cupboard in our bed-sitting room. I was righteously incensed and demanded my fair share of the drawer space. Alison stormed off to our tiny kitchen and waited for me to apologise. I, of course, being a paragon of virtue joined her after a while with the intention of affecting a reconciliation. She was at first a little reluctant, but we soon forgave each other for the heated words we had spoken and came to an amicable division of the drawers, and all was well. (What children we were! I was almost 21 and Alison almost 20!)

We had only one week to enjoy our honeymoon before I had to return to my job as a clerk in the office of BP (British Petroleum). So, we tried to pack as much into each day as we could. For a honeymoon event we boarded an aeroplane for a one-hour joy flight over Melbourne. The plane was an old DC3 which sat on the tarmac with its tail almost in the dust while its nose pointed skyward at an alarming angle. When the engines started with a terrifying roar the entire plane shook and trembled and Alison thought it was going to fall apart. Being somewhat nervous myself I gladly accepted her clutching hand and we sat together bracing ourselves for the ordeal of take-off. The plane lurched forward, quickly gathered speed, and was soon high in the air flying comfortably level so we could look out the window and admire the stunning lights of Melbourne shining brilliantly through the night sky. Melbourne's lights were unusually bright that night because it was the week of the Queen's visit. Unfortunately, we never saw her majesty in person as she had already left Melbourne and flown to Adelaide.

Alison said, "Boo!" to a lion at the Melbourne Zoo during that same week. I found her exclamation quite charming, was delighted by it, and burst out laughing. She took instant umbrage at what she deemed as mockery and began to rebuke me, but I quickly interrupted, assured her it was a laugh of love not of scorn, and we shared a quick kiss, and all was forgiven.

I suppose there were many other things we did during that week and Alison has one very happy memory of me purchasing a bunch of violets and presenting them with my deepest love. From then on they became her favourite flowers and thereby hangs another tale.

But on this we agree, our week together on honeymoon was wonderful and now, 70 years later, produces only a warm glow of happy memories.

Let him lead me to the banquet hall and let his banner over me be love.
Song of Solomon 2:4

1954 VIOLETS

I have always been an irremediable romantic with an attraction to Regency days when men of wealth wore immaculately tailored jackets and the softest cotton shirts with lace at their sleeves, flowing neckcloths, a single gold signet ring on their hand, and inscribed pocket watches and snuff boxes. These were the days when women were cherished beyond price and lived to please their husbands. The clergy were drawn from the upper classes and lived lives of distinction. It was the golden age of manners and decorum. Of course, this is a romanticised view, there were also many indignities and suffering amongst the people of that era. But suffice to say the romantic view of life often sustains us through the hardships that we all experience.

During my courtship of Alison, she was the beneficiary of this romantic side. Long walks on the jetty, little attentions and compliments designed to please, I was deeply in love. This pleased her mightily. However, once we were married, I relaxed any romance and settled down to staid married life. At first Alison was puzzled and then indignant and finally resigned to the departure of the previous romantic gestures as I focussed on the business of building my ministry. There was one area that she felt would not tax my focus too much – she wanted flowers. I had discovered her favourite flowers were violets and during our engagement had indulged this wish as often as I was able.

Buying flowers had descended to the depths of oblivion as the work that was ahead of me was constantly before us. Her complaints about my lack of romantic zeal achieved what happens to most men, a resistance to be pressured to conform to expectation. Little did she know that she was frustrating what I was already planning to do, that is, purchase her a bunch of her favourite flowers - violets! But, of course, no sooner did she present her repeated requests than I had to scratch my plans lest she feel there was no spontaneity in my gift. This happened on numerous occasions.

When our daughter Sharon turned twelve years of age, she realised what had been happening. So, she arranged with her mother not to hint that she would love a posy of violets or any other flower. Consequently, after a while when some special occasion arose, I was able to spontaneously give Alison her heart's desire. Ironically, when the right occasion arose, violets were not in season, so I had to purchase an African violet in a pot and give it to her with many expressions of unfailing and undying love.

Since that day it has been my delight to give Alison many more flowers and other gifts over the years we have been married. A wise and circumspect man will freely give the women they love – mothers, sisters, wives – the honour due to these givers of life. And to remember that old adage, 'happy wife, happy life'!

Husbands, love your wives, as Christ loved the church and gave himself up for her. Ephesians 5:25

The way of a fool is right in his own eyes, but a wise man listens to advice. Proverbs 12:15

1955 ORDAINED

Following our wedding we settled in Melbourne and began to attend Lloyd Longfield's CRC church. Alison and I were filled with godly zeal to begin our ministry together and it was not long before the elders and pastors gathered together and I was ordained for the ministry (at that time the wives weren't included). They also prayed for my speech impediment. This seldom troubled me when I was preaching but when conversing all speech would suddenly seize up and I would be left gaping like a codfish. I learned to overcome this obstruction by choosing different words to say which released the blockage. For many years I could still feel it hovering in the background, but it hasn't bothered me for a long time now.

Our first pastorate was to a small church in Ballarat. We travelled from our flat in Moorabbin each Friday night, taking the train journey of three hours, and returning on Sunday afternoon. This continued for seven or so months when we received the invitation to go ahead and take over the church. We moved to an apartment in Main Street, Ballarat. The church had 21 members and for the first year we enthusiastically engaged with this new life of pastoring, finding employment, producing our first child, and getting established. I found work at Myers in the Men's Department. As I waited for customers, I would often mentally review the coming Sunday sermon. One morning, while I was reflecting on a theme and accompanying Scriptures, gaining revelation and oratory, in the distance, I heard a little boy say to his mother, "Is that man real or is he a dummy?" Startled, I quickly straightened up and began tidying the shelves and the little boy got quite a shock.

We learned a great deal about human nature while ministering in this small town. Because our church was Pentecostal there were some folk in Ballarat who were highly sceptical of what occurred during our services. We hired a small building called the Fidelity Hall which was used through the week by the public and on Saturdays for parties. As a result, on Sunday mornings we made sure we arrived early as there was always a disastrous mess left from the night before. One Sunday I was standing on a chair straightening a picture when one of our detractors peered suspiciously through the window to see what we were up to. Much to our amusement we learned later the informer was convinced I had been 'crawling up the wall' in a Pentecostal frenzy.

So, our first year went by and we gained a few and lost a few and by the end of that year we still had a congregation of 21 people. The next year we had two breakthroughs. One was the unlikely event that a group from the Church of England, just up the hill, had started a prayer meeting seeking to be filled with the Holy Spirit. They were very earnest and prayed together early each morning before going to work. God answered their prayer by sending them down the hill to us where they were filled with the Holy Spirit one by one. After this glorious experience they were no longer acceptable to their Church of England congregation, so they joined us.

The second breakthrough was that the wife of the editor of the *Ballarat Courier* was healed from serious heart trouble. She was a great witness, praising God for his healing power, and brought many of her friends to our church to experience the power of God. So, we grew to around 60 people and things were going well, or so we thought. However, there were half a dozen original members who had decided they did not like the direction the church had gone and no longer valued our ministry. They called a meeting and told us the church wanted us to leave. This came as a shock, but in our naivete we believed them. We were still in our early twenties, young and idealistic. We had invested three years of ministry into the Ballarat congregation, and it was going well. Seeking advice from our superior, he suggested that perhaps it was time to gain further experience elsewhere. We tendered our resignation only to discover that the bulk of the church were highly dismayed. They urged us to remain, but it was too late and to avoid a split we decided we should leave.

So, with heavy hearts, we packed up our possessions and with our baby son, Dale, travelled from Ballarat to the Springvale/Dandenong area. I quickly found a job with a furniture store taking care of their accounting books and planted a church in Catani with a few other enthusiastic Christians from the area. These few years were a great training ground in developing pastoral and preaching skills, listening to the Holy Spirit, and serving God's people. But it was also a time of great sorrow in the death of our second son, Gavin James, who died shortly after birth. We questioned God during this time but realised the journey of any Christian is fraught with great joy and sadness, and we were not immune from this truth.

Following Catani, we were bidden to return to Adelaide as Leo Harris requested we take a full-time job serving back in the CRC Adelaide Assembly. We didn't know it at the time, but this was also part of God's plan to protect Alison's health and wellbeing during the pregnancy of our daughter, Sharon.

And we know that for those who love God all things work together for good, for those who are called according to his purpose. Romans 8:28

God is not unjust; he will not forget your work and the love you have shown him as you have helped his people and continue to help them. Hebrews 6:10

1955 PREACHING

When I first began preaching, I realised that my voice was set at an awkward pitch which felt strained after a while. I began to practise by striding through the house and declaiming the Word of God, Dante's Inferno, or a Shakespearean Sonnet. Losing one's voice to vocal strain is a very real concern for public speakers, singers, and actors. Leo had conveyed to me strategies on how to vary your tone from high to low, soft to loud, whisper to shout – to save one's voice from dreaded nodules that can lead to a total incapacity to speak. Sometimes I would  gargle with lemon juice and olive oil to alleviate any soreness. After some years of using these techniques, I was able to teach for an hour without even a glass of water!

Many preachers have found themselves in trouble preaching frequently and finding their voice to gradually fail. Several preachers I have known over the years have had to spend many months in silence to repair the damage to their vocal cords, writing down requests and responses using pen and paper (this was before the advent of tablets and ipads).

Whenever I heard Leo's sonorous voice and how he could throw his voice to the back of a crowded meeting, I would complain to the Lord for not giving me such resonant tonal capacity. However, I did what I could to improve my own feeble attempts and show that God can use for his glory even the most humble of preachers. I continued vocal exercises and made a conscious practise in my platform ministry to use a low register, or I would find myself screeching by the end of the sermon!

Eventually, I must say, through constant practice I became a very proficient speaker. I am sure those who heard my early attempts in younger days were now impressed by the practised ease of my preaching skills. I enjoyed painting vivid illustrations using the English language which, I am told, enthralled the listeners and brought to life Bible scenes. I was amazed that people remembered these sermons for many years which could cause some embarrassment. In New Zealand, many years ago now, I determined I would preach on a sermon that was well-received in Adelaide 20 years before, entitled *Shamgar and the Ox Goad*. Just before the meeting began a little old man approached and exclaimed, "I remember you! I heard you preach twenty years ago on *Shamgar and the Ox Goad*, and I've never forgotten it." He then proceeded to describe the whole sermon, every point, all the way through. Dismayed, I hastily changed what I had planned to preach that night to an equally appropriate sermon.

I kept a book, for many decades, which you can still find in the safe in my office. It holds records on the title of the sermon, the date, and church where it was preached. I'm sure there are many other ministers of the Word of God who do the same thing.

One thing which surprised Alison and me during our ten years in the USA was that travelling pastors would hone one series of sermons on one particular subject which they then repeated consistently as they travelled around America. They could do this as it is such a vast country with thousands of churches. These ministers of the Word became known for their speciality. Because of this tendency I was often asked, "What is your speciality, what do you teach?" To which I would reply, "I preach the whole counsel of God. Just tell me what your church needs and I will preach on that whatever it is." I have always been a strong believer on preaching the whole of God's Word, not just personal doctrine.

Another thing we noticed as I ministered in many states in the USA was that young pastors had not been taught the practical aspects of pastoring a flock. Many of them didn't know how to pray for people to be filled with the Spirit. They hesitated to preach on healing and to pray for their people when they were sick. This gave me many opportunities to teach and train on these essential roles of a pastoral ministry.

After discussing these issues with other Christian leaders, we realised that the Bible colleges were using theologians who had never had any practical training in running a church. As a result, the new pastors were well schooled in Scripture but not in practical understanding of how God works in the lives of the people in their congregations. A missionary might speak to the students but that was the only glimpse they had of the reality of spiritual warfare. This was a sad lack in the Bible colleges we had a chance to visit, in both mainstream and Pentecostal schools. In fact, some students had a deficit in Scripture also. They were taught themes and subjects but not how to unpack the Word of God, this was left for the students to develop themselves. Some of these new pastors were excited to learn about Vision College and the opportunity to study Bible-based texts that expounded on Scriptural understanding.

Preach the Word; be prepared, in season and out of season, correct, rebuke, and encourage – with great patience and careful instruction. 2 Timothy 4:2

1955 CHILDREN

It is only when you have your first child that you begin to understand, in some small way, the beneficent love God has for humanity. In the same ways you recognise that no matter what your child does, whether they are naughty or nice, this doesn't come into it. Your love doesn't change. When I held my first son, Dale, enclosed in my arms, I was overwhelmed with love for him. And I was somewhat concerned that if we were blessed with more children whether I would have enough love for them as well. When that time came, I discovered another truth. Love is exponential. No matter how many children there are, the heart expands to embrace them.

The trust an innocent child has in a parent is so fragile and precious. I remember in a busy department store Dale became separated from me for a few moments. He didn't hesitate but called loudly for his Dad. Of course, I swooped him up into my arms and he relaxed immediately, in complete trust that Dad would take care of him. As he grew and showed extraordinary cleverness, I was amazed at his capacity for understanding difficult concepts. I found myself able to discuss the theory of relativity with my young son, by then around eleven years of age. At twenty, he was convinced he already knew more than me! I have to acknowledge that he is highly intelligent and has outstripped me in several areas of expertise, achieving a Doctor of Philosophy degree at Melbourne's Monash University in his twenties!

However, we were by no means perfect parents in raising Dale, or our other offspring. There was not the information readily available on parenting that you can easily access today. Alison was told that, "No matter if you make some mistakes, as long as you love them all will be well." Well, that is naïve as any parent of a child will tell you. Mistakes can be costly in many respects, and it is a wise parent that seeks counsel, information, and benefits in wisdom from their own and others' failures.

One memorable occasion occurred when Dale was making a piercing cry of indignation and for good reason. Alison did not know what to do for him. Being the father, I was not expected to have any better wisdom but checking over his body I found that Alison had inadvertently pinned Dale to his nappy. He received an extra measure of love from both of us on that day!

When we were first married, one of my nicknames for Alison was, 'Bubaz'. Until Dale arrived and then he became my 'Bubaz'! Alison felt that she had taken second place. However, I had been unprepared for how much love I would feel towards my children. My little son generated a prevailing joy within me, and I took great enjoyment in hugging and kissing and playing with him. As Dale grew, I took delight in his growing intellect.

But as I said the parenting journey has many pitfalls. We were new at this role and as with any novice there are bound to be errors of judgment. Some of these had a lasting impact on Dale. We were aware of our role as leaders not just in the church but also in the community. In our enthusiasm to teach Dale good manners we did not see the ramifications. He had to fight off bullies at school, but we had taught him not to fight but to always find a peaceable solution. At one school, Dale complained that he had become a punching bag for the female students as we had taught him never to hit a girl. We modified this instruction so that in future he could warn the assailant that if they continued to assault him, he would respond in kind. Our children need to know that they can defend themselves. So, that resolved this problem but there would be others.

Our zeal for God and our service towards his people often took prevalence over family life. We moved frequently in our desire to fulfil God's will for our family, but this meant that Dale attended many different schools in his primary years. It never occurred to us to home-school which would have alleviated this issue, so it was Dale who had to establish himself over and over. Alison was unwell during these years with two failed pregnancies and then the death of our baby son, Gavin. This had a profound effect on Dale that we did not comprehend. The years following World War 2 were ones of soldiering on, no matter what crises were faced. So, we kept moving forward come what may.

After Sharon was safely born, we rediscovered our joy. Alison tells me that Sharon is a 'rainbow' baby, born after the loss of a child. (The term is attributed to author Shannon Adler who said – "After every storm, there is a rainbow.") Sharon's birth also followed nine months of Alison's confinement, unable to leave her bed for the fear of miscarriage, she spent her time knitting, reading and entertaining Dale, during this time I was busy ministering as the Senior Pastor of the Adelaide church while Leo was in the USA. We had prayed earnestly for a successful birth and when Sharon was born there was great hope after a time of distressing grief. She was indeed a rainbow in our world.

We did enjoy some happy family times – visiting the Fairy Penguins on Phillip Island, sitting quietly with Dale on the sandy beach waiting for the penguins to make their way to their nests for the night. Dale informed us that this was his earliest memory, so it made a deep impression on him as well. Later, when we lived in Tasmania, we had many winter trips to the snow to one of the mountains surrounding Launceston. Saturday was picnic day with other church families often joining us. These excursions were necessary as Sunday was always taken up with church ministry.

Our only pet was a cat, Bruffy, who was a close companion for Dale. Her name was a combination of the words brother and fluffy. We discovered she was a girl after she produced quite a few sets of kittens over the years; and lived to the ripe old age of eighteen years. She was very clever and always knew when we were packing to go away, trying to stop us by getting into our suitcase and lying on our clothes. Also, when I was trying to write she would come and sit on my papers so I would take notice of her.

Dale inherited my love of music and began playing the Spanish guitar around the age of seven and did quite well. When he became a teenager with some money of his own, he bought a machine called a 'fuzz box' to distort the sound of his guitar. He loved this sound, but it was not a noise we grew to enjoy! Dale has retained his eclectic style; music gave him an opportunity to relax away from the computer program suite he devised and sold around the world.

All the challenges Dale faced made him stronger and more determined. As he matured, he put himself through Hobart University and then Monash, finishing a PhD in Ancient Greek. He taught for a few years before finding an opportunity in computer software programming to enhance his skills. His extensive studies took him away from the family and we only saw him intermittently through the following years.

Ministry was all important to us and we found it challenging to combine family life and our work in the church. The needs of the congregation often came first, and our children spent many hours waiting for us to finish meetings, conversations, and events. Alison used many of our experiences to write a book, along with some fellow pastors' wives, called *Unsung Heroines* which has been, and continues to be of great help to young parents. These days, at least in the CRC Churches International, the education requirements to pastor are greatly changed. Now the pastor's wife often goes to Bible school and gets ordained along with her husband to work as a partnership in both home and ministry life.

It has always been a sadness to me that many Pastor's kids leave the church as adults and disappear into the world, angry and disillusioned with feelings of neglect. Our generation was focussed on building God's Kingdom with whatever sacrifice was necessary. However, as we are encouraged in the letter Paul sends to Timothy – as fathers and pastors we are commanded to be gentle, not quarrelsome; to rule our homes well so those outside of our families can give a good account of us. (1 Timothy 3:1-13) So our testimony begins at home – do our children feel loved and valued, do we take time to teach, listen and play with these small new Christians? Although church life is a ministry, it is also a job, and balance is critical for our offspring to value the Christian life.

Train up a child in the way he should go and even when he is old, he will not depart from it. Proverbs 22:6

Impress these commandments (the Christian way of life) on your children. Talk about them when you sit at home and when you walk along the road. Deuteronomy 6:6-7

1956 SAVED

There have been several moments in my life when I became contiguous to heaven's gates! During our third year of ministry in Ballarat we were given a small 1938 Hillman Minx with a Dickie Seat instead of a boot. It was so old it had a hole in the wooden floor which we jokingly called our air conditioner. However, we thanked God for his kind provision and threw ourselves with renewed vigour into the work of the church. By winter we were ready for a holiday and decided to visit our parents in Adelaide, 400 miles away.

We drove out of Ballarat along the magnificent *Avenue of Honour*, a memorial avenue of trees planted by the relatives of soldiers killed during World War 1. Alison remembers that our conversation centred on the puzzling aspects of divine guidance, which subject I have reflected upon many times. Alison wanted to know - How can you be sure that you are in the will of God? How can we know that this trip is part of his will for us? Does God expect us to ask him about every little thing, or should we just live our lives normally, and only ask his guidance for specific or important things?

I pondered these deep questions and finally said, "I asked an older pastor about that very thing recently and he gave me an answer I'll never forget.

It's like this - you should first pray and ask for God's guidance, and then simply believe that he has heard your prayer. After that, it becomes God's task to make sure you are in his will." And then Alison questioned, "But what if you aren't in his will?" To which I responded, "Then our Heavenly Father will manoeuvre circumstances until you are in his will. So long as you trust God, the obligation is no longer yours, but his."

Sometimes revelation comes through wrestling with the principles in God's Word – this answer satisfied Alison, but I can tell you that, over the years, I have grappled with Scripture until I was satisfied that I had the correct interpretation. I never relent until I have the peace that passes all understanding. As we sped through the vast Australian countryside, I thanked God for his Word and all the wisdom that it contains if we but search for his truths. As it happened it would not be long before this faith and wisdom would be put to the test.

A few days after arriving in Adelaide and sharing a joyful reunion with our families, we decided to take a trip to Victor Harbour. This is a beautiful part of the South Australian shoreline, and a popular picnic spot. The air was chilly, but the sky was blue, the sun was brightly shining, and it was a perfect day for a country drive. We motored through the hills, revelling in the glorious views of the rolling hills and ocean vistas stretched out before us.

The time together at the beach, with our little son Dale, was everything we had hoped for, and when we finally packed up to return home, we were weary but rejuvenated. It had been delightful to play on the beautiful white sands, and to paddle with him in the salt water. As we travelled through the twisting winding hills on our return journey we noticed a sign on the side of the road, 'Steep incline around next bend'. Naturally, I expected to find a sharply rising hill after the next turn in the road so accordingly accelerated to accommodate the slope. Alas, instead of an upgrade we found to our horror that we were plunging down a steep decline! Not an incline! Our car only had mechanical brakes, and when the drums were hot after a long trip, as they were now, they failed to stop the car. We were travelling too fast. We were gaining speed. The brakes were ineffective, and we could not make the next corner. I was sure our time had come, and we were about to meet our glorious Lord by plunging over the edge of the cliff to smash on the valley floor below. Alison remembers me distinctly crying out, "Lord, here we come!"

But God had not finished with us yet! Just as the car was about to go over the precipice it stopped! Just like that! We sat there, shaken but alive, praising God for deliverance from a terrible death! There was absolutely no reason why our car should have halted at that moment. We could only suppose God had intervened to arrest the vehicle. One moment we were travelling at high speed, and the next we had come to an abrupt halt - yet we were not jolted, nor hurt in the slightest. We backed up slowly and then, with trembling but thankful hearts, travelled the remainder of our way home. How grateful we were to the Lord for this sign that we were indeed in his will and under his protection! This would not be the only time we experienced such a strong example of his hand on our lives.

Sometime later we were travelling back to Ballarat through the Adelaide Hills and looking forward to another year of fruitful work for the Lord. Suddenly we saw a car wheel roll past us, trundling to a stop and leaning crazily on the fence that bordered the road. At the same time, our car lurched, and we realised with startled surprise that we had been watching one of our own back wheels! I stopped the vehicle and jumped out to view the damage. Alison remembers me thanking God it was a back wheel. Had it been a front wheel we could have been killed or been the cause of a horrifying accident with oncoming traffic. To my embarrassment I had never learned the mechanics of maintaining or repairing a car. I did not even know if we had any tools onboard, or even a carjack. We began to look.

But God, who is always watching, intervened once more by the arrival of a police car which pulled up beside us. They had seen the whole thing. You can imagine my dismay when I had to confess what a novice I was this being our first vehicle but also realising I had failed in protecting my family from potential catastrophe. Alison remembers with relief the policeman chuckling and retrieving their wheel jack and tools showed me how to return the wheel back to its proper place, and furthermore, gave me a lesson in mechanics on how to tighten the nuts on all the other wheels, patiently explaining that it is a good idea, before starting on a long journey, to check your wheels - especially on a car built in 1938!

Feeling a little foolish, we thanked the two officers heartily and continued on our way. How blessed we felt that it was a rear wheel, and not one of our front ones, that had come off first; and how grateful were we for understanding policemen with a sense of humour. Did the Lord arrange for the police car to travel behind us or was it a fulfilment of the promise to trust him in all things. These things are a mystery, but I say along with the psalmist and Paul –

For he will command his angels concerning you to guard you in all your ways. Psalm 91:11

And we know that in all things God works for the good of those who love him, who have been called according to his purpose. Romans 8:28

1958 SHOTGUN

Getting a belly full of shotgun pellets is, I should imagine, a terrible way to die. That peril confronted me when the pianist of our newly planted church in Ballarat came to me saying that her husband was angrily opposed to her attending the church. He had shown her a double barrel loaded shotgun and told her that if I dared to visit their home, he would shoot me like a wild pig. She begged me not to go to her house but of course I could not let this unbelievably foolish man prevent me from doing what I considered my pastoral duty. I told her that I would visit them that very night.

Resolutely, I turned up at the appointed hour, knocked politely on the door, which in a few moments was opened by my pianist. She showed me the loaded shotgun leaning against the wall just inside the front door and tried to persuade me to go away. I had to refuse this request and insisted that she allow me to enter and to confront her husband, which I did. Entering their lounge room, I found him seated there and began a conversation which (I think) continued for some time. What did we talk about? I can't remember. I do recall, however, that I discreetly ignored the shotgun peril, not because I was afraid to mention it, but because, if I may echo Paul in his second letter to the Corinthians, I find it hard to tolerate fools. Having called the man's bluff, he continued to stay away from the church and my pianist continued attending and playing for services without any further interference from him.

About a decade later, when I was pastoring in Launceston, Tasmania, I had to confront another man, this time with a .303 rifle, who threatened to blow my head off my shoulders. His wife attended our church, along with their children, but he was an unbeliever and refused to attend any of our services. He sometimes hid her car keys so that she could not attend unless she could find a friend to pick her and the children up, bring them to the Sunday morning service, and take them home again. On this particular day, he was standing aggressively outside the church with a rifle in his hands, yelling out my name, saying he would shoot me if I dared to show my face.

We were in the middle of a church service and merrily singing a popular hymn. An anxious elder from the church approached and told me about the rifleman and his threats. To use the proverbial expression, this was to me like a 'red rag to a bull'. At once I decided to go out and confront him. I told the elder what I planned to do and bade him that as soon as I had left the building to ensure that all the doors and windows were locked and to keep all the people safely inside until the crisis had been averted. I also told the elder as soon as the hymn was finished to interrupt the service, tell the people what was happening, and call them to prayer.

In the meantime, I marched outside half expecting that the whole matter was a hoax. I soon discovered my error! The man was there alright and carrying a deadly weapon. I was familiar with this rifle as I had used the same in the army when I was training as a soldier. Also, during my time on my uncle's farm I had often gone shooting rabbits and other pests with a .22 rifle. As soon as he saw me, he began to raise the gun, but I was quicker than he expected. Striding straight up to him, I seized the gun and wrenched it out of his hands. I opened the breach, removed the bullet that was in there and then emptied the magazine. Putting all the bullets into my pocket I handed the gun back to him and then threatened him with the severest penalties the law could impose unless he left the church grounds immediately.

He was so bewildered by this reversal of his intentions that he obeyed my words, turned around, and stalked off. When I saw him get into his car and drive away, I waited another minute or two to make sure that he was truly gone then went back into the church to the relief of the congregation and told the people that all was well. That man had never crossed my path before, nor have I ever seen him since. My rebuke and my fierce anger at his stupidity must have been enough, if not to make him afraid of me, at least to display the wrath of God. He continued to prevent his wife from going to church but she managed, in the main successfully, to defy him in this way. Eventually they divorced so she was then free to attend church without any opposition.

I've often wondered whether I would still be so brave as I was in these two instances. My feeling is that I would not. There is a popular saying to the effect that God gives to every believer whatever they need to complete his purpose for their lives at the time. I needed the courage to confront possible, if not probable death on those two occasions. The threats they embodied no longer face me, so I no longer need that same measure of divine grace. That is why I can look back on those two fools and those essentially empty threats with a degree of amazement at the courage that imbued me each time. So, right now I don't have that level of intrepidness. If an occasion should today arise in which the service of Christ or his church demanded that I risk possible harm; then whatever grace I need for this occasion I would embrace it and sally forth to do my duty. That is, if I could, considering my present frail body and ninety-one years, the angels would need to assist me.

Do you not know? Have you not heard? The Lord is the everlasting God, the Creator of the ends of the earth. He will not grow tired or weary, and his understanding no one can fathom. He gives strength to the weary and increases the power of the weak. Even youths grow tired and weary, and young men stumble and fall; but those who hope in the Lord will renew their strength. They will soar on wings like eagles; they will run and not grow weary they will walk and not be faint. Isaiah 40:28-31

1958 MIRACLE

While we were ministering in the Springvale/Dandenong area I came down with a bad attack of a jaundice-like illness. The doctor was called as I was unable to get out of bed. I truly felt like I was dying. The doctor examined me, went to the foot of the bed, and pronounced I would be dead before I was thirty if I didn't get out of the ministry and take on a less stressful job. He then turned on his heel and left with no comforting word or alternative suggestion leaving behind two very shattered young people. Alison was holding my hand at this dire pronouncement. After he was gone, we prayed for God's intervention as I had no intention of giving up preaching for one weekend, let alone a lifetime! I resolved to submit an advert to the local press, advertising that I was going to preach on, *Christ the Great Physician,* the following Sunday. Alison posted this off to the newspaper and it was duly inserted in Saturday's newspaper, advertising that the next day I would be preaching at the hall we were using for our meetings at that time.

I resolved to remain in bed for the rest of the week and rest until Sunday morning. The elders of the church came to my bedside and prayed vigorously for healing. I arranged for one of the elders of the church to pick me up on Sunday morning. He dutifully arrived at the appointed time and I climbed slowly into his car still feeling more dead than alive, and he carried me off to preach.

Struggling into the service I collapsed into my chair where I found I could barely sit up. I was still feeling very ill, but I had resolved by the grace of God to preach and believed that he would strengthen me and enable me to continue. And so it happened. When the time came, I stood up, staggered to the platform, propped myself with both hands on the pulpit, and announced I was going to preach on, *Christ the Great Physician.* I gave my text from the gospel of Luke, still leaning heavily on the pulpit and began to preach! Almost at once, the life, strength, and grace of the healing Christ began to flow through me. And within a few moments I was able to let go of this support, stand back, and (as my habit was in those days) began marching from side to side of the platform every moment preaching with more and more passion.

Without doubt that was a miracle of answered prayer! And, of course, an extraordinary demonstration of the truth of the good news and the powerful promise of divine healing. (James 5:13-14)

Praise the Lord, my soul, and forget not all his benefits - who forgives all your sins and heals all your diseases, who redeems your life from the pit and crowns you with love and compassion, who satisfies your desires with good things so that your youth is renewed like the eagle's. Psalm 103:2-5

1958 CADAVER

The Big Bad Wolf would have known exactly what to do. After all, he knew precisely how to blow down a house made of sticks. "I'll huff, and I'll puff, and I'll blow your house down!" he had roared at the three little pigs who were cowering inside. Admittedly, the house in which a dozen or so of us were gathered for a prayer meeting had several bedrooms and was made of timber not of sticks, but it still shook and trembled when the group of hearty farmers began to pray in earnest.

I was pioneering a new church in Catani, a Victorian country town. Perhaps a dozen or so people gathered there for a weekly prayer meeting to support the Sunday morning service I was conducting in a local rented hall. News of those noisy and enthusiastic prayer meetings began to spread around the countryside along with scandalised reports of orgies conducted around a cadaver lying on the kitchen table. Orgies? Cadaver? Evidently one of the neighbours had crept around the shaking house one evening and looking through the window had seen what they thought was a cadaver lying under a sheet on the kitchen table. The reporter had been deceived by the incidental way in which our supper banquet was arranged and placed under a sheet to keep the flies away. It looked exactly like a dead body because there were three bumps - the smallest at the bottom, the fattest in the middle, and the roundest shaped cake at the head, the whole then covered with a sheet!

Another oddity about that prayer meeting was that often the demands of the farmers schedule would be disturbed so that some of them would arrive half-way through my Bible study. Nothing would suit the latecomers but that I should start off all over again. I indulged their request, hoping that the second version of my message would be as good if not better than the first.

We had to leave the Catani church when we were invited by Pastor Leo Harris to come to Adelaide, but it continued on under Pastor Baker and his wife. The reason Leo invited us to come back to Adelaide was due to some differences with Lloyd Longfield. He and Leo had parted ways due to Lloyd's new belief that only those who were filled with the Holy Spirit and spoke in tongues were genuinely saved. Both Alison and I were saved before we were filled. Alison in the Church of Christ and myself in the Baptist church so we could not accept Lloyd's new teaching and parted from him with some sorrow. This new doctrine had caused a split in the Victorian CRC churches with some aligning themselves with Lloyd but most, including our Catani church, agreeing with Leo that this teaching was not biblical.

It was good for us to get away from the controversy and put it behind us for five very important and wonderful years of training in Adelaide. After five years there, Alison and I moved to Tasmania and spent fifteen years ministering in Launceston. While we were there, I planted four CRC churches but more on that later.

My goal is that they may be encouraged in heart and united in love, so that they may have the full riches of complete understanding, in order that they may know the mystery of God, namely, Christ, in whom are hidden all the treasures of wisdom and knowledge. Colossians 2:2-3

I urge you, brothers and sisters, to watch out for those who cause divisions and put obstacles in your way that are contrary to the teaching you have learned. Keep away from them. Romans 16:17

1958 LEO

What a commanding platform presence! What a preacher! What an astonishing sonorous voice! Leo's knowledge of Scripture was profound, though he made no pretence to be an actual theologian. He left such endeavours to others such as myself, my brother Barry, and some others as well. But what a man of God! Leo Harris was all those things and more.

Around the end of the Second World War (1945) and still a young man, Leo ministered as an evangelist for the Assemblies of God. On one of his campaigns, he met Pastor Tom Foster who was a promoter for the British Israel World Federation. They hold the view that the ten lost tribes of Israel migrated across Europe to eventually become the British Commonwealth of nations and the United States of America. This view depends heavily on Jacob's prophecy that Ephraim would become a company of nations and Manasseh a great nation. (Genesis 48:17-20) Tom persuaded Leo to embrace the British Israel message and they joined forces and began to preach a combined message embracing Bible prophecy with a focus on world events, allied to British Israel dogma. They took their message to Melbourne where on several occasions they preached to thousands who were keen to understand what was happening in the world. A significant number asked them to begin a church in Melbourne as they wanted to remain under their ministry. So, Tom planted a *National Revival Crusade* church in Melbourne and another pastor, Don Dawson, planted one in Frankston, Victoria. The NRC later became the Christian Revival Crusade, and finally the CRC Churches International.

In the meantime, Leo flew to New Zealand to promulgate the same message there, receiving a positive response wherever he went. In one church a pastor stood up and delivered a prophecy which said that Leo would return to Australia, travel to Adelaide, and there establish a movement that would girdle the globe. Feeling much elated Leo returned to Australia, and to Adelaide, and began to bring the words of the oracle into fulfillment. He remained a firm believer in the British Israel concept for many years but moved away from it before his death at 58 years of age in 1977. And in fulfillment of the New Zealand oracle, Leo's ministry founded what is now the CRC Churches International. Their current faith goal is to 'have 500 churches in Australia, and a CRC ministry presence in every nation of our world by 2045' which I heartily endorse.

It is my view that Leo was Australia's greatest preacher, or at any rate I have never heard better. His influence on me and on my ministry style was profound. I absorbed deeply his love of Scripture and his insistence that everything we believe and teach must be subservient to the divinely inspired message of the Bible. If a doctrine or dogma or practice could not be supported by biblical chapter and verse, he would reject it out of hand. It is a standard by which I have measured my whole adult life and ministry.

His wife, Belle, was a magnificent support to him. Because she had a strong and forceful character not everyone got along with her, in fact some were even frightened of her forthright manner. But Belle and I got on quite well, and apart from an occasional tiff which I ignored, we never had any serious disagreements. I loved her, if for no other reason than because she loved and deeply supported her husband, Leo. However, I do remember a couple of significant altercations. One of them related to a young people's camp. I advocated that the teenage girls, in preference to skirts, should wear jeans, shorts, and other similar clothing akin to male garments. Of course, they were not male in any real sense only in similarity because they were designed for females to wear. I wanted to see this change as shorts and slacks were more appropriate for camp activities and preserved the dignity and modesty of the young ladies than to wear skirts and dresses. I won this bout, but another squabble Belle and I had was about my untidy desktop. No doubt it looked untidy, but I knew precisely where everything was. However, the matter was too trivial to make an issue of it and I easily agreed to do as Belle wanted and kept it somewhat in good order.

Another matter was perhaps more serious. A large statue of Michaelangelo's David was put on display in an Adelaide department store. It was an exact full-size replica and therefore completely naked. You can find the original statue today at the Accademia Gallery in Florence, Italy. Belle was deeply affronted that I had taken the young men and women in the Crusade Bible College, where I was a teacher, to look at and admire Michelangelo's stunning sculpture. It was perhaps unfortunate that the more intimate parts of David in the displayed sculpture were almost exactly at eye level and could not be avoided! Were any of the young people scandalised? I doubt it. You may wonder why I took the class to see the sculpture? I thought it was appropriate to the theme of my current lectures in the college. This is one instance in which I refused to yield to Belle and told her that she was being foolish beyond measure.

In the meantime, Leo and I continued to get on well. I had moved to Adelaide at Leo's invitation to become his visitation pastor. This was not my forte! The more people I visited, the more I tried to counsel, the more I prayed for the healing of the sick, the worse people seemed to get! Support and comfort are not one of my strengths. So, I looked around for another role. I boldly snatched some work off Leo's desk, saying he had too much to do, and I could relieve him from a number of jobs. He wanted a Bible college so I told him I would set it up for him and write the curriculum. This was a successful enterprise. I became principal of the college and the main lecturer. I would spend my days writing the curriculum and with Leo's help we lectured for two hours each night from Monday to Thursday. At that time, we had no other classes. From memory we had about thirty students in the beginning.

Leo was then publishing and editing the CRC journal, which in those days was called the *Revivalist*. I took that off his desk as well and set myself to write a key article every month and to collect articles, news stories and other material from other writers. In other words, while Leo was the titular editor, I was the real editor of the magazine. This is not so brash as it sounds as during my high school years, under the tutelage of a teacher, I had enthusiastically functioned as the editor of the quarterly school newspaper, and of the annual school journal.

My labours, I hope, were a real help to Leo, at any rate he raised no protest against me clearing his desk of several onerous tasks. As I have said, Leo's influence on me was far reaching. He was the best mentor I ever had, and I owe him limitless respect and gratitude. And so, we continued happily in ministry together for some five years.

After we had been ministering together for about three years, Leo trusted me enough to put his large church under my control and took himself and Belle to the United States for twelve months. He found himself addressed and advertised by sundry churches as Dr Leo Harris. A Doctor of what? None of us ever learned. He preached all over the country including one Southern church on a steamy summer night where there were swarms of mosquitoes. Leo began slapping at the obnoxious biting insects whereupon many of the people began shouting, "Glory! Hallelujah! Praise God!" and the like. They thought his gesticulations showed that the power of God had fallen on him.

During that same twelve months I fell into a deep depression. My wife was bedfast at her mother's home with her body threatening to birth Sharon far too early. I had taken over Leo's nation-wide weekly radio broadcast, I was editing the Crusade journal and of course running the church. Then I came under a Satanic attack. I found myself on Sundays preaching alongside a voice in my mind saying, "What a load of claptrap! What fools these people are to believe anything I say. What nonsense to expect that anyone will be healed of any sickness just because I laid my hands on them and prayed." The voice was cynical and unbelieving. It was an awful experience. What could I do about it?

In the end, somewhere deep inside I knew those words were lies, and that if I continued doing what I was expected to do the bout of cynicism would vanish. And so, it happened. After a couple of months, the depression completely lifted and I was able to continue my ministry with joy, with many committing their lives to Christ, and many others wonderfully healed. Why did God allow this horrifying experience? Was God testing my faith and whether or not I could be depended upon to do my duty whatever the circumstances? Or was it because I was pushing myself too hard and growing weary. God knew what lay ahead in my life though I did not. I would need a deep faith to achieve what he had in store for me.

Leo was often warned by new American friends that when he got back to Australia he would find himself ousted from his church by the pastor, that is myself, who had been put in charge of it. But he was unafraid and confident the church would flourish under my leadership and would be handed back to him on his return to Australia, which of course proved to be true. In fact, the congregation had grown by about one hundred people to an average attendance of around six hundred. Leo became leader of the church again and I reverted to being his associate pastor without any issue.

However, a couple of years later Leo became enamoured of exorcism which eventually resolved itself into a weekly session every Wednesday morning. There he would endeavour to cast demons out of people who claimed to be possessed. There were a few spectacular recoveries but mostly the same people would come back week after week which resulted in Leo trying to cast out dozens of devils with wild and sometimes disgusting manifestations. The worst part of it was that many times those people would go home, tell their friends with great excitement what had happened to them, so that on the next Wednesday they too would arrive at the deliverance session and produce the same and even worse externalisations.

I raised an occasional gentle protest, but Leo refused to heed me. Eventually I felt I had no choice but to voice my objections vigorously. I insisted that what he was doing seemed to me like a violation of what he had taught for years about the realities of the new creation that God has made us in Christ and of the innate authority over Satan and all the powers of darkness that God has given every believer in Christ. Spending hours every week trying to cast demons out of people in order to solve their problems and their spiritual failures, mocked the truth of those very biblical and strong beliefs.

Since I could not in all godliness remain in Leo's church while opposing him, I resigned. I told Leo why I was doing this, and he agreed it was the correct decision. We remained excellent friends, and he told me about a small church in Launceston Tasmania that was looking for a pastor and that he would recommend me. So, we parted amicably, and he gave us a wonderful send off and agreed to pay our salary in Launceston for the first few months. The irony in all this was that not much more than twelve months after I had left Adelaide, Leo himself came to realise the folly of what he had been doing and to revert to his former emphasis on the believer's throne rights in Christ, our righteous identity, and our proper authority over sin and hell, and so on.

One remarkable consequence of this dramatic change in my life was that living in Launceston, initially with only a small congregation, I had the time and circumstances to conceive the idea of a Bible College built around correspondence students and satellite campuses that would be attached to the *Launceston College of Theology*. At this time there was no mail order Bible study course that I knew about. Had I stayed in Adelaide with Leo I would not have seen the need for such a correspondence course. More on this later.

Let me also include here a list of scriptural references I prepared for people who felt they were under some kind of satanic attack.

Prepare the way for your deliverance with these powerful Scriptures!

- On the believer's authority - Luke 10:9; Revelation 12:10-11; Acts 10:33; Philippians 4:13.
- On the assurance of sins forgiven - Isaiah 1:18; 1 John 1:9; Romans 10:9-13.
- On submission to the will of God - James 4:7; Romans 12:1-2.
- On the power of Jesus name - Mark 16:17; Philippians 2:9-12; Acts 3:6,16; John 16:24.
- On your legal position with Christ - Ephesians 2:4-6; Colossians 1:27; 2:10; Romans 6:11.
- On the power of the Word of God - John 8:32; Ephesians 6:17; Hebrews 4:12.
- On casting out demons - Mark 16:17; Acts 8:7; James 4:7; 1 Peter 5:7-11.
- On your right to freedom - Luke 4:18; Acts 26:18; Galatians 5:1; Colossians 1:13-14.
- On the strength of Christ within you - Romans 8:31; 2 Corinthians 2:14; 9:8; Ephesians 6:10; 1:19-20; 3:20; Philippians 4:13; Colossians 1:11, 27; 2:13-15.
- On the power of a right confession - Romans 10:9; Hebrews 3:1; Romans 4:17-21.

- On the ministry of the Holy Spirit - 2 Timothy 1:7; 2 Corinthians 3:17-18.

Instructions -

You should copy the above Scriptures from your Bible and then write them out again in your own words. Personalise them by using your own name. Write them in a way that relates to your own circumstance and need. Pray over them. Open your heart to them. Keep on working with them until they become powerfully alive in your spirit. (Ephesians 1:17-20) Thus, you will build a foundation of spiritual authority upon which you can both gain and retain a striking victory over the works of the enemy!

Following these instructions, I would not pray for anyone unless they could prove they had done the work required! This worked remarkably well. A few people who really did have some kind of demonic problem did as I suggested, came back to me for prayer, and in every case were delivered within a few minutes. Many others I never heard from again as they presumably gained personal victory in their life.

Although Leo was a deeply inspiring pastor, preacher, and mentor, he did have four deficiencies which is worthwhile noting (and he would not mind in the least):

First - While Leo was a profoundly godly man, he was not a good manager and often had difficulty handling any forceful elders and leaders in the congregation. I wasn't much better than he was on these matters so I could not help him in his frequent difficulties.

Second - Leo loathed confrontation and would do almost anything to avoid it. When I arrived on the scene, I was an instant scapegoat. I didn't much like confrontation either, but I didn't shrink from it. I approached this task most reluctantly but gritted my teeth and did my duty.

For instance, there were several occasions in the life of Leo's church when people had committed some misdemeanour and as a junior member of the team, I was given the task of imposing some discipline upon them. Mostly people graciously accepted the rebuke or correction, such as the man, let's call him Joe, who delivered a supposed prophecy one Sunday morning, and in the process quoted almost verbatim the words of a popular book which I had read only recently. He tried to deny it but soon capitulated and admitted his fault thereby continuing in good fellowship.

Then there was another man, let's call him Fred, who also delivered two or three prophecies in the church on a Sunday that were atrocious, full of negativity, gloom, despair and harsh criticism of the people. This was a violation of the purpose Paul gives prophecy that it should be focussed on spiritual edification, comfort and positive exhortation (1 Corinthians 14:3). So, I had to rebuke him and tell him that he was forbidden to deliver a prophetic oracle again until he had received a pastor's permission. He was three times my age, quite well built, and he was furious at receiving such a command from myself. He said with much anger, "If you were my son, I would take a whip to you!" Whereupon I said, "I am not your son, you are not my father, and you will do what I say as your pastor, or I will have you bodily removed from the church!" He left the church voluntarily!

Third - Leo hated losing and loved winning. He often played tennis with my brother Barry, sometimes winning, sometimes losing. Watching from the office window I could always tell what the result had been. If Leo had won, he would march briskly back to the office grinning from ear to ear. If he had lost, he would droop along looking dejected!

Fourth - Despite his profound conviction that every doctrine had to be measured against the Word of God, Leo retained a firm belief in the aberrant British Israel theory. Although to be fair in his later years he sidelined any use of the dogma. This was a remarkable retreat because in the early years he always decorated the wall behind the pulpit with the Australian, British and American flags, and often began a meeting with the British National Anthem.

However, nothing can remove from Leo the splendour of the achievement of writing several influential books and more importantly in establishing the CRC Churches International which has had a significant impact around the globe.

All Scripture is God-breathed and is useful for teaching, rebuking, correcting and training in righteousness, so that the servant of God may be thoroughly equipped for every good work. Timothy 3:16

1958 BW

BW stands for Boogie-Woogie, which is an unsanctified kind of music I began to teach myself to play when I was about sixteen. Why Boogie? For no better reason than in pop circles it was the current rage. I liked the sound of it, and I estimated it would be fairly easy to learn. Apart  from the banjo mandolin, which taught me the rudiments of music, I never had any lessons on the piano but taught myself how to play, probably not well, but sufficient to give much pleasure to myself and joy to many others. I eventually purchased a book on chord structure and instruction on when each cord was appropriate. But that was several years after I had developed some skill in Boogie Woogie which I often used to entertain young people at youth camps and other similar events.

For several years in Adelaide, I organised an Easter Camp for our young people at Sandy Creek, some sixty kilometres north of Adelaide. It was an ideal location for a youth camp being several kilometres from the nearest shops and virtually isolated. There were several large barns in the paddock that we were able to organise into separate dormitories for the girls, and the boys had tents. Another of the sheds provided dining facilities. We provided as many large sacks as needed and enough hay for each of the young people (aged between 15-25, all unmarried) to fill their sacks to make mattresses. Some much older married couples volunteered to cook and to act as parents for the camp. These camps attracted at least two hundred young people from the CRC churches in Adelaide and Victoria each year. We held a church service on Good

Friday afternoon, a camp concert on Saturday evening, and a church service Sunday morning. Along with a devotional time for a half an hour in the mornings along with a special speaker for a plenary meeting.

The youth were required to remain within the large boundaries of the paddock, which was no problem, since there was nowhere else to go. They occupied themselves with various sporting activities and other games. I set a few other simple rules, among them being after lights out the boys and the girls had to remain apart. Each night, being suspicious of human nature, I patrolled the sleeping areas for half an hour with a powerful torch. On one occasion I caught two young men wandering around the girl's barn. I reprimanded them sharply, telling them that they would have to go home the next morning. They protested hotly, as also did their parents, but I was adamant and home they went. After that I had no further occasion to bring disciplinary action against any of the youth, they knew I was a man of my word. Every camp was truly successful with many of the young people finding Christ as Saviour, many filled with the Holy Spirit, and even a few miracles of healing.

Saturday night concerts were called, *Amateur Howl* (after a then popular radio broadcast *Amateur Hour*). All those concerts were hilarious and kept us laughing so much it hurt! I received many accolades from the young people for my Boogie Woogie efforts except on one occasion when some of them apparently thought I needed taking down a peg or two. So, one morning they heard me asking for a cup of coffee and managed to intercept it before it reached me. Instead of the sugar I had ordered they put two or three teaspoons of salt and stirred it in vigorously. Unbeknownst to them I had observed what they were doing, and when they handed the coffee to me, I accepted it without comment and drank it down (though it tasted ghastly!) without any indication that anything was amiss! The coffee doping jokesters were startled and amazed! They did not know if I was altogether without tastebuds or even worse had such a weird taste preference that I didn't notice the coffee was salty. In any case they were filled with admiration and shared the story with their friends so that they became perhaps the most responsive group I had ever preached to at a youth camp!

In the meantime, my prowess at Boogie Woogie continued to the point that every time I spoke at a youth meeting, I was required to entertain the audience with at least one or two Boogie pieces. However, as I got older, became a pastor, and began to speak at prayer meetings and other gatherings where youth and adults were mixed together, I felt more and more uncomfortable playing Boogie. So, I dropped it and instead, using a couple of music manuals, taught myself the circle of twelve chords in all their variations (major, minor, seventh, augmented and diminished) with all their various positions on the piano keyboard. From then on, I could play any chorus or hymn by ear, and this was a great help in my ministry as a pastor. But I was never more than mediocre on the piano, whether playing Boogie, choruses, or hymns. Nonetheless, it was a mediocrity that still managed to bring pleasure to those who listened and far more importantly those who sang along with me at various gatherings.

Still, there were times of great frustration, such as when our church pianist, Linda Thorpe, who played entirely by ear, would strike a chord that stunned me with its beauty and harmony. I several times hastened to ask her what she had just played but she could never tell me, since she couldn't read music and played entirely by instinct! More recently I have come across YouTube music and have watched a number of Boogie Woogie videos. The wizardry of the performers leaves me with my jaw dropping and almost ashamed that I ever dared to play Boogie myself. But not quite, for I did enjoy playing it and judging from comments that are still being made to me decades after I stopped, I must have played well enough for others to enjoy it too.

Happy are the people whose God is the Lord. Psalm 144:15b

1960 APPLICABLE

"You can't be serious!"

A young couple had come to me for advice on their upcoming wedding service. I asked them what hymns, if any, they would like sung. Without hesitation they named as their first choice, *Dear Lord and Father of Mankind*.

"Are you sure," said I, "You want to sing that hymn at a wedding service? It is indeed one of my favourite hymns too, but I certainly would not choose to sing it as part of a wedding service." They were surprised at this and protested that it was a great and powerful hymn. "No doubt it is," said I, "and I would usually thoroughly enjoy singing it but not when facing a couple waiting to be married." Again, the young couple asked me to explain myself.

I opened a copy of a hymn book, found the hymn, and began to quote some of the lines, such as –

- Forgive our foolish ways
- Reclothe us in our rightful mind
- In purer lives thy service find
- Breathe through the heats of our desire
- Let sense be dumb let flesh retire

Having drawn their attention to such lines from the hymn I said, "Those sentiments are true enough for all of us, and I suppose we need a constant reminder of them and many injunctions to cast them away from our lives but not at a wedding! They are simply not appropriate." Happily, the young couple chose another hymn that was far more suitable to a joyful and lovely event.

This highlights a problem I have often found with Christians. They think that every verse in the Bible is applicable to them at all times. For example, we used to sing, "Every promise in the book is mine, every chapter, every verse, every line, all the blessings of his love divine, every promise in the book is mine." But, of course, that is simply not true. Every promise in the Bible may indeed be yours but each promise has its own time and place to be fulfilled. It is our task to pray and seek a divine inner quickening by God on the promise we wish to claim, so that we know with absolute certainty, rid of all doubt, filled with sure faith that the promise we are claiming has already been fulfilled. Even though we may not yet see any evidence of it we must stick firmly to our faith. We need this inner revelation of God, which enables us to believe, as John says in his first letter –

This is the confidence that we have in him, that if we ask anything according to his will, he heareth us: And if we know that he hears us, whatsoever we ask, we know that we have the petitions that we desired of him. 1 John 5:14-15

There have been times when Alison and I have been able to grasp a promise to good effect, but those times have been rare and thrilling, as you will find in the pages of this book. So, be careful and responsible in the way you quote the Bible or claim the fulfillment of any of its promises. I have found that things for which I could easily believe days ago, or years ago, I cannot believe for today. Divinely quickened faith is simply not present on this occasion, yet I may well find that invincible faith is restored to me tomorrow.

I keep asking that the God of our Lord Jesus Christ, the Glorious Father, may give you the Spirit of wisdom and revelation, so that you may know him better. I pray that the eyes of your heart may be enlightened in order that you may know the hope to which he has called you. Ephesians 1:17-18a

1961 BRISBANE

While I was ministering with Leo in Adelaide, he sent me up to our Brisbane CRC to hold an Evangelistic Tent Campaign with his father, Cecil Harris's church. This was a remarkable experience as described in this letter to Alison written on April 15th, 1961 -

> Darling Alison,
>
> Contentment fills me this Sunday morning. In the distance the bell of an ice-cream cart is ringing cheerily, dogs are barking, the sun is shining, a gentle breeze is rustling the palm trees, breakfast sits satisfyingly in the inner man, good health fills me – life is wonderful!
>
> Just at this moment my only sorrow is that you are not with me, and little Dale and Sharon. I say 'just at this moment' because later on when the next meeting begins some other causes for sorrow may appear. More of this in a later paragraph.

Yesterday morning we spent time visiting various shopping centres and buying the weekend groceries and meat. One shopping centre was of great interest. It was at Coorparoo, a new two storey drive-in centre (with a roof top parking area) jointly owned by Myers and Woolworths. This centre is a pleasure to visit and shop in, and has every modern convenience, including a large and well-equipped playroom for children, under the care of three trained assistants. As far as I know there is nothing like it in Adelaide. This store at Coorparoo is one of four owned by Myers in Brisbane – two drive-in shopping centres, and two large shops in the city.

Your voice was very sweet to hear the other night, though it was only a few brief words …

More than two hours have passed by since I penned the last sentence, and in that time we have attended the morning service and are now home again. Perhaps I should tell you about the meetings now. I don't know whether to laugh or cry about them! The folk are undoubtedly all very sincere, but they seem completely oblivious of the impression their services must convey to newcomers.

First, the tent: it is a very good tent, well designed, pleasantly situated, and furnished with seating for about 120 though it could be adapted to seat twice that number. At 7:45 Brother Harris stands up and begins leading choruses – he has a voice like a trumpet, but a little old and scratched, and his thunderings completely swamp the handful of people in the congregation. On Friday, seventeen were present, and last night twenty-two, all Christians, so there were no decisions but there was good blessing on the prayer line both nights.

Allied to Brother Harris is dear old Sister Harris, pounding away with great gusto on their old, out of tune piano and joining in with her are the other musicians – saxophone, cornet, piano accordion, all playing and blowing as hard as they can, each trying to outdo the other, and blissfully unaware of the awful cacophony they are creating! Over this overwhelming onslaught of sound, the pitiful handful of people have no hope of making themselves heard! To make matters worse they sing the choruses written by Sister Harris which, while they are very good, are quite unknown to strangers or visitors from other assemblies.

After a few choruses, Brother Harris announces the first hymn which he and the orchestra thunder forth with great enthusiasm, usually singing the chorus, if any, two or three times at the end of each verse.

And at most meetings he has asked the men, and then the ladies, to sing the chorus on their own – fortunately only at the end of one verse and only with one hymn in each meeting, as you can imagine what seven or eight men, and then ten to twelve ladies sound like.

Having sung a hymn, Brother Harris then prays, and promptly announces another hymn, after which he calls for testimonies. For the most part the same people testify each meeting, with some variation of subject matter: some of the testimonies have been good, but others have made me shudder. The testimonies are followed by the announcements and then the offering while another hymn is sung. By this time it is 8:30, three quarters of an hour has gone by and I have Brother Harris introducing me to the people and saying how much they are looking forward to my ministry that night. It is at this point the Lord has wonderfully undertaken each time; for I have been alternating between interest, annoyance, pleasure, frustration, blessing, oppression, amusement, and indignation, until finally finding myself quite despondent by the time I step up to the platform. But when I look at the people, just a handful of them, I find that I love them and want to give them the Word of God, and the Lord has graciously anointed the Word and given me a great blessing in preaching.

This is the strangest anomaly of this incredible campaign – I find myself preaching with greater liberty and pleasure than I have known for a long time! Well! Glory to God!

The people have obviously enjoyed the meetings (that is the people belonging to the assembly here: as for outsiders it is impossible to say what they think) and are richly enjoying my ministry.

At this point I must say that in all of the above I do not mean in any way to be sarcastic or unkind. Brother Harris and all the people of his church who are attending the meetings, very clearly love the Lord and are putting all their heart into the meetings and are desperately eager to see the tent full and a harvest reaped for the Lord. But they seem to me to be amazingly unaware of the fact that almost everything about the conduct of the meetings is surely more likely to keep outsiders away, rather than attract them.

I have tried very hard to enter into the first part of the meeting and to put my faith behind it but have been compelled to give up the unequal struggle and let each change in the meeting have its proper effect on me – of pleasure or frustration!

A communion service was held in the hall this morning. Seventeen people were present, and I shudder at the memory of the clattering din made in that big hall by the orchestra and Brother Harris! It made no difference that two or three of the hymns should have been sung softly and reverently; the sax, the piano, the pastor and the people all agreed in creating (to my ears) a bedlam of sound! However, they all enjoyed themselves. There was good anointing on the gifts of the Spirit, and at the end of the service I gave a brief message of no more than four or five minutes. I suppose to the people present this morning there was nothing untoward in the meeting, but I am certain that a visitor would have been appalled: there is no doubt in my mind that the conduct of these services must be greatly altered if there is to be any growth in the work here. I have no hope at all of the attendances in the tent increasing much above what they are at present: it will be a miracle of God's overriding goodness if they do!

This afternoon seventeen were present in the tent, and the meeting went on just as described, except that at testimony time a very odd, obviously mental lady came up to the platform, stepped up to the pulpit, and launched into a crazy rigmarole about nothing. She occupied the pulpit for about three or four minutes before Brother Harris made a move toward her, upon which she stopped and went back to her seat.

However, despite all, God anointed my message, and apparently everyone enjoyed themselves. It is nearly time to leave again for the evening service so I will have to close in a few moments.

Do not think that I am miserable here, far from it, even the meetings with their very difference and offence to my sense of what is necessary and proper are fascinating. I am loving every minute! Brother and Sister Harris are treating me like a king; the people are wonderfully appreciative of my ministry, and I know the Lord is bringing them blessing. My whole heart and soul is behind my preaching, and all my faith, but as far as a campaign to save souls and bring increase to the church is concerned, for that I have no hope, and have left the result to the Lord. Nonetheless I know the Lord has brought me here and has a purpose in my coming, and in this I am happy.

Brother Harris hasn't (and won't) spare himself in taking me to every place of interest. Already he has shown me most of the Brisbane city and suburbs, and he has an extensive itinerary planned for every day of the coming week that I am sure will take me over half the state. Because there are some places which will require a whole day to reach, he urged me to postpone my departure to Thursday: I have taken the liberty to do this and hope it will not place any extra burden on Leo and Alan.

The Lord is blessing me wonderfully here, giving me a very enjoyable break, and I am really looking forward to the next ten days, they should be thoroughly enjoyable.

Once again, several hours have passed by and we are home again after the evening service. The meeting followed the set pattern, but I must be getting used to it: I almost enjoyed the music and singing tonight!

About forty-five were present and I preached with great anointing and liberty on, 'The Measure of a Man'. However, there were no decisions because all those present were Christians. It still does not seem likely that there will be any spectacular results in the remainder of the campaign probably about twenty or so attending during the week and perhaps fifty to sixty on Sunday, the last night of the campaign. However, one never knows what God will do as our Easter Camp at Sandy Creek so wonderfully demonstrated. I fervently trust and pray that the blessing and deep meaning of that camp is continuing in the witness of the young people.

Give a big kiss to Dale and Sharon, love to all the folks, but especially to you, my darling wife,

Love Ken

And we know that for those who love God all things work together for good, for those who are called according to His purpose. Romans 8:28

Come, let us sing for joy to the Lord; let us shout aloud to the rock of our salvation. Let us come before him with thanksgiving and extol him with music and song. Psalms 95:1-2

1962 WOLVES

They called it the 'House of Prayer'. It was nothing of the sort. Rather it was the 'House of Seduction'! The organisers had gathered a group of young people, whom they exhorted to believe they would actually hear the voice of God, telling them what to do. This was an enticing fantasy and while a number of the young people had the good sense to vanish like terrified rabbits from the scene, there were perhaps a dozen others in whose eyes the red fires of fanaticism burned fiery bright, and they yearned with a terrible yearning to hear God speak to them.

It all began well enough when the young people heard a voice speaking out of nowhere (perhaps a hidden microphone) about the fact that nothing exists on earth or heaven greater than the love of God. "Nothing", said the persuasive husky voice, "can surpass a person's love for God and for the people of God." (1 John 5:1-2) "So," went on the voice, "find someone you can love with my love." The voice kept on speaking in this fashion becoming even more intimate and erotic, declaring that if the love of God was the most noble expression of divine love, then the most exalted expression of human love could not be more blessedly expressed than through two people joined together in an intimate sexual relationship.

At the time, I was an associate pastor in Leo Harris's large church in Adelaide and was unaware that some of the young people in our church were involved in this grotesque scene. I only learned what was happening because one of the victims was a beautiful 19-year-old girl. Her father (who was himself not a Christian believer) came to me to lodge a bitter complaint. He threatened many different sorts of legal action against the failure of the church to exercise proper duty of care over its young parishioners. I was utterly dismayed by the report and promised to take swift and stern action. That same day I drove to the home in which these unauthorised meetings were being held and promised I would shut them down and would see to it that the senior couple involved who were leading this so-called disgusting 'house of prayer' would be driven out of the city. I'm not sure how much authority I really had, but what I lacked in jurisdiction I certainly added to in spiritual authority. In any case, my angry commands were heeded by those vile procurers. Unfortunately, when they left our state, they took with them the beautiful 19-year-old who married one of the perpetrators who was 60 years of age and so she was lost to her family. After this I had no further contact with them.

In the meantime, within our local church we had learned a sombre lesson. From then on, we discouraged people from holding any meetings unless they were endorsed by the eldership of the local church and gave even more attention to encouraging people to be especially wary of wolves garbed in sheep's clothing. (Matthew 7:15-20) They may seem to be shining with the radiant truths of Scripture until you measure them against the hard dictum –

To the law and to the testimony: if they speak not according to this Word, it is because there is no light in them. Isaiah 8:20

All Scripture is breathed out by God and profitable for teaching, for reproof, for correction, and for training in righteousness, that the man of God may be complete, equipped for every good work. 2 Timothy 3:16-17

Watch out for false prophets. They come to you in sheep's clothing, but inwardly they are ferocious wolves. By their fruit you will recognize them. Do people pick grapes from thornbushes, or figs from thistles? Likewise, every good tree bears good fruit, but a bad tree bears bad fruit. Matthew 7:15-17

1962 TOURS

Although Tasmania is an integral part of Australia, we would refer to the other states across Bass Strait as the 'mainland'. During my years planting churches in this great state, I would often undertake ministry on the mainland to keep abreast of what was happening in the CRC and other denominations. Our only means of communication with the rest  of the world was a black and white television and a dial phone, apart from the mail. Sometimes I would be away from the family and the church for two or three weeks at a time. Looking after the church in Launceston and starting other churches in Devonport, Burnie, and Hobart was not enough to keep me busy!

As well as these tours, I flew to Flinders Island in a little one engine, two-seater plane to hold meetings there as the island did not have a fulltime church minister. This was a hair-raising experience, bouncing over the sea with the pilot beside me. I used to watch carefully how he flew the plane just in case something went wrong with him, and I had to land the plane myself! We did have one hair raising experience when the engine began to fail, and we had to land on a beach instead of the landing field. The pilot fixed whatever was wrong and we took off again and finally made a successful landing on the Flinders Island airfield.

Once I remember we were over Bass Strait, and my door flew open. Fortunately, I was fastened in with a sturdy seatbelt but for a moment my heart was in my mouth as I viewed the sea far below. Then I was able to close the door successfully and we flew on to our destination.

Alison thought I was very brave and would not even contemplate getting into a one engine plane! I was not brave so much as determined to preach like Jeremiah of old, and knowing I had another congregation to preach to spurred me on -

But if I say, 'I will not mention his Word or speak anymore in his name,' his Word is in my heart like a fire, a fire shut up in my bones. I am weary of holding it in; indeed, I cannot! Jeremiah 20:9

When Sharon was four years of age, we discovered that she thought I spent the whole of my absences from home in whichever aeroplane she had seen me enter for my trip. We found this out as she pointed to an aeroplane flying overhead and said confidently to Alison, "My daddy's up there!"

At first when I came home from trips away the children would all rush to the front door to greet me and to give me hugs and kisses. However, the time came when they no longer ran to greet me and scarcely looked up from what they were doing. I was deeply hurt but realised I was going away too often and had to curb my frustration and concentrate on my family. This was around the time we began family church camps and took more personal holidays.

Fathers do not exasperate your children; instead, bring them up in the instruction and training of the Lord. Ephesians 6:4

1962 ABSENT

While I was away preaching and teaching, Alison kept herself busy with projects – painting a room, sewing, knitting for the children and building relationships with the women who offered to help her and fellowship with her. In return she would assist them when they needed it. Our church was a community of friends which has lasted despite our now forty years away from Tasmania. On our regular visits to preach there we were greeted with great fondness. Friendships you make in your early adult years often remain deep and abiding.

Meanwhile, Alison tells me that she saw me operating as a 'father in the faith' which helped her bear the lonely nights. I would visit young pastors and give them Biblical advice and wisdom. These zealous young men were so intent on building a ministry to the glory of God but were neglecting their wives and family. On nights when the meetings would pause, I encouraged these husbands to buy their wife some flowers and take her out to dinner while I did child minding duty. I had learned how important a little romance can be from my own mistakes.

Alison trained me to drop everything and take her out whenever she had had enough of the hours I spent in the office writing, calling herself a 'computer widow'. Whatever she asked for was hers! Feeling that love and appreciation on occasion was the oil of joy in our marriage. Fortunately for me Alison is a very patient and longsuffering female who did not require constant attention. And she has filled her time successfully in later years by researching topics and writing her own books!

These ministry tours often had added bonuses. In the 60s and 70s, Tasmania had very few international concerts. One had to fly to the mainland to see anything of calibre. While ministering in Sydney I discovered that Verdi's grand opera *Aida* was being performed at the Sydney Opera House. My heart soared, for although I had a deep love of music, I had never before had the opportunity to experience a live opera in all its magnificence and splendour. I invited my pastoral friends to go with me, but unfortunately opera was not to their liking, so I found another friend who loved music and off we went.

Having made earlier enquiries, I knew that the theatre had been booked out for months, but I was vibrantly optimistic that we would find two seats together. Of course, the lady at the box office laughed when I made this request, but she had no objection to me hovering nearby, hoping for the best. In fact, I was divinely assured that the Lord would provide! And sure enough, within a few minutes a man approached the box wanting to return his tickets and claim a refund. The lady said that she could not oblige, but then she kindly pointed to me, saying, "That gentleman may be willing to buy them from you."

I was at first hesitant to accept these tickets, on the chance they were in a poorly located position. But to my delight I discovered the seats were right in the middle of the main floor, two of the best positions in the house for seeing and hearing an opera! And the performance was sublime! At one point, the lead soprano had to sing above a vast array of soloists and choristers, in addition the entire orchestra was at full strength, but she soared above them all, and I would not have been surprised to find myself being lifted right off my seat. We went home afterward, deeply satisfied, and grateful to God for a marvellous evening, remembering that Verdi himself claimed that he wrote all of his music for the glory of God.

Verdi said this about his requiem in a letter to his childhood friend, Piroli, on the March 7th, 1871:

> I've been here since the beginning of the year and haven't done anything but write notes upon notes for the greater glory of God, and perhaps for the future annoyance of my fellow man. But be that as it may, the music is now finished, and I'm pleased that I've done it.

On my arrival back in Tasmania, I shared with Alison about God's amazing provision and the superb opera that had so moved my spirit. Sometime in the future it was shown on television, and I was able to share my joy in this operatic work with Alison. It was another wonderful example of God's great love and provision in something that was of immense value to me. Even in the small things, in the minutiae, God's hand can be seen in answered prayer.

All things, whatsoever you believe, when you ask in prayer, you shall receive. Matthew 21:22

It is good to praise the Lord and make music to your name, O Most High, proclaiming your love in the morning and your faithfulness at night, in the music of the ten stringed lyre and the melody of the harp. For you make me glad by your deeds, Lord; I sing for joy at what your hands have done. How great are your works, Lord, how profound your thoughts. Psalm 92:1-5

1965 ART

My lounge room at home, and where I am sitting in my reclining chair, is a mini art gallery. Currently eleven original artworks festoon its walls and there are several artworks behind me, and indeed in other rooms in our house. Some of them are gifts from the renowned Australian artist, Pro Hart, who was given a state funeral when he died in 2006. Some fifty years ago, I often preached in Pro and Raylee's hometown, and in their home church in Broken Hill. They were both committed Christians, and Alison and I stayed with them on several occasions.

As a devout Christian, Pro helped us financially with Vision Bible College. He painted an original artwork which we were able to use for the cover of 300 hardcover copies of our book, *Discovery;* this raised $15,000 for scholarships. He also gave us permission to sell some of the paintings he gave us which raised more finances for the College. He was our largest donor and now the College is in 150 countries, and we have had more than 2 million graduates in the 50 years the College has been in existence. Pro's help was invaluable and did a great amount of good.

Pro owned perhaps the largest private collection of famous artworks in Australia from many famous artists. These were housed in a two-story purpose-built brick Art Gallery for which he charged an admission fee. He was also a brilliant artist with a style all his own. Once you have seen a Pro Hart painting if you see another one somewhere you will recognise the style instantly.

Pro was a true Australian eccentric who often employed unorthodox procedures to produce his original works -

- Using a small cannon, he would shoot paint onto a canvas thus creating his version of abstract art.
- He invented a car that would run on water, among many other strange and remarkable inventions.
- For a commercial advertiser he painted dragonflies on a piece of expensive carpet. Indeed, he had many variations of his *Dragonfly and Ant* paintings, of which we have a few smaller versions.
- He scattered ironwork sculptures around Broken Hill that you can still enjoy today.
- He bought a Rodgers Pipe organ for his gallery and enjoyed playing it.
- At the Pro Hart Gallery in Broken Hill, you can view a *Rolls Royce* completely painted in Pro's unique style.

There were always people walking in and out of Pro and Raylee's home, despite that its walls were garnished with many costly paintings. Pro seemed to be indifferent to the damage they might suffer, though admittedly I never saw any of them harmed, probably because the visitors knew they were expensive and took care not to rub against them. Pro and Raylee were very hospitable, loving, and generous to all who came their way. We remember them with great fondness and great respect for all the good they did in Broken Hill. Their home was a kind of Mecca for a host of diverse people, and his paintings were bought by such famous people as Prince Philip of England.

One of his sons now runs his gallery and carefully controls how his works are released and sold which suits us very well, because it means that our Pro Harts are steadily rising in value! At the time I am writing these words (2024) his beloved wife Raylee still lives. May she enjoy many more pleasant years!

Pro and Raylee are wonderful examples of the diversity that exists among the servants of God. The Lord chooses from the vast array of personalities and characteristics. He does indeed not look upon the outward appearance but on our hearts and whether or not we truly love and serve him. I've no doubt that Pro Hart was such a man.

The Lord does not look at the things people look at; people look at the outward appearance, but the Lord looks at the heart.
1 Samuel 16:7b

1965 COUNTESS

She was born a Russian aristocrat and was a Countess in her own right. Her family was rich and had extensive properties in a Southern Russian province, but under the tyranny of the Soviet Union her lands were all confiscated, and she and her family had to flee for their lives. Once away from Russian control she Anglicised her name to Vicki Beaumont, which was the name she was still using when somehow in the providence of God she and her husband came to Launceston, Tasmania, where Alison and I were pastoring a church. She later proved to me the authenticity of her story by showing me her patent of nobility, which stated that she was born a Countess.

She and her husband, whose name both Alison and I have forgotten, kept on attending our church and soon surrendered their lives to Christ. From this point I will allow Vicki to tell her story in her own words.

"When I was nineteen years of age an Xray examination showed that I was suffering from a hole in my heart. Over the years this condition caused me much pain and misery, and I was told that only an operation would bring me any relief. Every two or three months I would suffer a severe blackout and would have to spend three or four days in bed. The whole condition left me weak and exhausted, greatly hindered my enjoyment of life, and interrupted my work. But nine months ago, my husband and I both attended the CRC church meetings in Launceston, and accepted Christ as our Saviour. Later on we were both baptised and I asked Pastor Chant to pray for my healing. The power of God moved on me in a wonderful way, and I was instantly healed. That was over six months ago, and I have not suffered the least discomfort from my heart in all that time.

"Along with my heart condition, I also suffered from a perforated eardrum. This made me practically deaf in one ear and caused me very great pain if any water got into the ear. It also made me very dizzy and faint when I was travelling in a car over a high hill. However, since prayer (although doctors have told me it is impossible) I can hear perfectly, water no longer causes me any pain, and heights no longer make me dizzy."

(Reprinted from *Divine Healing – The Wonder and the Mystery* by Alison Chant, Vision Publishing, 2006).

Vicki and her husband continued in the church for some time but then chose to move to New Zealand for reasons of employment.

At that time we more or less lost contact with them until some five years later on a preaching tour to my delight I found them still joyful in Christ and attending one of the churches in which I preached. Vicki told me that she was still completely free from the ailments mentioned in her testimony. Meeting them again and hearing about Vicki's ongoing health and the Christian witness of her and her husband made my day!

It is not often that a lowly Pentecostal pastor has an opportunity to lay hands on and pray for an aristocrat!

I heartily thank God for the privilege of praying for sick people to be healed. Sadly, not everyone does recover when I pray for them. This remains in the providence of God, but I have followed the rule: If I pray for no-one, then no-one gets healed, but if I pray for many at least some will recover, to the glory of God, and the building of his church.

Why do I wish to pray for the sick even though I am often disappointed by the result? The answer is simple: Scripture commands us to do so!

Bless the Lord, O my soul, and all that is within me, bless his holy name! Bless the Lord, O my soul, and forget not all his benefits, who forgives all your iniquity, who heals all your diseases, who redeems your life from the pit, who crowns you with steadfast love and mercy, who satisfies you with good so that your youth is renewed like the eagle's. Psalm 103:1-5

Is anyone among you sick? Let them call the elders of the church to pray over them and anoint them with oil in the name of the Lord. And the prayer offered in faith will make the sick person well. James 5:14

All things, whatsoever you believe, when you ask in prayer, you shall receive. Matthew 21:22

1966 HEALING

We had a sudden explosion of signs, wonders, and miracles! I had discovered that if one wants to see miracles of healing one must preach it day and night, which I was doing. At the same time, I was writing three key books, which were also faith inspiring -

- *Healing in the Whole Bible*
- *Throne Rights*, and
- *Faith Dynamics.*

These books are still part of the world-wide Vision College curriculum. My personal faith was mightily stirred and for a period of about three years miracle after miracle occurred among the people in my church. Here are some of them -

- Fifteen years ago, I had a double tooth extraction which left a puncture through my gum and jawbone and into the antrum. This perforation was discovered when I rinsed my mouth with water because the water trickled into my nose. The dentist expected the hole to heal naturally but it didn't, and eventually it became infected and painful. I received various kinds of unsuccessful treatment, culminating in an operation to place a plastic flap over the decayed bone. This proved unsatisfactory and another operation was needed to put a drainage hole at the back of my mouth. However, after twelve months this hole closed, necessitating yet another operation. But this too failed and my mouth remained infected and painful. Then one Sunday night Pastor Chant (who did not know of my problem) said he felt impressed by the Lord to pray for someone (1 Corinthians 12:7-8) with an infected sore in the roof of the mouth. I indicated I was probably the person concerned, and the pastor prayed for me. Within a short time, all trace of the problem left me, and my dentist has confirmed that the hole has closed, and the infection is gone. Praise God for his divine power. (Mrs. J. Harvey)

- For nearly twelve years I suffered greatly from a diseased gall bladder. I was hospitalised for treatment but was not cured. Time and again I had to walk the floor at night because of the severe pain, and there were many things I was unable to eat. Three doctors X-rayed me and told me that only an operation to remove the gall bladder would bring me any relief. However, about nine months ago I stepped out in the prayer line and asked Pastor Chant to lay hands on me and pray for God to heal me. From that time on the pain and sickness disappeared, and now I have no need of an operation. Proof of my healing is that now I can eat anything I like without the least discomfort. (C. M. Hayes)

- For three years I suffered with a very bad infection in my eyes and throughout that time I was not able to gain any relief from the drops and ointment given to me by the eye specialist. Then twelve months ago in the CRC meeting in Launceston I asked Pastor Chant to pray for me. The next day my eyes were much better, and during that week they were completely healed. How wonderful to be rid of that wretched infection. (B. Connors)

However, the most wonderful miracle for us was the birth of our children. I will let Alison relate that story (taken from our book, *Discovery*) -

Something was seriously wrong! Ken and I had always wanted a large family. During our courtship we had joked about having twelve children after our marriage and had both eagerly looked forward to lots of babies. We had one dear little son, but he was growing older, and we wanted to give him a brother or sister to enjoy.

Tragedy struck! I became pregnant only to lose the baby at two months. Later, I became pregnant again only to lose yet another child. Looking back now over the years I can recognise the deep spiritual work done in us by these happenings, but at the time I could not see the coming heartbreak, nor the overwhelming joy of God's final triumph over all our despair. I know why God will not let us look too far ahead: we could not bear the knowledge! I can also see how our heavenly Father uses tragedy to build character, compassion, and toughness of spirit into his people. His goal is to refine and mould us into strong men and women of God if we let him.

God does not personally send illness or accident. These are just part of life. But he does use them. Nothing is wasted. The Lord weaves every thread of experience into the fabric of our personality as we learn to yield ourselves to him and to rely on him totally.

My doctor discovered I had some small fibroid tumours, and he wanted to operate, but I refused. I preferred to believe God for my healing and began to fast and pray. God had healed my body and met our physical needs often, each in a new and different way.

I felt wonderful after my fast and had boundless energy. Scriptures filled my mind. I allowed no negative thoughts to enter. Life was good. Months later I learned that God had answered our prayer, and that the tumours had disappeared. But by then it didn't seem to matter very much. A new sorrow had fallen upon us, casting a bleak shadow over our happiness. Our home would never be the same again. Our second little son, Gavin, was born six weeks early by caesarean section due to placenta previa, and he only survived for two days.

We were devastated. As I lay there in hospital, all I could say was, "Why, Lord? Why did you allow this to happen to us?" Ken tried to encourage me that one day God would explain everything, and we would be satisfied. Clinging to this thought brought comfort to me over the next painful weeks and months. Each time I closed my eyes I was given a picture of Jesus holding my little baby close in his arms. He seemed to say that baby Gavin was safe with him; and with that I must be content.

If Ken and I could have seen into the future during those dark days, we would have been consoled. God would recompense us for the suffering we were going through. He was to grant us not only a darling daughter, but also two more precious sons to give us much happiness. Before then, however, we had to work through a great test of our faith, and to gain an enormous victory for the Lord. It would be a vindication of God's healing power, which he would allow us to take around the world. Through this testimony many other couples, yearning for children, would find faith to have their prayers answered by God. You will find that story later; but meanwhile, I needed a period of healing and recuperation. The doctor assured me I had no tumours. The reason for my miscarriages was still a mystery. During the following year I built up my strength. We also moved back to Adelaide, where Ken was asked to become an assistant pastor in our home church, under Pastor Leo Harris.

Finally, when Dale was five and a half years of age, we were able to place in his arms a little sister, Sharon Elizabeth Rae. Through that pregnancy I had to remain bedfast for seven months (from when I was six weeks pregnant until she was born at eight and a half months). Many times, it seemed we would lose her, but always God intervened, and at last she was born safely. The mystery of my miscarriages was also revealed. I had RH Negative blood and had built up antibodies against my babies. Sharon had to have a blood transfusion when she was just two days of age. After that all was well. We were happy and contented. Our little family was growing.

We had been living in Adelaide for two years when we decided to move to Launceston, Tasmania, once again following the call from God in answer to a need! There was a small church in Launceston needing a pastor, and we were ready to go. We did not know it at the time, but here God would teach us some vital lessons in faith, and by assimilating those lessons we would gain two miracle sons!

After we had been in Tasmania for some time, I began to feel the urge to become a mother again. It was an enormously strong desire, and we began to pray about it. On the surface it seemed madness to attempt another pregnancy. I had spent so much time in bed, and had suffered so much to have Sharon, and now had two children to look after as well as a busy church schedule. But I did become pregnant again, only to lose yet another child, once again at two months. This time my specialist doctor told me that from now on all my babies would terminate at two months. I had too many antibodies to bear a child, and in those days (1965) no one knew how to overcome this problem. Ken and I spent some time talking this over. How could we continue to preach that 'Jesus was the Healer' if we could not have any more babies? If I hadn't wanted a baby, there would be no problem - but I did!

The God who gave me the yearning to have more children, and who allowed me to become pregnant, surely could work a miracle and help me to overcome this difficulty in my body. I reasoned this way - if God didn't want me to have any more babies, all he would have to do would be to close up my womb as he had with Rachel in Old Testament times. Since he hadn't done that, but had allowed me to get pregnant, that to me was sure proof he would help me. He who had given me the desire for motherhood would also give me another baby I wanted so much.

Despite these rationalisations, I wasn't going to rush in and conceive again without a definite Word from God. Not only was there a strong probability of another miscarriage, but now, observed the obstetrician, my own life was at risk. I might die myself if I tried to have another baby! What I needed was the faith of God, an unwavering certainty that he was with me, and that I had nothing to fear in attempting another pregnancy.

Finally, after much prayer, I said to Ken, "If I discover another couple who have had a similar problem, and it is established that God intervened in their life, granting them a baby, then I will go ahead." We continued to pray. Some time passed. Meanwhile, God gave me a Scripture to cling to –

So, do not throw away your confidence; it will be richly rewarded. You need to persevere so that when you have done the will of God, you will receive what he has promised. Hebrews 10:35-36

One day in the mail we received a magazine from the USA that we had not ordered or subscribed to. In it was the following testimony from an American physician, Dr William Standish-Reed -

> QUESTION: My wife and I have an RH incompatibility. As a result, my wife has lost her last two children by miscarriages. Do you believe that we can hope to have children? Or should my wife or I have an operation to prevent any further conception?
>
> ANSWER: A very dear friend of mine, a minister, at one time had this same problem. When his wife again conceived, they faced long months of anxiety, wondering whether they would have a normal child, or even if she would be able to carry the pregnancy through to its entirety. At that time, I had been studying the church's ministry of healing. I advised the minister to lay hands on his wife daily, and pray in the name of Jesus of Nazareth, asking God to allow her to have a normal pregnancy and a normal child ... It is my feeling that a pregnancy, carried through with husband and wife praying together, would produce wonderful results. The minister's wife had a normal child. Only God knows how he could 'juggle the genes' to cause such a result.

We were overjoyed! Here was the guidance for which we had been asking. We set ourselves to pray for each other. Every night Ken laid his hands on me and prayed for me; then I would pray for him. This seemed so right to us. God had answered our prayer and given us specific instructions through a medical doctor, which gave us the extra confidence we needed. For us, it was like another verse added to the Bible; a promise of healing with our names on it! God would do for us, what he had done for others!

After some months I became aware that I had conceived again. I was excited, though a little apprehensive. I rang my doctor, and she was horrified, despite my assurance to her that this time all would be well. She examined me, and to my astonishment told me that I was already three months pregnant. She took some blood from me and had it tested. I still had my antibodies, but they were not harming the baby. She took some of Ken's blood, it had not changed. In fact, nothing had changed! Except that against all probability I was having a successful pregnancy, with no sign of losing the baby! She kept asking me what we had done, and I kept telling her that we had prayed about it, and God was giving us a miracle baby. She was a Christian doctor, so she had to accept what was happening; even though, as far as she knew at that time, it was not possible.

Later on we were to discover that God had intervened to 'juggle our genes' and to give us a baby with the same blood group as myself (RH Negative). In due time, and without being obliged to spend even one day in bed, I gave birth to our third son, Eric. While in hospital I spoke to my paediatrician who was caring for Eric and I asked him, "Doctor, do you understand how this could have happened?" He admitted that he did not know, but he did give me a warning, "This was a one in a million chance. Don't try to do it again. It won't work another time."

God must have heard him and decided to do it again! Four and a half years later our fourth son, Baden, was born. So, after the trauma of three miscarriages, and placenta praevia when our second son died, we finally had our family of four children. From Dale (our first born) to Baden (our last born) covered a period of seventeen years altogether. In those years we learned so much about faith and saw many healings.

Now we were able to rejoice in our God who does all things well. Ken began to pray for others who had a desperate longing to bear children but who, for some reason, were unable to conceive. There are many such testimonies, but the one I will share with you happened in Perth, Western Australia. Ken was preaching in a church there and had a sudden insight, A 'word of knowledge' that there were two women in the congregation who wanted a child but were unable to conceive. Two young ladies came forward, weeping; one had been married six years, and the other eight years. God had cared for them enough to reveal their deep longing to a visiting preacher! Ken prayed for them and then left Perth to return home. Ten months later we received a letter from their pastor. They had both had baby girls. One after nine months and one week, and the other after nine months and two weeks! Praise God!

Why was God teaching us such mighty lessons of faith? Looking back, we can see that God was growing a teacher! It takes perhaps only five or ten minutes to grow an evangelist. Anyone who has been saved can become a soul-winner, burning to tell others about Jesus; but it takes God twenty years to grow a teacher.

(Ken continues here!) Four years passed before Alison once more expressed a desire to have more children. I was unwilling to put Alison's life in danger just to prove a dogma about divine healing or that I was a great man of faith. Her pregnancy with Sharon had been a stressful time, Alison was confined to her bed and although her mother was there to assist, it was difficult for us all, especially for little Dale. (It can be dangerous for both mother and unborn child when the mother's blood type is negative, and the father's is positive. The baby has a 50/50 chance of having the mother's blood type. If the baby is positive, then the mother's negative antibodies will attack the foetus causing a miscarriage. Today we have injections to stop this from happening but when Alison was pregnant there was no cure.)

So, I needed to hear from God personally. I needed him to quicken some promise of Scripture to me so powerfully that I could not possibly doubt its final fulfillment. That Word came to me in a passage from Romans where Paul refers to Abraham's faith that God would give him a son through Sarah even though both were too old to have children –

(Abraham) *did not waver through unbelief regarding the promise of God but was strengthened in his faith and gave glory to God, being fully persuaded that God had power to do what he had promised.* Romans 4:20-21 NIV

And another promise - *As it is written, I have made thee a father of many nations, before him whom he believed, even God, who quickeneth the dead, and calleth those things which be not as though they were.* Romans 4:17b KJV

These passages of promise flamed off the pages of Scripture. I knew with certainty that God was speaking to me through them and that I too could speak life into my wife's womb and that she would conceive and safely bear a child. I no longer felt there was any risk to Alison in a pregnancy.

With an inner conviction that we were in God's will, and filled with faith, we joined together in prayer each day with me laying hands on Alison, and she, with her hands on me, we agreed together in the name of Jesus that she would conceive, carry the child to full term, and be safely delivered of a healthy baby. I will concede that taking four years to reach this point probably was a sign of deficient faith. I cannot, and do not worry about that, I am just glad that finally Alison and I had found a sure way to believe God, and to lay hands upon each other every day and gain a miracle. All we needed was for the Lord to 'juggle the genes' for us!

Notice how carefully Paul expresses himself in Romans 4:17 (see above) - he does not say that God calls into existence something that had not existed. Any cook baking a new cake can do that. Rather, Paul says that God calls those things that do not exist as if they already do exist. That was the concept that gripped us and upon which we acted. So, I did just that. Night after night laying my hands on Alison in Jesus' name, I spoke to her barren womb, and declared it filled with life, and carrying a lively foetus. So, we prayed, and God spoke our son Eric into existence. He honoured our faith!

Four and a half years later, to our surprise this time, God gave us another miracle of 'juggled genes', and another perfect pregnancy without any sign of miscarriage and a fourth son, Baden Matthew. Both our sons had Alison's negative blood type! Not my positive blood type which would have caused a miscarriage. (Alison had three miscarriages and Sharon was nearly added to that number. Today women can receive an injection to prevent miscarriages from an RH negative mother and an RH positive father. But back in the 60's and 70's this was a real issue of concern for many women.)

Even though we had so much success in the healing ministry, perhaps I am too much a teacher to be able to focus consistently on one doctrine. I felt compelled to extend my knowledge and explore the many different aspects of the Bible and its theology.

At the time, I was travelling widely as an evangelist, preaching the gospel and praying for the sick. However, I made a conscious decision to abandon this ministry life and instead focus on a wider teaching ministry which included writing the books we would need for the Correspondence Course, and later the Bible College. I have written more than fifty such works. There are many evangelists in the world, but not many can write theological textbooks.

Jesus was able to be all things - master evangelist, prophet, healer, and teacher. He could and did, with equal emphasis, achieve astonishing success in all these areas. He prophesied accurately many times. One such prophecy was:

- **The destruction of the temple which fell to the Romans in 70AD.** *Jesus left the temple and was walking away when his disciples came up to him to call his attention to its buildings. "Do you see all these things?" he asked. "Truly I tell you, not one stone here will be left on another; every one will be thrown down."* Matthew 24:1-2
- **He had the Holy Spirit without measure.** *For the one whom God has sent speaks the words of God, for God gives the Spirit without limit.* John 3:34
- **God was with Jesus.** *God anointed Jesus of Nazareth with the Holy Spirit and power, and he went around doing good and healing all who were under the power of the devil, because God was with him.* Acts 10:38
- **He healed them all.** *When evening came, many who were demon possessed were brought to him, and he drove out the spirits with a word and healed all the sick.* Matthew 8:16
- **He taught not as the scribes.** *When Jesus had finished saying these things, the crowds were amazed at his teaching, because he taught as one who had authority, and not as their teachers of the law.* Matthew 7:28-29

When we walk in the fullness of what God has for each one of us the impossible becomes possible. We only need to believe and put our faith into action!

Truly, truly, I say to you, whoever believes in me will also do the works that I do; and greater works than these will he do, because I am going to the Father. Whatever you ask in my name, this I will do, that the Father may be glorified in the Son. If you ask me anything in my name I will do it. John 14:12-28

1968 DEMONS

"Ken Chant is coming! Don't let him near me!" This screech came from the mouth of a woman from our church. But the voice was coming from a demon.

It was a Saturday, and I was in the front garden, pulling out some weeds when a sudden urge seized me to go inside, put on some more dignified garments, and as quickly as possible visit Joan (not her real name). The command was imperative, allowing no delay, and requiring instant obedience. Happily, I owned at this time a new and reliable car; so, nothing loath, I obeyed what was clearly the voice of God and rushing inside told Alison the Lord had just instructed me to visit Joan and pray for her.

When I got to Joan's home, I found her husband leaning over their front gate. Mobile phones were unheard of in that time, so I was surprised to see him waiting there. When I asked if he had been waiting for me, he simply held a finger to his lips, turned toward the house and said, "Just listen." I did as he bade me and at once in the distance, I could hear Joan's voice screaming, "Ken Chant's coming! Don't let him in!"

"That is Joan," said he, "she has locked herself in the bathroom and won't come out." I requested he take me to her and after talking to her through the bathroom door for a few minutes she agreed to come out and speak to me.

Her story is quite dramatic. She had suffered greatly during the Second World War, personally experiencing the devastating effects of bombs, bodies strewn in the streets, living with terror and fear of what the day would bring. This led to a gradual building of nervous terror that would seize her from time to time without warning. For example, she would be washing the dishes or engaging in some other household chore when a terrible sensation would overwhelm her. She could feel two hands going around her neck and squeezing as hard as a navvy (a construction worker). She felt she could no longer breathe and would quickly reach a point when she was straining agonizingly to catch her breath again. But the more she strained the more she felt herself suffocating, utterly unable to take that next breath. The only way she could find to relieve her agony was to turn her back to the nearest wall and press hard against it until she had convinced herself that it was impossible for any creature to be there. Many times, her husband would come home from work and find her nearly collapsing from exhaustion from standing for several hours pressing hard against the wall.

The stress and misery this was causing her was driving her relentlessly toward a complete breakdown. Even telling me the story was deeply disturbing her. I persuaded her to come into the lounge room, find a comfortable lounge chair in which to sit while I read some peaceful Scriptures to her. I then asked her husband to pray with her, and himself read a couple of suitable passages from the Bible. I then told her about the reality of demons and how this could only be a demonic attack. I told her also about the authority and power in the name of Jesus Christ, and that when we use that name, we gain complete control over all the power of the enemy.

I asked if she were willing to place her own faith in the wonderful name of Jesus. She agreed heartily that she would indeed trust in the Lord alone. I then asked if she would let me pray for her and command, in Jesus' name, the evil spirit to come out of her. She would then be free from this awful bondage. She agreed and so we stood up, the three of us holding hands, asking the Lord in his grace to show Joan an abundance of kindness and at my command that the demon would be cast out of her.

No doubt many different explanations could be given by sceptical thinkers for Joan's experience, and I would not say that even I had sufficient intellectual powers to refute their naturalistic arguments. I know only that casting out the demon in Jesus' name worked. For as Scripture commands, I laid hands on Joan, prayed for her in Jesus' name, rebuked the demon, commanded it to leave her, never to return. And this command was obeyed. The demon left.

Forgive me if I quote here the Egyptian Pharoah's dictum (as shown in the movie, *The Ten Commandments*) -

"So let it be written, so let it be done."

I felt, at that moment, that the authority God had given me in Christ was indeed irrefutable.

The wonderful result of all this was the deliverance Joan felt in reclaiming her life. She had not felt safe having children before this but now she and her husband could begin a family which they did with the blessing of the Lord on their life together.

Several sayings, both biblical and secular jostle for supremacy.

Secular: "There are more things in heaven and earth, Horatio, than are dreamt of in your philosophy." *Hamlet* by William Shakespeare; Act I, Scene V

"You can tear apart the baby's rattle and see what makes the noise inside, but there is a veil covering the unseen world which not the strongest man, nor even the united strength of all the strongest men that ever lived, could tear apart." Francis Pharcellus Church (1839-1906), an American war correspondent for the New York Times during the Civil War.

Biblical: "Submit yourselves, then, to God. Resist the devil, and he will flee from you." James letter to the New Testament Church, Chapter 4 Verse 7.

I saw Satan fall like lightning from heaven. I have given you authority to trample on snakes and scorpions and to overcome all the power of the enemy; nothing will harm you. Luke 10: 18-19

Finally, be strong in the Lord and in his mighty power. Put on the full armour of God, so you can take your stand against the devil's schemes. For our struggle is not against flesh and blood, but against the rulers, against the authorities, against the powers of this dark world, and against the spiritual forces of evil in the heavenly realms. Ephesians 6:10-12

1970 KELSO

At the mouth of the River Tamar there was a building which someone in my church discovered and declared it good for a church camp. Turns out it was previously the Bathurst Infantry Training Camp with cabins, a kitchen, and  meeting area. It was no longer being used so I announced to the church that we would hold a camp for a week or so during the coming Christmas season. A sufficient number of people, mostly young families, were eager to attend, and so I began to plan for our first Christmas Camp at Kelso. This was not an entirely new venture for me because I had organised several similar live-in camps for as many as 200+ young people at Sandy Creek, for the South Australian CRC churches. (See 1958 BW)

Nonetheless, organising the Kelso Camp required a massive effort. How many beds would we need? How many would bring their own tents? How many would bring their own caravan? How much cooking apparatus would we need? How much milk, cheese, butter, and other similar perishables? How much fruit and vegetables? What kind of refrigeration was available? How many packets of lollies, what variety, and would chocolate survive the summer heat? How many bottles of soft drinks, and cordials and many other similar items? (Alison set up a small lolly shop and sold drinks and lollies in little white bags to the children for a few pennies.)

We had a couple of camp cooks, who were helped by a roster of ladies, while other campers were rostered to set up a dining table, wash the dishes, and so on. Perhaps miraculously, no-one ever got sick because of the food, or the primitive environment.

The days were free, but each evening we sat around a campfire, sang choruses, shared anecdotes and then I gave a short homily.

There were no existing toilets, so we had to dig our own outside long-drop toilets. Here my army experience in setting up military camp hygiene was useful. So, we dug two long-drops, put some protective covering around each of them and voila! We were set to go.

We had only one potential tragedy with the toilet. There was a young man at the camp who was mildly intellectually challenged. He did not want to join us one day when we decided to walk further up the river. So, we left him behind and asked him to dig another hole for a toilet because the other two would soon be unusable. When we returned early in the evening, we found he had dug in the sand an enormous hole nearly twice his own height. There was a great mound of sand heaped up all around. All we could see was a spadeful of sand flying into the air, but no human body was visible! We hurried over and found that the pit was in imminent peril of collapsing on top of him! To this day, apart from the providence of God, I do not know how it failed to do so. We hastily pulled him out, helped him dust off the sand, and then filled the hole in again and packed it down. What a relief! We were all very grateful to the Lord for protecting our friend!

Another story, not so dramatic, was with the water heater. It burst! There was a plumber among the campers. He told us to hand out all the chewing gum from the camp lolly shop. So, we vigorously chewed the gum, standing in line, and handed our offerings to the plumber who plugged the hole. The rough remedy proved to be remarkably successful so that we had hot water again until the camp ended.

Another aspect of Kelso Beach were the thousands of soldier crabs emerging every afternoon from the wet sand when the tide receded. The soldier crabs had a body about one inch (25mm) wide. They were white with blue on their backs. We had great fun, especially the children, running up and down the beach trying to catch them without treading on any of them. Mostly successfully but with an occasional mishap. In each of those camps, on the Saturday evening, we put on a concert featuring the campers as the artists to which we gave a spoof name that was a mockery of a popular programme in the Australian media at that time. The programme was called the *Australian Amateur Hour,* but we called our concert, *The Kelso Amateur Howl.* I don't really remember any of the concerts, or any particular act being a fizzer.

But, if I may boast a little, I do remember at one concert our daughter, Sharon, and her friend Vicki, who were then about ten years old, charming everybody by dressing themselves in raggedy peasant garments, with charcoal on their cheeks singing a duet by Harry M Woods (1927) -

> Oh! We ain't got a barrel of money,
> Maybe we're ragged and funny
> But we'll travel along
> Singing a song
> Side by side.

Some performances were serious but mostly they were hilarious. Another skit that was performed at a later camp was recounted to me by my son, Eric. Here it is in his own words -

"I recall a skit where one of the elders of the church, Austin Hudson, for some reason had his hands tied behind his back but was then unable to speak his lines. It was discovered that he was so used to gesticulating while talking, that with his hands tied he was barely able to utter a word. There was great merriment in the audience as we saw that no matter how hard he tried to remain still and speak without moving, his arms would start twitching again and he couldn't get out more than a word or two before stuttering into incoherence."

For us, one memorable day a strong wind caught the huge beach ball we had given to one of our sons for Christmas. He had to stand in howling frustration watching the tide carry it out to sea and away from him forever. One of the sorrows of childhood.

However, living together so happily and amicably was a little foretaste of heaven. We were all together, enjoying each other's company, loving and serving one another, singing and rejoicing each day. All the camps were great fun and Alison and I look back on them with nostalgia.

How good and how pleasant it is when God's people live together in unity! It is like precious oil poured on the head, running down on the beard, running down on Aaron's beard, down on the collar of his robe. It is as if the dew of Hermon were falling on Mount Zion. For there the Lord bestows his blessing, even life evermore. Psalm 133:1-3

1970 GARDENING

"When Adam delved and Eve span who was then the gentleman." *John Ball 1338-1381*

In the 14th century, John Ball was a prominent Roman Catholic priest. He became an enthusiastic supporter of the radical Lollardists, thought to be one of the earliest expressions and the earliest rumblings of the English Reformation, which itself was a provocative forerunner of the Protestant Reformation. He believed in social equality and promoted Adam and Eve as equals in the Garden of Eden.

The issue of delving (dig or shovel) confronted me when we moved into our new home in Riverside, a suburb of Launceston, Tasmania. I loathed gardening! And none of my children had at that time, any more liking for the enterprise than I had. Nonetheless we set ourselves to do our duty, and the garden with its concrete walls and paths, confined the flower beds sparkling like jewels in a tidy cabinet of a jeweller's shop.

Of course, every gardener knows that gardening is arduous. No-one can create a garden without toilsome labour as declared by a popular poem, *The Glory of the Garden,* by Rudyard Kipling -

> Oh, Adam was a gardener, and God who made him sees,
> That half a proper gardener's work is done upon his knees,
> So when your work is finished,
> You can wash your hands and pray
> For the Glory of the Garden that it may not pass away!
> And the Glory of the Garden it shall never pass away!

However, here is a story told by someone who built a beautiful garden and was showing it off to a friend. The friend said, "What a beautiful garden! Isn't God a wonderful creator to produce such beauty?" The gardener replied, "Huh! You should have seen it when God had it all to himself! It was nothing but weeds and stones!"

My apologies to whoever coined this story and please forgive me if I am breaking some copyright. This familiar story has both some serious and comedic aspects. On the one hand it is just a funny story, and most would chuckle at it. Others would find in it a serious challenge to fulfil one of the first demands of Scripture, that it is our responsibility as caretakers of the planet to do all we can in helping nature to flourish.

The heavens declare the glory of God; the skies proclaim the work of his hands. Day after day they pour forth speech; night after night they reveal knowledge. Psalm 19:1

Let the heavens rejoice, let the earth be glad; let the sea resound, and all that is in it. Let the fields be jubilant, and everything in them; let all the trees of the forest sing for joy. Psalm 96:12

1970 HORROR

There was a hideously loud crash, followed almost instantly by the awful screams of our four-year-old son, Eric. He had been sitting on the edge of the footpath next to a parked car, exploring something he had found in the gutter.

There was a steep hill in front of our house at the top of which the brakes of a parked car had failed. The vehicle plummeted down the hill and crashed horribly into a large Ford V8 just where Eric was playing.

The sickening noise of the crash told us of the catastrophe and both Alison and I rushed to see what had happened. I had been working in our front garden, so I got there first. Picking up a length of framing timber, I thrust it under the bumper bar of the V8. With an almost superhuman strength I was able to move both cars sufficiently back from the gutter so that Alison could pull our wounded son away from danger. He had deep lacerations on both legs that had left his bones exposed. The skin of his head had also been slashed open as the impact had driven him backwards onto the gravelled path. Alison wrapped Eric in a blanket, and we raced in our car to the local physician.

On the way, Eric, who was in shock but still conscious, looked up at his mother and said, "Mummy, may I cry." It was enough to bring us both to tears. Alison had been teaching him to be brave whenever he hurt himself, and to not cry over a little scratch. Those were the days when mothers taught their sons to - "Keep a stiff upper lip and be brave!" (Nowadays we realise that it is far better to let children recognise and express a range of emotions to benefit their mental health and ability to empathise with others.)

The doctor called an ambulance and bound up the boy's wounds while we waited anxiously. Once we were in the ambulance and heading for the hospital, Eric, who was still conscious through this whole episode, imperatively demanded if the driver could please sound his siren. It was against their rules, but the driver chuckled and turned on this warning to other drivers. When it began wailing Eric was delighted. His time in hospital was not so pleasant. He was anaesthetised and his legs which were deeply cut were sewn up. Likewise, his scalp which had to be shaved and sewn.

Fifty years later our son is still sensitive about this story. He still bears the scars of this accident. He can sense when people walk up behind him as his scar tingles. His big sister, Sharon, is also still emotional about this incident. She slept in our room each night and held our hands until her brother came home.

I hear how other people have found supernatural (or hysterical) strength to call upon, when faced with a sudden emergency. For myself, I am more inclined to believe that the strong arm that lifted two cars, was not mine but God's. I cannot believe that the spaghetti that passes for muscles in my arms was strong enough to move those heavy vehicles. The power of the Holy Spirit was indeed evident in this case. This reminded me of the time my uncle Bob saved my life by a similar superhuman miracle when he directed a heavy windmill away from my prostrate body. (See 1948 Farming)

Did I learn anything from this miracle of divine intervention? Primarily, I learned that no matter what crisis one is facing, you can trust in God to provide whatever strength, wisdom, or miracle is needed to meet the exigencies of the time.

God is our refuge and strength, an ever present help in trouble. Psalm 46:1

The Lord is near to the broken hearted and saves the crushed in spirit. Psalm 34:18

1971 ACCIDENTS

There are memories charged with emotion that you never forget.

The River Torrens runs alongside the Adelaide Zoo. It is more a lake than a river, as it is dammed up to keep the water from draining away during the dry summers. It is so muddy that nothing is visible below its surface. Despite this many people hire a boat and have a pleasant time rowing up and down. Alison and I did this one day with our family but when the time approached to row the boat to the shore and we were stepping onto the landing, Eric, then around two years of age, slipped into the water and instantly disappeared from our sight. At once I leaned over the edge of the boat, reached into the water, and because he had long hair, I was able to find him fairly quickly and haul him out. Our little son sat on the bank shaking, our hearts were pounding, but as he had taken in very little water, he soon expelled it and in a short time was fully recovered for which we heartily thanked God.

We lived in Launceston, Tasmania, for some 15 years and occasionally we would drive 50 minutes west of Launceston to a local creek for a family picnic. On one occasion, Eric, who was about three years of age, was running along the edge of the creek when he fell into a hole he could not see and vanished from our sight. I was too far away from the bank to be aware of what was happening, but our older children were there, and Dale was sufficiently quick witted to reach into the water, locate Eric, and haul him out with help from his other sibling, Sharon. Once again Eric sat on the bank gasping for air, he had swallowed only a little water and once again soon recovered.

Eric seemed to have a propensity for having accidents. There was another occasion about the age of seven years, when he joined a school excursion. The children were to learn about fishing. Almost inevitably among all his fellow students, Eric was the only one who managed to ram a fishhook through one of his fingers. The teacher had no idea how to remove it without causing too much pain, so he took Eric to a nearby physician who quickly solved the problem by cutting the hook into two parts. This enabled him to lift the hook out of Eric's finger by pulling the straight shank horizontally out. He then wrapped the finger in a bandage and Eric was able to rejoin the excursion and returned home without further mishap.

Sharon recalls that Eric once put a peg on his ear lobe and finding this uncomfortable pulled it off with great vigour. Blood gushed from the subsequent tear, and she never forgot this ghastly sight.

Many years later Eric bought a motor bike. Sure enough, while riding down the highway, the motorbike slipped on the road and he had an accident, breaking one of his collarbones. He told us how, in the midst of that terrifying feeling of flying down the road, the motorbike on its side, he felt God's hand hold his head up from the concrete surface. So, the accident was not fatal.

I have no doubt there were other times which he didn't bother to relate to us. For these rescues we were, and remain, deeply grateful to the overriding providence of God.

Baden was our other miracle son born with RH negative blood like Alison's. Baden only had one accident in his childhood! For a father could there be any sight more sickening than to watch his nine-month-old son falling from the second storey of his home, past his office window. There were concrete pavers below and to fall from that height was a death sentence. I had been working at my desk when I heard a cry from above made by Baden's four-year-old brother, Eric. The upstairs window in the lounge room was open, the baby was encouraged to wave to his sister who had run down the stairs to wave up to him. The curious baby leaned out to see what was below and toppled over, falling to the ground one storey below.

I saw something falling past the window and heard Eric crying out that he had killed his brother. Realising with horror that my baby son had fallen to the ground I rushed out of my office yelling for Alison. We found Baden suffering from shock and obviously winded, with his face white as a sheet, but otherwise unharmed. We rushed him to the local doctor who deduced that Baden had been saved by his winter clothing - two jumpers, and double cloth nappies - had preserved our son from a fatal injury. No-one was more relieved than Eric and his sister! As a consequence of this event, I had all the windows in the upper storey fixed so they could not open more than 6 inches!

There are times when God so obviously saves us from something that would be more than we could bear, and others where we suffered profound sorrow. But through all of life's anomalies, we give thanks for his saving grace. In this case, with profound delight and gratitude to God, our family drove home from the doctors, loving Baden even more than we had before.

There are many more stories that I could relate but suffice to say that our children have grown into exemplary adults and have brought us great joy throughout their lives, as have our 17 grandchildren and 19 great grandchildren!

Fear not, for I am with you; be not dismayed, for I am your God; I will strengthen you, I will help you, I will uphold you with my righteous right hand. Isaiah 41:10

Children are a heritage from the LORD, offspring a reward from him. Psalms 127:3

1971 DEGREES

Wow! What a year 1971 was! So many important life and ministry changes occurred that I can hardly sort them all out. Among these changes was a commitment to higher learning. I decided that if I was going to present myself as an expert in Christian theology and Biblical theology, I needed to gain credibility by obtaining some higher education awards. I won't weary you with the details but will say at least this, having decided to begin with a Bachelor of Arts, with a major in theology, I searched for a school that would enable me to do this as an external student. The only one I could find that was truly suitable was Berean Christian College, in Wichita, Kansas. USA. They graciously gave me a scholarship as an external overseas student which made it possible for me to afford the studies.

My first degree took me four years to complete. It was a Bachelor of Ministries degree, and it was presented to me on behalf of Berean by the Rev A. S. Holmes BA, BD, MRE, Dip Ed, MACE, who was Principal of Oakburn College, Launceston, on April 20th 1975.

Of course, I didn't stop there but kept on researching and writing for another four years, to add a Master of Religious Education to the baccalaureate. Yet still I pressed on until six years later I was able to add a Doctor of Ministry to my awards. That was a proud moment, I can't deny, when the renowned American actor, Buddy Ebsen, handed me my doctorate as part of a special Berean Christian College celebration held in the ballroom of the great sailing ship, the Queen Mary, which is still permanently moored at Long Beach, California. How brilliant! How much I enjoyed the ceremony and was delighted to receive my award from the hands of such a famous American actor and Christian. The Bible reading for the service came from 2 Timothy 2:1-15 (Jerusalem Bible) where Paul encourages Timothy to standfast in the faith; and to remember that nothing worthwhile is achieved without hard work and sacrifice. I had applied that Scripture diligently to my studies and received my reward.

The following quote from a letter I wrote to the President of Berean, Dr Charles Bachman, gives the steady progression of my education with Berean -

> Do you realise that our association goes back 14 years, to 1971? I took four years to complete the BMin, another four years to obtain the Master of Religious Education (MRE), and now nearly six years to reach the level of Doctor of Ministry! The labour that has gone into the books and assignments I have sent you over those years has been immense, especially as it was all done in the midst of a busy program of teaching, preaching, and pastoring. But I certainly do know a lot more now than when I began.

Four years later, again I resolved to upgrade from a Doctor of Ministry (DMin) to a Doctor of Theology (ThD) which I earned from Logos Graduate School, Jacksonville, Florida.

That goal being achieved, I would have been content to rest on my laurels, except that my younger brother Barry had the temerity to gain a fully earned Doctor of Philosophy (PhD) from Macquarie University. This was more than my pride could endure, so back to school I went, this time to Logos Graduate School, and after a massive effort gained my own Doctor of Philosophy (PhD).

How did I manage this with a wife, four children, and a church to run? I did it by turning my essays into sermons, and my sermons into books, and I began the Launceston Bible Correspondence Course (now Vision Colleges) in tandem with my studies. I used everything and wasted nothing. And all this writing was by hand! I must have written more than a million words. Finally, I was able to buy a typewriter and then later a computer. Then I had to learn to type!

I did finally gain a volunteer secretary, Mary Shadbolt, with an electric typewriter who was able to assist by typing up my written work neatly and another volunteer secretary, Lois Mackey, who helped by marking the exam papers for our correspondence students and sending out new books.

I had many other helpers to correlate the books after they were printed on our first Gestetner Machine. How much easier it is these days when we can order a few, or many books, from the large printing companies who receive our latest PDF via email. Somehow, they enter the current book into their enormous printing machine at one end and then the completed book, printed, with binding and cover all complete, comes out the other end. What a blessing this is for us after many years of struggle with various printing machines.

You then, my son, be strong in the grace that is in Christ Jesus. And the things you have heard me say in the presence of many witnesses entrust to reliable people who will also be qualified to teach others. Join with me in suffering, like a good soldier of Christ Jesus. 2 Timothy 2:1-3

1972 MARIA

What an exhilarating ride! Myself, Alison, our children, plus a significant number of people from my Launceston congregation were roaring across the sea in a large motor launch to Maria Island, located off the East coast of Tasmania. We had decided to have our church camp here, rather than Kelso. The trip took us about 40 exciting minutes.

Before we left the mainland, however, several annoying things happened. On my way to the launch, my car dropped its muffler, leaving only the open tail pipe and a roar like a jet plane taking off. It was a most embarrassing noise. My daughter, Sharon, says that I lost my temper and stood on the side of the road raving against the universe! I, of course, deny that categorically. I'll leave you to choose whom to believe! Nonetheless, I had to put up with the ghastly racket for several kilometres before we reached the wharf where we parked the car and boarded the motor launch. In this small town there was no mechanic available to repair the muffler. So, a week later, we journeyed back home enduring the ghastly noise all the way back to Launceston. Was that legal? Probably not! But I got away with it until I was able to get a new muffler fitted!

Maria Island, apart from one or two state appointed rangers, was uninhabited, and only a few simple buildings were provided for shelter from the elements. One of them was a large shed surrounded by a veranda. Toilet facilities were primitive, but they were enough for us. The shed was too big to partition, so we all had to sleep there together. We did separate the sexes into two groups – we had sleeping bags and each night the ladies and girls would retire first and then turn their backs while we men retired. It worked quite well, and I can't remember any scandalous behaviour.

In the meantime, all the children (and there were a number of them) snuggled into their sleeping bags on the veranda, so they could shine their torches into the bush to observe the many native creatures that emerged in the darkness. Among them were wombats, emus, kangaroos and wallabies, as well as musk ducks and blue billed ducks. The animals moved freely among us as this was their island and we were the interlopers. They had no fear of us humans and the emus would steal our food if given half a chance. Alison remembers an emu reaching over her shoulder and grabbing her lunchtime sandwich right out of her hand on one occasion. What a shock! But great fun all the same.

There were no shops of any sort anywhere on the island, so we had to carry all our food, water, milk, and the like, with us on the ferry. But we didn't bring enough, so halfway through the week we had to ask for a couple of volunteers to go back to the mainland to replenish our supplies. We brought giant blocks of ice in Eskys to keep food cold as there was no electricity either. None of us got sick or starved, so this must have been enough to work adequately. In the meantime, we no doubt all benefited from the fresh and health-giving air.

We stayed on the island for 7 delightful days, and occupied ourselves by swimming, hiking, and playing cricket. The children had a wonderful time exploring, climbing trees, gathering sticks, playing together, and telling stories to one another around the campfire. Every night we cooked damper and potatoes in silver foil over hot coals, and toasted jam jaffles with a jaffle iron in the ashes. The rest of our food we cooked in the primitive barbeque area. We barbecued sausages, bacon, steaks, eggs, onions, and so on. There was always plenty of food as everyone shared and there were some fine home cooks in our church.

On one occasion we visited a 19th century cemetery, overgrown with weeds, a broken short iron fence and gravestones tilting in many different directions, some broken, and some toppled over. It showed that a hundred years before there had been some people living and working on the island. We later learned that the gravestones commemorated convicts who had died while serving their sentence in a penitentiary built in 1825.

Happily, no one suffered any hurt during the week we were there, neither adult, nor perhaps surprisingly, any child. After a happy week on the island, and with great satisfaction, we boarded the launch again for another exhilarating ride back to the mainland. We are grateful to the Lord for such a delightful holiday and for keeping us safe while we were there and for safe travel to and from the island. I am reminded of the Scriptures -

Some went out on the sea in ships; they were merchants on the mighty waters. They saw the works of the Lord, his wonderful deeds in the deep. Psalm 107:23-24

God made the wild animals according to their kinds, the livestock according to their kinds, and all the creatures that move along the ground according to their kinds. And God saw that it was good. Genesis 1:24-26

1973 ORU

I was wallowing in deep misery and despair, on my knees at the lowest point I could find on the Oral Roberts University grounds. I was at the bottom of a bowl-shaped garden bed where I was surrounded by a profusion of flowers, shrubs and other kinds of glorious expressions of God's creative power. But I was barely aware of them. I was reeling from the impact that had come upon me. I was surrounded by the splendid buildings, the ultramodern architecture, and the multi-storey administration block of which the entire top floor was devoted to Dr Roberts private office, apart from the entrance corridor in which sat his secretary behind a magnificent desk equipped with a variety of almost futuristic secretarial gadgets.

The secretary guarded the way into her employer's private domain. But I had been given permission to explore the whole building, including the top floor. So, I marched boldly down the corridor and into the revered office itself, whose floor was covered by a very thick and very expensive carpet. I was stunned to discover that the entire ceiling consisted of gorgeous, brightly lit panels of stained glass. There, too, sat Oral's magnificent desk, which at first sight seemed to me to be almost as big as my entire office back in our humble home in Launceston, Tasmania.

By the time I had explored all eight floors of the admin block where every desk was equipped with the latest possible office technology and then explored many of the marvellous university buildings with their very up to date furnishings and equipment, and had reflected on the smallness of my own ministry achievements in comparison with those of Dr Roberts, I felt so crushed and humiliated that I was driven to seek the lowest place in the university gardens. There complained to God about the unfairness of life, asking why he would give so much to one man and so little to another. I continued my complaints in one shape or another for perhaps a half an hour when suddenly, it seemed to me that God seized me, shook me violently, and demanded, "Chant! How much longer do you think I will put up with this nonsense?" At once, I understood what the Almighty was saying to me. He might as well have quoted the proverb, 'Comparisons are odious!'

I knew the Lord was telling me to shake off my depression, accept what he had called me to be, to do, and to become. I understood also – better than I ever had before – that had God wanted me to be Oral Roberts, or Billy Graham, or John Wesley, or any other famous religious leader, he would have made me in that fashion. Since he had not, he wanted me to be happy living within my own skin and gladly fulfilling his plan for my life, whether that led to global fame or utter obscurity.

That lesson was reinforced to me by a book that came into my hands, *Twelve English Reformers*. It described twelve men in Great Britain who had had a powerful impact on the English Reformation of the 16th and 17th centuries yet showed how vastly different they were from each other. One was an extrovert, another was an introvert; one was very scholarly, another barely literate; one was highly sociable, another shyly withdrawn; one was a fiery preacher who used few if any written notes, another depended upon a sermon that was written out in full; one was irascible, another was friendly and sociable. Yet they were all quite powerfully used by God for his purpose in the English Reformation.

Of course, the principle of gladly accepting yourself for who you are and what you have is not restricted to preachers. It is a salubrious rule for everyone; for a housewife as well as the CEO of a great corporation; for a bricklayer as for a renowned architect; for the rich and poor alike; for those who are well-educated as well as those who are barely literate; and so on.

So, learn how to live well, love well, laugh often, knowing that you are the very person whom God designed and sent into the world to fulfil a specific eternal purpose. Never forget that for a Christian the only conceivable definition of success is to find the will of God and do it!

Teach me to do your will, for you are my God! May your good Spirit lead me on level ground. Psalm 143:10

1973 USA

A health food store in an excellent location and selling products at a good price was an attractive proposition. After being in full time ministry for some twenty years why was I thinking about buying a health food store? Mostly because I was disappointed and frustrated. Not because I had failed as a local church pioneer and pastor, for I had successfully planted several churches. The church I pastored at the time was the one in Launceston, Tasmania, a CRC congregation which had about two hundred people in its membership, and who attended more or less regularly, except that on an ordinary Sunday probably 30% of the congregants would be absent or delayed (some of them being farmers who were milking cows and came late). Nonetheless gloom enveloped me.

Why? Because I deeply sensed that my real capacity would never be achieved as a pastor. So, I had to find another expression of my ministry skills. My thought was then to buy the shop, build it to the point so that a manager could be put in charge of it while I travelled the country preaching and teaching. Would that plan have succeeded? Probably not! In any case God made it plain to me that he would not allow it. The voice God used was Dr Ralph Wilkerson's, who was then senior pastor of the Melodyland Christian Centre, Los Angeles. The auditorium was wholly circular with its pulpit in the centre, surrounded by around 4,000 seats. I was there attending a conference when Dr Wilkerson who had never met me, or knew anything about me, suddenly stopped speaking and said, "God has just shown me that an Australian pastor is present who has been called to ministry but who is contemplating leaving it." He then went on to say that God's judgment would fall on such a man.

I was shocked almost beyond belief!! Who would have thought that the Word of God could pursue one around the planet! I left that meeting a shaken man knowing two things, that my health food store fairytale had come to an abrupt end, and that God would find another way to help me fulfil my potential. And he did so remarkably.

Another attendee at the Melodyland Conference was evangelist and prophet the late Dick Mills. God brought us together and we arranged to have breakfast the next morning. I have forgotten everything else about that conference except that breakfast with Dick Mills. Prior to this meeting we were unknown to each other although I soon learned that Dick was well acquainted with my brother Barry. They had shared several meetings during one of Dick's earlier visits to Australia. But I had never met him. Anyway, we began our breakfast, and I ordered my usual stack of American pancakes with butter and maple syrup – a dish I had never had an opportunity to enjoy before my arrival in the USA.

How surprised I was when Dick downed his knife and fork, looked at me and said, "I have just received a word from God for you." Then under the powerful inspiration of the Holy Spirit he devoted nearly an hour to telling me more about myself than even I knew! Dick must have wondered what impact he was making because I continued munching through my pile of pancakes while his breakfast grew cold. Actually, I was falling apart inside. Dick told me things that I knew only God knew, that not even my wife knew. It was a staggering miracle of divine revelation. Some 40 years later I still have an outline of that stupendous oracle in my office files. Among other things, Dick told me that when I got back to Tasmania, I would begin to develop a Bible college that would become worldwide in its scope. He also warned me that the first couple of years after my return home would be among the darkest I would ever experience in my life, but if I pressed bravely on and did not doubt the call and promise of God, I would prevail over all opposition.

How sadly true that was! Anyway, more of that story later. (See 1975 Warnings)

Dick also told me that having predicted a new career for me as a teacher of theology he would like to put some money where his mouth was, so he arranged for us to visit a large warehouse which had on its shelves a massive collection of theological, historical, doctrinal, dogmatic books, with hundreds of other works dealing with Christian life and belief. The books I chose cost Dick a little over $200US, which in today's currency would be equivalent to possibly $2000 Australian. Here was a rare thing indeed! A modern prophet who had such confidence in his oracle that he was able to back it out of his own funds.

Astonishingly, that morning a man had approached Dick wanting to repay him money that he had borrowed several years ago. He owed Dick very close to the cost of the books Dick had purchased for me but had not had the funds to return the loan until that week. Dick had forgotten all about it and was astounded to have his generosity returned to him. He then passed on these funds to me through the purchase of the books and arranged for them to be shipped to Australia. It was God's provision. Dick and I remained lifelong friends.

The books included all the volumes in the Anti-Nicene and Post Nicene Church Fathers. There were also several history collections, Bible dictionaries, and other reference works. Altogether, it was an amazing gift and when the shipment finally arrived, it wonderfully increased my then small library. Over the years this book collection kept growing until it numbered more than two thousand doctrine and reference works, along with several hundred volumes of fiction, poetry, and a couple of encyclopedias. So, the love of reading which first began in my childhood was strongly enhanced and I have ever since been a voracious devourer of many kinds of literature.

Dick had predicted that I would go back to Tasmania, overcome several seemingly insuperable problems and would in time set up a Bible school. In anticipation of a future teaching ministry and to gain credibility for books I wanted to write for a future Bible college. I continued to study for many years working my way up to a Doctorate. (See 1971 Degrees)

All scripture is God breathed and is useful for teaching, rebuking, correcting and training in righteousness, so that the servant of God may be thoroughly equipped for every good work. 2 Timothy 3:16-17

1973 WRITING

It was the most frustrating thing. As mentioned in Degrees, I had decided that I needed at least a Bachelor degree if I were to have any sort of credibility as a Bible teacher, which meant that I would have to write at least one thesis of book length to attain it. My first obstacle to this noble aspiration was found in a number of my fellow pastors. They saw some of the modernist and critical writings I was researching for my thesis and expressed either scorn or alarm at such an endeavour. In any case they all thought that I would at least either destroy or seriously weaken my faith in God if I kept on absorbing such stuff. But when one is pursuing God's will one knows it and has not the least fear of being hurt by it. So, I laughed at their protests and continued researching and writing.

When I began writing, I realised that initially I would have to do this by hand since I couldn't afford even a manual typewriter let alone an electric one. But I soon found that deciding to do something and then actually doing it were vastly different. So, I would purchase a ream of lined paper, which I think in those days was itself up to 500 sheets and then found myself deeply reluctant to tackle those white sheets, which seemed to stare at me with defiant eyes. Whenever I resolved to begin writing I found that I could think of a thousand things to do that were more important! The result, I was well into the year before I finally sat down and began to put words on those challenging pages. But then another surprising thing began to happen. I discovered it was rather like preaching - scary to begin with, but one soon grows in confidence as the Holy Spirit inspires and you end in the full flush of divine glory. I found it was like that with writing – arduous, or even scary to begin, but the more one wrote the more one felt the quickening grace of the Holy Spirit.

That does not mean there is any infallibility about my writing. I am no Paul! I freely accept that even the best of my writing has blemishes. So, when I talk about, 'divine glory' and, 'quickening grace' I do not mean that I have ever written without error. So, don't blame me if you treat anything I say, or write, as being totally inspired by God. A sensible person will consider carefully before attributing infallibility to anything that I, or any other ordinary human being says is free of error. Indeed, if I may paraphrase the apostle Paul, "We are all like people looking through a dark glass." (1 Cor. 13:12) He adds that even the best of us can, "See only in part and know only in part." There were after all a multitude of things past, present, and future about which even Paul did not, and could not have even the least knowledge. Then there were those other times when Paul just as plainly knew that God was talking to him and revealing to him those truly infallible words.

My expertise, if I had any over the many years I have been writing the textbooks for Vision Colleges, consisted in being a good editor. The Lord gave me the ability to read difficult theological books, think deeply about them, and then reproduce the theology and complex ideas in layman's terms so even the average student could grasp easily the wonderful truths of the Word of God.

I made a short video on the subject of writing for one of my students a decade ago. Here are some of the principles –

- You need a hunger to write just for the joy of the task, an innate skill and a love for words for their own sake.
- Look for opportunities to write and submit articles.
- Attend writing workshops to build on your knowledge and skills.
- Gain a fluency of words by reading a wide variety of books.
- Develop a creative mind that can find new ways to present familiar things.
- You will need a measure of self-confidence and a belief that people will want to read what you have written.
- Acquire the discipline and patient persistence needed for writing.
- Above all you need a sense of God's call to write; that this is something that the Lord wants you to do.

- So, start pounding the keyboard or scratching your pen across the page and start writing!

You can watch this video at https://www.youtube.com/watch?v=I_1odwGft8U (Retrieved 20/01/2025)

Therefore, brothers, be all the more diligent to confirm your calling and election, for if you practice these qualities you will never fall. 2 Peter 1:10

Therefore, my beloved brothers, be steadfast, immovable, always abounding in the work of the Lord, knowing that in the Lord your labour is not in vain. 1 Corinthians 15:58

1973 CONFRONTATIONS

I don't enjoy confrontation as do others who like the battle of wits and wills. However, there have been moments when something arose within me, and I was able to not only stand my ground but also speak sternly to the perpetrators. Here are some stories to ponder.

"If you think I am going to walk through that iron grill to see any pastor on the face of the earth you are very wrong!"

As a visitor from Australia, and as a magazine editor, I arranged an appointment to see the pastor of a large church I was then visiting in the United States. On the appointed day I arrived at the church and discovered that to see the pastor I had first to get past a controller. She sat behind a large desk with an iron grill stretching out each side of her. When it was opened the grill led to a corridor at the end of which there was another grill with a secretary sitting at a desk. I looked at the first girl, I looked down the corridor at the second girl and then demanded to know if I had to get through those two grills in order to see the pastor. She agreed that such was the rule. In my opinion any pastor who so isolated himself from his people hardly deserved the title. I told the controller that she would have to cancel my appointment and give whatever excuse she chose to the pastor. She was distressed protesting that I should keep the appointment. But I declined, telling her that under no circumstance could I be persuaded to negotiate those two grills in order to see any pastor. So, once again I politely declined to keep the appointment and left the church.

During my years in America there were several times where I faced ministerial arrogance. Another was in Southern California where I made an appointment to see a pastor but was then told when I arrived that he was busy, and I would have to make another appointment. This I graciously did choosing the next day when I was met with the same excuse. Being an equitable man and knowing that there are many unforeseen pastoral demands that can pull one away from a busy schedule, I once again made an appointment for the following day only to be told when I arrived that the pastor was too busy to see me. Upon this third rejection I told the receptionist that I was going to see the pastor regardless of how busy he was. I started to walk past her desk. "You can't do that," she said, rising to her feet. This was ignored and I walked past her to the pastor's office just beyond.

Knocking on the door, I peremptorily opened it and found the pastor with his feet on the desk reading the newspaper and drinking a cup of coffee. As you can imagine I was deeply affronted by this sight and angrily told the pastor that he was rude and arrogant and that the next time I made an appointment I would not tolerate any delay in him keeping it. Why was he so boorish? It was nothing but a power play, trying to prove that despite biblical teaching on equality, he was more important than me. He was following a secular model of hierarchy and control which has no place in the family of God, nor in his church. That pastor knew when he was in the wrong and accepted my judgment. Later he was, probably inevitably, caught embezzling church funds and engaging in other unseemly activities.

I was due to preach at a country church in Minnesota but when I arrived there, I found that a number of the church team were unhappy. The pastor had a very large and opulent office, but the members of the team were barely allowed broom cupboard space. The pastor was also paid at least twice as much as the next member of his team. He never visited the homes of his team members nor had them visit him on a social basis. He largely isolated himself both from them and from his congregation. Well, you know what's coming! I confronted him and told him that running a church on secular power play principles was a recipe for disaster. And so it happened, within a short time after my visit he ran off with the church secretary, abandoning his wife and children, and making a shipwreck of his ministry.

On another occasion in a church where I was scheduled to preach, I arrived on the appointed day and at once notified the pastor of my arrival, ready to discuss a programme of ministry. Once again, I arrived after making an appointment only to be told that the pastor could not see me. However, I happened to observe him hurrying past a window. Obviously, it was going to be the old power play over again. But since I had seen him through that window, I knew that I could catch him. I found him in another room and told him what I thought of his behaviour. He would not accept my rebuke, so I also told him he was headed for disaster. You may hardly credit this, but it is the simple truth. Not long afterwards he too was caught in adultery with one of the ladies in the church and was obliged to resign.

In America, there is a nation-wide television network with scores of outlets, and many famous people striving for exposure. While there Alison and I were scheduled to feature in one of the programs and we were interviewed about my ministry but especially about miracles of healing. Two of our sons, Eric and Baden, were with us, and we were able to tell the amazing story of their birth, despite the fact that my wife and I had a blood incompatibility. (See 1966 Healing) This rather gripping story was recorded and successfully used in the TV network across America.

I made no comment on that occasion but talking to a friend of the network I observed that the manager of the network was a kind of one-man-band - that is despite having many staff members he really did not delegate true responsibility to any of them but preferred to micro-manage the network himself. This could only lead to disaster, which of course happened. Same old story! Those who take on an impossible load in arrogance will surely crumble and fall. His ministry became a shambles, he ended up in prison, and the whole network collapsed.

Such tragedies should provide a salutary warning to all pastors. While churches do need to be well organised, they cannot be run solely like a business, nor on rules of power-play. There is no room for dictatorship, tyranny, or any such ungodly behaviour. The church is above all else a family and should operate and be governed like a family. Families too, need to be run properly, but also with an all-encompassing mutual love and respect. As Paul said -

Therefore, as God's chosen people, holy and dearly loved, clothe yourselves with compassion, kindness, humility, gentleness and patience. Bear with each other and forgive one another if any of you has a grievance against someone. Forgive as the Lord forgave you. And over all these virtues put on love, which bids them all together in perfect unity. Colossians 3:12-14

1974 MOTTO

"That's a bit arrogant, isn't it?" My brother Barry asked this question when we were preparing to launch the Launceston Bible Correspondence Course. The motto Alison and I had chosen - *The whole Word to the whole World.* Since at that time we had not a single student, nor even the first page of a textbook written, nor any money to launch any sort of a school, I suppose that motto did sound a bit pompous.

However, I had a deep feeling that somehow God would bring it to pass. So, I began to write the first textbook, which we printed in 1974 and advertise for students in a few Christian outlets and initially called our school The Launceston College of Theology - which was hardly less arrogant than the motto. After all, we still had no students, nor any significant funds, but at least we had the first part of a curriculum, a book I had just published, *The Authority and Authenticity of the Bible.*

Over the next four years, I wrote another ten books to add to the first one. My brother Barry graciously helped by writing two books for us also, *Typology* and *The Church,* and those 12 books became the basic curriculum for a Diploma in Biblical Studies. By the end of 1975 we had just over one hundred students, which continued to grow steadily.

To my surprise the student body spread far beyond my own denomination. We had Pentecostals, Baptists, Uniting Church, Salvation Army, and others, including even some Roman Catholic priests. Nobody was more surprised than I was at the widening appeal of the books I was writing. Of course, it was far from being any genius of mine that gave our new school such wide attention. Inadvertently I had launched the LCT in the heart of the charismatic renewal, which gave great appeal in many denominations to anything charismatic or Pentecostal.

The charismatic renewal was initially universal in its constituency. I reaped the benefit of that universality. Sadly, the renewal by the end of the 1980's had become denominationalised and broken into many different segments. This certainly slowed our growth for a while, but not entirely. The LCT continued to increase its enrolments. Indeed, when we carried the College to Sydney in 1978, we had five hundred enrolled students. In Sydney we decided to change the name to Vision Bible College, which later became Vision International College as we gained students from around the world.

Before we began down the road of establishing the Bible school, we had some remarkable confirmations of our plan that I would like to share with you.

The first: The phone rang. It was after midnight, and an excited voice came over the wire. It was our good friend Pastor Peter Vacca, calling from 600 miles away. He had been praying and had seen a vision of a map of the world with a light glowing in our city of Launceston. As he watched, the light spread all over Australia, then across to New Zealand, and then around the world. Peter was so impressed and stirred by this vision that he had to ring us and let us know. Could we explain what it meant? We weren't sure, but we said we would certainly pray about it.

The second: Mary Shadbolt, a member of our church travelled across to Perth, and while there she heard a prophecy that a tree would grow out of Launceston, and its branches would spread over Australia, then across to New Zealand, and on around the world. A remarkably similar prophecy! But some months would pass before we would understand what God was saying to us.

For twelve years we had laboured in Tasmania, and through this period God had blessed us with great miracles, some of which are mentioned in Alison's book, *Divine Healing: The Wonder and the Mystery*. Many people had found healing in Jesus' name, our own congregation was growing, and we had helped establish four other churches. They had been years of laughter and tears, sunshine and sadness, happiness and frustration. There had been both defeats and triumphs. Much had been done, but I was deeply troubled by a feeling that I had not fulfilled the full purpose of God for my life.

I believe God himself caused this, for it made me seek him earnestly about what my future should be. I was denied complete satisfaction in local church ministry because God had a different path for my future.

The third: I became convinced that God wanted to speak to me, to direct me in some way, and that I would find the answer in the USA. Alison agreed to let me go as she knew I was deeply entrenched in a struggle to understand what God wanted for my future ministry. So, I booked myself in to a School of Ministry conference in Melodyland Church, California, and also into one on church growth at Robert Schuller's, Crystal Cathedral, in Orange County. Two other pastors wanted to go with me, so they also booked for the same conferences.

For both Alison and me this whole idea was unusual. It was a dramatic departure from our normal way of understanding God's will. Why go to the USA? Couldn't the Lord speak in Australia? Yet we both knew this decision came from God, though in the past guidance had always come to us through prayer and Scripture and the wisdom God had planted in us over the years. Even so, it was only by a series of miracles that I was able to go to America. Perhaps Satan was standing against us, sensing that this was a turning point in our lives. So, we had to contend with opposition from some church members who could not understand why I had to go to the USA; a lost visa that turned up at the last moment; a plane that was not scheduled to fly; a pilot's strike; and many other unusual happenings.

When I finally arrived in the USA, I was ready to give up full-time ministry. I had given the Lord twenty years of my life, and though God had been very gracious and taught me many things, I was deeply dissatisfied, feeling that something vital was lacking from my life. Perhaps it was time to find a new way to serve the Lord?

But what did God want me to do? How would those prophecies about the 'light' and the 'tree' be fulfilled? I was perplexed and unsure, yet still hopeful that during my time in America the Lord would give me insight and understanding and enable me to make a decision. Did God want me to write the books I felt I should write? Was it important to God? I was to receive some stunning answers to my prayers over the next few days as this letter I wrote to Alison will show.

14th August 1974

Sweetheart,

The time is 11pm Wednesday and I have just returned to my room after attending the evening rally at Melodyland. The speaker was Agnes Sandford, and she was most entertaining – a sprightly and gay-hearted 75 year old! Her message was not focused on healing, but rather on the power of prayer in the areas of life – and particularly on prayer for the salvation and healing of the nation, its government, homes, and schools.

Melodyland is an extraordinary place. Each night this week it has been packed to the doors with about 4,000 people, perhaps more. And, of course, through the day several hundred people have been attending the clinic sessions. Several sessions are being conducted at the same time, some for pastors, some for young people, some for women, some for Sunday school teachers. The delegates are free to choose which sessions they wish to attend.

The evening rallies are more like concerts than church rallies. They are run very professionally (although they allow time for worship and praise) each person on the platform is highly skilled, from song leaders, to announcers, to singers and instrumentalists, to preachers. No one has appeared amateurish or made a poor presentation. The lighting effects, the sound system etc. are all the best money can buy. The soloists and the instrumentalists are absolutely top class. The audience also behaves more like a concert audience than a church congregation. They applaud all the items and sometimes demand an encore. The preacher is applauded as he comes onto the platform, and quite often during his sermon when he has made a statement that enthuses the people, he will be interrupted by applause. Some of the preachers have received standing ovations at various points in their sermons. But it all serves to create an atmosphere of excitement and of eager response to the Word of God. Certainly, there have been scores of decisions and of people filled with the Spirit so far this week.

The study sessions through the day have been intensive and useful. There are at least 200 ministers and their wives attending the ministers' sessions. God has been dealing with me. I was very depressed and restless for a couple of days and I felt driven to prayer. I'm sure Ralph Wilkerson had a word of knowledge about me today, although he himself did not know to which pastor he was speaking. Anyway, time will confirm whether or not the word he gave for "one minister in this group" was in fact me.

In the meantime, God is slowly giving me answers. Because of this I have cancelled arrangements I had made to travel down to Mexico on Friday with Leon and David. They will still be going with someone else to take my place, but I want to take advantage of having the hotel room to myself to spend the day in prayer. I will have to forfeit at least some of my part of the combined fare, but it will be well worth it if I can gain some definite guidance from God. Tomorrow morning I am having breakfast with Dick Mills and am looking forward to being able to share fellowship with him and his wife.

I am hoping a letter will arrive from you tomorrow or Friday. Don't forget to send photos of yourself and the children. Pray with me that the Lord will bring me home with clear and definite guidance as to his will for you and me and for the church. Please convey my love to Philip and Brian and to their families and to all the saints. I'm sorry I can't write more often or in more detail, but the programme is so demanding that it leaves little time or energy for letters.

An ocean of love to you and the children,

Ken

P.S. The prophecy given by Pastor Ralph Wilkerson was this: "There is a preacher here who is thinking of leaving the full-time ministry. If you do that, it will be a very costly mistake. God has called you and still has a work for you to do. The Lord forbids you to go back into secular business."

Since I had been contemplating buying a small business in Adelaide, I had no doubt this warning was directed at me! So here was something different from the usual silent prompting of the Holy Spirit!

Three days later I wrote to Alison again.

17th August 1974

Sweetheart,

Some incredible things have happened to me since I last wrote to you. On Thursday morning I had breakfast with Dick Mills, not with any attention of seeking spiritual counsel from him, but simply to thank him personally on Barry's behalf for all the books he has sent Barry. But while we were eating breakfast he suddenly received a word of knowledge about me, and he described with astonishing detail the spiritual struggles I had been undergoing, my present spiritual position, and what directions my ministry was taking and would take in the future.

I was stunned. My mind as it were, was falling apart! If I had been the kind of person who weeps easily, I would have howled like a smacked baby. (As it was, I must admit, I just calmly continued eating my muffin, and Dick did not know what a staggering effect he was having on me until it was all over.) He continued discussing my past present and future (with virtually no help from me) for about an hour, and he gave me several Scriptures which he said were from the Lord, and which point out the directions the Lord wants me to take.

I cannot share with you here what he told me, and in any case, I am still trying to absorb and evaluate it all, but I will tell you all about it when I return. Suffice it to say it was a stunning answer to my restless cry for divine guidance and it was a remarkable vindication of my belief that somewhere on this trip through America I would find the direction I was seeking from God about my future, and about the future of the work in Tasmania. But I was admittedly not expecting the answer to come so quickly nor in such an entirely supernatural form. Praise God for his goodness!

After breakfast I went back to Melodyland for the morning service, which every Thursday is a worship and healing service. Usually about three thousand attend but on this morning the clinic delegates swelled the service to 3500.

Dick Mills had offered to take me to lunch also, so after the service I met him once again, and he drove me off in his Chrysler. On the way to lunch Dick stopped at a bookshop and staggered me a second time by telling me the day before (Wednesday) the Lord had told him to buy me $200 worth of books. At the time Dick had no money, but during the day a person who owed him that amount paid him. To Dick this was confirmation of God's will, so he insisted I choose books to the value of $200 (including freight cost to Tasmania) I uttered a few feeble protests, but it was obviously pointless to resist, so I did as I was told. The books are now on the way! What an incredible man! He has also given me several books and tapes which I have with me. I am still trying to recover from it all! Praise God with me.

With all my love to you all,

Ken

Here is the outline of the prophecy given to me in Los Angeles by Dick Mills.

Concerning my own personal attitudes –

- 2 Ch 15:7 - *But you take courage! Do not let your hands be weak, for your work shall be rewarded.* An exhortation to boldness, which Dick linked with a prayer that I might be delivered from the fear of man.

- 1 Co 15:58 - *Therefore, my beloved brother, be steadfast, immovable, always abounding in the work of the Lord, knowing that in the Lord your labour is not in vain.* A declaration that the days of difficulty are not yet over, but that eventually the full harvest will come.

- He 6:9-10 - *In your case, beloved, we feel sure of better things that belong to salvation. For God is not so unjust as to overlook your work and the love which you showed for his sake in serving the saints, as you still do.* This was a rebuke of my dispirited feeling that God had forgotten me, that all my efforts had been largely in vain, which had led me seriously to consider resigning from the ministry (which Dick knew even though I had not intimated anything).

Concerning my future ministry -

- Ecc 6:9 - *Better is the sight of the eyes than the wandering of desire.* A rebuke of my feeling that distant fields might be greener, and a demand that I be satisfied with a ministry based in Tasmania, plus a demand that I rejoice in the church God had raised up in Launceston and not be envious of other larger churches.

- Re 3:7-11 - *I know your works. Behold, I have set before you an open door, which no one is able to shut ...* This is a message addressed to the church in Launceston, and the church is to accept it as a special word from the Lord. But it is particularly addressed to me, for I am as "the angel of the church at Philadelphia" (Launceston). In this capacity I must apply the particulars of this passage to myself. I should see the passage also as requiring I remain bold in exercising leadership in the assembly, within the framework of the role God has given me. However, though I must retain a leadership role in Launceston, I must be prepared to be less closely associated with the local church. In the fulfilling of this and of the promise of an 'open door' <u>I must keep myself ready for my ministry to take new and as yet undisclosed directions.</u>

After this stunning answer to prayer my depression lifted and I was able to enjoy the rest of the trip, learning many useful things for my ministry. I travelled home to Launceston a new man, confident that I was in God's will to pursue the path to education and writing. Everything I had learned was put into practice slowly but surely. I spoke to the church council, and they agreed to me spending more time in studying and writing books. They looked for an assistant to help with the church and Pastors Philip and Heather Baker were led to come from the Faith Bible College, New

Zealand. Philip and Heather fitted in perfectly and the church continued to flourish.

From the age of 34 I had been studying for degrees in theology through Berean Christian College, Kansas, USA. I believed that because of my writing ability God wanted me to write books and I needed a theology degree to gain credibility. (This was stunningly confirmed by Dick Mills.) As well as this, our church was continually losing our best young people to mainland Bible colleges, and they were not returning. I reasoned that there must be other pastors like me who would like to keep their young people in the church and train them themselves. These different aspects came together in the idea of starting a correspondence course on theology. My trip to the States and my encounter with Dick Mills gave me the courage to go ahead with this plan, knowing I was in God's perfect will for my life.

So, here I have written the background of why we were brave enough to take the motto, *The whole Word to the whole World*, which has been taken up enthusiastically by all those who have helped us spread the College around the world.

Ask and it will be given to you; seek and you will find; knock and the door will be opened to you. For everyone who asks receives; the one who seeks finds; and to the one who knocks, the door will be opened. Matthew 7:7-8

So, do not fear, for I am with you; do not be dismayed, for I am your God. I will strengthen you and help you; I will uphold you with my righteous right hand. Isaiah 41:10

1975 WARNINGS

Several times over the years of my ministry, God has given me a specific warning concerning a Christian leader, and a mandate that I had to deal with the situation.

"He is involved in an act of adultery! Get to his house straight away! God knows what he is doing! The Lord will judge him harshly for his behaviour unless he repents and changes his ways."

Not once, not twice, but three times that warning came to me starkly as a prophetic oracle from heaven to the three churches and their pastors who were engaged in ungodly activity. So, these were three astonishing miracles of divine revelation. I would like to give more details but am reluctant as I could unwittingly cause hurt to innocent family members.

Suffice it to say this, we should all remember –

Be sure your sins will find you out. Numbers 32:23

If we confess our sins, he is faithful and just and will forgive us our sins and purify us from all unrighteousness. 1 John 1:9

Do not go!

This was a fourth occasion when even more stunningly, God spoke to me while I was sitting at my desk. This time it was to stop me from keeping a 5pm appointment I had already made. Instead, I learned that my associate pastor and his wife were about to make a similar visit in that direction and that I should hand the problem to them. They cheerfully agreed and I happily went back to my office desk.

My fellow pastor and his wife arrived for the appointment and to their astonishment were greeted at the parishioner's front door by the lady herself - standing there stark naked! At once my fellow pastor's wife took control. Pushing her husband aside and leaving him on the front veranda, she rushed inside and slammed the door. She wrapped the woman in a blanket and sat her down to find the reason for her behaviour.

The parishioner was a beautiful Spanish lady who was plainly making ready to give herself and all her exquisite charms to me. I was kept blissfully ignorant working at home while the pastor's wife with marked fury, but also remarkable Christian grace, tried to show the woman the error of her ways. She was indeed much ashamed and truly repentant and being on the edge of a nervous breakdown she later yielded to her despair and submitted herself to an admission to a mental hospital.

I thank God for warning me, keeping me from these dangerous waters in the first years of my ministry.

He holds success in store for the upright, he is a shield to those whose walk is blameless. For he guards the course of the just and protects the way of his faithful ones. Proverbs 2: 7-8

Trust in the Lord with all your heart and lean not on your own understanding; in all your ways submit to him, and he will make your paths straight. Proverbs 3:5-6

1976 FRIENDS

People in leadership tend not to have a great many friends as authority roles don't lend themselves to being the life of the party! Over the years, my best friend has been my brother, but there have also been a few men who have persisted in maintaining friendship despite my self-contained persona.

One of these friends was one of our first converts in Launceston, Austin Hudson. He was a jovial man, a jokester, and perpetually cheerful. He had a habit of phoning me using a foreign accent, pretending to be some dignitary or other, "This is Doctor Fondu from the Morgue, here." I got used to this and responded with a quip or two. However, this humorous propensity went too far on one occasion when the phone rang and a voice said, "This is the Fire Chief speaking." Thinking it was Austin, I reciprocated with a joke whereupon an angry voice said again, "This is the Fire Chief speaking!" I realised to my dismay that it was not Austin with one of his joking phone calls and hastily apologised to the Fire Chief who was phoning us about a permit we had requested for our new church building. I requested Austin to promise not to phone me ever again with one of his trick accents!

As Austin was such a good friend I decided to introduce him to the glorious wonders of classical music. Consequently, I took him along to a recital of the *Tasmanian Philharmonic Orchestra*. Austin knew nothing of classical music, so he listened carefully to the orchestra tuning up ready for the performance then turned to me and said, "I don't think much of classical music, it sounds very discordant!" I despaired then and there of Austin ever enjoying the concert. The music of Grieg's piano concerto that moved me so deeply, even to tears because of its beauty, was to Austin just a noise he did not like at all. He could not keep still but squirmed this way and that, obviously very uncomfortable, all the way through until the end whereupon he breathed a sigh of relief. I did not try to take him to a classical concert again recognising that one can still be friends and not share the same enjoyment.

Austin and his wife Freda were faithful friends while we ministered in Launceston and when we moved to Sydney and then the USA, kept in contact with us over the next forty years, supporting us through times of sorrow and rejoicing with us in every success. They were also a practical help, keeping an eye on our physical and emotional wellbeing. Austin supported my decision when I travelled to the States to seek God's direction, insisting that I be given permission from the church to follow this deep desire. Austin and Freda remained faithful members of the Launceston church, seeing it through many years of change. Now one of his sons, Scott Hudson, is the Pastor of the church and Austin continues to be supportive even in his old age. His wife and daughter both died of cancer, but his faith has never failed, and he remains faithful still in his eighties. Occasionally he phones us even after all these years and it is grand to hear from him that our church in Launceston continues strong in faith and is an ongoing witness for the glory of God.

My last friend who remained faithful during our years in Sydney is John Schild. In the last two years he has visited me faithfully every Wednesday on his way to play golf with another fellow believer. We solved the problems of the universe and discussed theology and anything else that took our fancy. Sometimes I was too unwell for any visitors, but he took this in good part and always called before his visit to see if I was up for company.

There are many other people I could share with you whom God has brought in and out of our lives to help us on our journey. Some friends were for life and some for a season. And some have already attained their reward and gone before us. I thank God for them all.

Perfume and incense bring joy to the heart, and the pleasantness of a friend springs from their heartfelt advice. Proverbs 27:9

1978 WITCHES

She was the most gorgeous looking girl - long red hair, sparkling blue eyes, luscious lips, and massive sex appeal!

Who was she? I have forgotten her name but not her beauty. I was a local pastor in Launceston, Tasmania, and she had made an appointment to see me for counselling. She began by telling me about two or three other ministers in the area with whom she had had intimate relations. Of course, she blamed the men. I knew all three of them and that they had been obliged to leave their churches. And indeed, to leave Tasmania altogether. Now I knew why!

Perhaps I am naïve, but it eventually dawned on me during our conversation that she was setting me up to be her next victim. This infuriated me. Much incensed, I rebuked her and her sleazy lifestyle, telling her to get out of my office and never to come back! I had no wish to ever see her again. She then revealed her true nature when she turned on me with fierce vituperation, pronounced herself the leader of a coven of witches, and that she would call her cronies together that night and they would perform some kind of demonic dance around an upside-down crucifix which they had stolen from a church. "At midnight," said she, "we will slaughter chickens and sprinkle their blood over the crucifix while cursing you, your wife, your children, and your church!" She then predicted many terrible evils that would assuredly fall upon us.

The church had a prayer meeting scheduled for that very evening and perhaps twenty or more people attended. I told them about the witch and her coven and suggested that we should set up a barrier of prayer against them, which we did. Then, to my astonishment, almost the entire group suggested we should keep on praying until after midnight! I hardly knew whether to laugh, or weep. It seemed to me scarcely believable that people who had received continual and strong teaching on the believer's position in the heavenlies in Christ and authority over all the principalities and powers of darkness, should be in the least fearful of the maledictions of a bunch of crazy females! I said to them that any of them who wished to do so were welcome to keep on praying for another three or four hours, but as for me I would declare the meeting closed no later than 9:30pm, and as I usually did, go home, have a cup of coffee, watch some tv to wind down, go to bed around 11pm, and by midnight would be peacefully and soundly asleep. Somewhat ashamed of their fear, they accepted these biblical truths of which they had heard many times, stirred up their faith, and agreed with me to go home, go to bed, and enjoy a restful and untroubled night.

What happened then? Nothing! From that day to this I have never heard a single word from this woman. Did her curses harm us? Of course not! If any Christian is silly enough to believe such superstitious nonsense, they will live a deeply troubled life. And they will get no sympathy from me! Read your Bible, operate in faith, and stand on the Word of God!

This was not the first time I had been threatened. I have heard that a large group of witches held a special forum on top of Mt Barrow overlooking the whole of Launceston and pronounced valedictions against all the churches in that region. But with as little result as the smaller group that tried to ineffectually curse us. My God is greater!

Over the years, I have had several different experiences of the preternatural, which have included poltergeist activity – that is (in my case) objects levitating from a shelf and moving around the room seemingly of their own volition. I presume the intention was to frighten us into stopping our prayer meeting, an attempt at spiritual obfuscation that utterly failed! I have also experienced demonic apparitions, spiritual phenomena, and other similar weird happenings. None of them ever caused me the least anxiety.

But I need to retract that last statement. Early in my ministry there was one occasion when I was home alone and had decided to spend some hours in fasting and prayer. Evening had come. The shadows grew darker. I had left the lights off. The blackness grew ever deeper. Suddenly it seemed to me that Satan himself had walked into the room. He was standing just inside the door. He was hideous! Malevolence surrounded him and flowed out towards me. He was clad in garments of many stark colours that struck terror into my soul. Somehow, I found the courage to stand up and walk toward him and the light switch on the wall. As quickly as possible I flicked the switch while opening the door and telling the devil to depart. Of course, the apparition vanished and along with it the nauseating dread that for a few moments had gripped my spirit. I must confess that divine aspirations had departed from me as quickly as the devil had done. I abandoned the time of prayer and fasting, kept the light on, and found something else to do. Succumbing to fear on this occasion was indeed disgraceful. Hence, a day or two later I promised God never again to surrender to such infantile fear. Nor have I.

I have also been asked on two or three occasions to exorcise a house that seemed to be in the possession of a demon. So, I devised an appropriate routine and prayed my way through the house putting a block on all the troubles that the inhabitants had been suffering. How real was this? I truly don't know, except that on each of the few occasions I have done this the families have thanked God for the divine peace and happiness that thereafter characterised their home life.

There was also the occasion when a room that had been used across several years for exorcism, had been turned into a bedroom. When Alison and I arrived to stay at the home, we were told by the owners that everyone who had tried to sleep in that bedroom was troubled during the night by some kind of demonic force, so much so they were thinking about changing it back to an office space used during the day. Both of us laughed and requested that the room be left untouched, and we would be happy to sleep there, which we did for an extended period. We were never troubled by any evil phenomena.

In the end, Satan and his minions have only as much power as we allow them. So, if you are ever confronted by similar threats, stir up your courage and your faith, and declare your complete trust in the goodness and love of God.

Submit yourselves therefore to God. Resist the devil, and he will flee from you. James 4:7

Finally, be strong in the Lord and in his mighty power. Put on the full armour of God, so you can take your stand against the devil's schemes. For our struggle is not against flesh and blood, but against the rulers, against the authorities, against the powers of this dark world, and against the spiritual forces of evil in the heavenly realms. Ephesians 6:10-12

1978 BUILDINGS

Over the years in Tasmania, we used several buildings for our church purposes. We began in the Ex Navalman's Hall which was very cold and had steel seats, so the first thing I did was to go out and buy sheets of foam to cut into appropriate squares for the chilly seats. The excellent seamstresses in the church covered them with leftover colourful fabric. These lent a cheerful note to the rather plain building, and the people were very grateful for the warmth the cushions gave them. The cushions were also helpful when we prayed on our knees for divine intervention in the growth of our church meetings, healing, and other needs.

The only distraction we found in this first meeting space were the toilets which were unfortunately situated on either side of the platform. This meant that everyone who needed to use the facilities had to brave the stares of the whole congregation. I remember one little old man who, unable to contain himself through the whole service, eventually had to make his way to the facilities which always arrived at the highest synchronic moment of the sermon. This was a mild irritation, however, we all felt humbled and rebuked when he died suddenly. And if that was not enough, stricken to discover from the local paper that he had died of malnutrition! Why had no-one invited him home for lunch or visited him in his home? His scruffy appearance should have alerted us to his welfare. This situation haunted us for some time, and I resolved to be more aware for the wellbeing of each member of my congregation.

After we had been in Launceston for a few years and the church had grown sufficiently we had enough money to put a deposit on a building. Around the corner from the Hall, we discovered a Georgian Cottage, which in early days had been a school. It was in good  repair, so we moved in and took out a few walls to make an auditorium to seat around 75 people. The church people worked hard together getting the place painted and ready for our first Sunday. It is unfortunate then that we had not enquired if there were any historical rules that we had to follow as the building was over a hundred years old. We found ourselves roundly rebuked by the Tasmanian Historical Society. We had removed one of the chimneys of the building and as a result spoilt its symmetry! Erecting a false chimney was the remedy, as this would restore the outline of the building to their satisfaction. After this was completed, they were happy with the result and sent one of their members to grace our opening meeting and dedication of the Georgian Chapel, the name we had given the building. Leo Harris was the speaker, and he followed this up with many visits to Launceston over the sixteen years we were there.

The Chapel served us well for a time with a small basement for Sunday School and an upstairs room for a pastor's office that was accessed via a beautiful curved wooden staircase. There was a large space at the back for parking, but this was obscured by several dilapidated outbuildings. This was our second mistake. Pulling these down we sent the remnants to the tip only to discover later they had been built by convicts, each brick bearing the thumbprint of a labourer which was worth a substantial amount of money as historical artefacts. We had to move on from this experience, older and wiser.

The church grew steadily and after some years we began to look around for new premises. There was a magnificent old Congregational church building in Launceston just adjacent to the city park which had fallen vacant. (Launceston has a church building on every corner as the city was built on the riches of the wool industry and therefore the architecture in all the key buildings is magnificent and worth visiting.) The population in the town had grown to a point of around 72,000 and had now plateaued. It barely changed at all during our time there and many of the older churches suffered as the congregation died out and was not replaced with new members. So, I began to pray and speak a word of faith over this church which no longer had any congregants. Every time I drove past, I would claim it in the name of Jesus. The building was a fine example of its type with stained glass windows and ornate stonework. What a wonderful building in which to worship our mighty God, the music and praise of all who had gone before resonating in the magnificent wood pews and iron work. It also had a glorious 19th century raised lectern that was reached by a short curving stairway. This gives greater visual acuity and audibility for the congregation below in the vast and cavernous stone space. I imagined myself extolling God's Word to a church full of people eager to grow in Christ from that splendid platform! Eventually, after some negotiation, we had permission to move in at an agreed rent we could afford. Not everyone was happy about this move, but I stubbornly insisted, and so they reluctantly agreed.

This was my third building mistake, and it cost me dearly being an unmitigated failure. It was a bitter lesson in allowing vanity to override good judgment. I had been cautioned and closed my ears, knowing better than those around me. God knew it was a dead end for my ministry but had the grace to allow me to learn this for myself. My faithful congregation sat in a church which could seat 1200 as it was built in a time where everyone went to church, master and servant alike. But now our small congregation of 75 or so were perched in one corner of the vast nave, intimidated by the sheer size of the space. Their voices were small in comparison so there was no gift of prophecy, or encouraging words, no exhortation from the people. The pulpit was six feet in the air so that was abandoned, and I preached from the floor, but it was no good. It took some time for me to let go of this program but eventually I had to acknowledge this catastrophic mistake. The people who had been faithful enthusiastic followers now voted with their feet. One by one they refused to attend the Sunday service.

We still owned the Georgian Chapel and to this familiar place we returned. Word spread quickly and the first Sunday back the Chapel was packed with people filling every seat, sitting on the floor, and standing around the walls. I wish that it was possible to describe the deep satisfaction that attends being in the centre of God's will, but you will know it when you are in it. The enthusiastic praise and deepfelt worship of the people gladdened the soul and I imagine was especially pleasing to the Father.

There have only been a few times I can recall where I have gone ahead of God and obstinately insisted on my own way. But these are seared into my soul, and I have never forgotten them. Fortunately, we serve a merciful God, and he had our future firmly in mind. The Chapel was too small, and we looked around again for a larger building. God led us to a large shopfront on one of the main streets in the town, it had a corner shop already rented, a large meeting area, kitchen and toilets, and space for the future offices of the Launceston College of Theology. There was a large parking area across the road which was empty on Sundays. The walls inside, once painted, housed a gallery of local artists which beautified the space and encouraged the public to visit during the week and purchase these pictures.

Using the sale of the Georgian Chapel we were able to secure financing, by God's grace, and the building was ours. It had plenty of room for growth. *Gideon's 300* was our slogan to attract new members to God's Kingdom and over the years we came close to that goal. (You will find the inspiring story of Gideon and his 300 soldiers in the book of Judges.) This building served us well and when we left Launceston at the end of 1978, we praised God for the goodness and faithfulness he showed us. Pastor Phil Baker continued pastoring this work, and it remains today with Pastor Scott Hudson (son of my good friend Austin Hudson mentioned elsewhere in this book).

Oh, the depth of the riches of the wisdom and knowledge of God! How unsearchable his judgments, and his paths beyond tracing out! Who has known the mind of the Lord? Or who has been his counsellor? Who has ever given to God, that God should repay them? For from him and through him and for him are all things. To him be glory for ever! Amen.
Romans 11:33-36

Therefore, I urge you, brothers and sisters, in view of God's mercy, to offer your bodies as a living sacrifice, holy and pleasing to God – this is your true and proper worship. Do not conform to the pattern of this world but be transformed by the renewing of your mind. Then you will be able to test and approve what God's will is – his good, pleasing and perfect will. Romans 12: 1-2

1978 SINGAPORE

It was unmistakable, more like a catcall than an alarm! But it rang out across the entire audience of several thousand people who were attending a great Pentecostal Convention in a stadium in Singapore.

I was thrilled to be one of the invited delegates although somewhat humbled when I discovered that my invitation was originally issued to Pastor Leo Harris who was then head of the CRC churches in Australasia. He told me that he was unable to accept his own invitation but had recommended myself in his place, which the organisers of the Convention accepted.

Several other Australian Pentecostal pastors and leaders had also been invited by a group of renowned senior Pentecostal leaders who headed up the World Pentecostal Fellowship, founded in 1947 in Zurich, under the leadership of Swiss Pastor Leonard Steiner, along with Mr Pentecost, David Du Plessis. (Not to be confused with Charles H. Parham whose nickname was the Father of Pentecost.) Night after night our joyful friend's raucous cries spanned the huge arena without any difficulty.

At that Convention I made something of a name for myself by writing a letter of complaint to the organising committee. Two things irritated me. Originally our hotel accommodation was a plebian and low-cost motel which had mouldy walls, damp floors, and numerous other blemishes. But then Dr Yonggi Cho turned up with his entourage, and if my memory serves me correctly, they had booked out an entire floor of the best hotel for himself, his guests, and his staff members. He declined to 'humble himself' by staying in the plebian premises that had first been selected by the committee. His choice fell instead on the luxurious and splendid Shangri La Hotel. I thought it excessively humorous that an attempt by the Western Churches to show humility to their brothers from South-East Asia failed so dismally. But I do remember walking down the corridor of our motel and being irritated by the mouldy smell of the walls and damp carpet while our humble brethren from South East Asia spent the week in luxury.

However, I was even more irritated and strongly objected to the practise adopted by the Western organisers in the running of the Convention meetings. They swiftly abandoned any organised program and began to structure their meetings by following a kind of Christian Quietism. This was a practise that was adopted and rejected centuries ago by Christian leaders and organisers. In reality, at the Convention it meant that there was actually very little control from the leadership, and the meetings followed a slap-dash order with no principles whatsoever.

I was scandalised! I had attended the expensive Convention expecting to hear well-structured and thoughtful addresses by some of the top Pentecostal theologians in the Pentecostal movement. Instead of which I had to endure a mishmash of slap-dash orations by people who were sufficiently brash to push themselves forward and seize the platform.

I wrote a letter of stringent complaint to Dr Du Plessis and other members of the program committee saying that 'quietistic' practices had been tested and found to be disastrously wanting centuries ago. Two or three days later I was carpeted by the programme committee and sternly rebuked for my rude solecisms toward a group of men and women, Pentecostal leaders, who were much superior to myself in Pentecostal rankings. This incident had an amusing follow on.

Quite a few years later, along with Dr David Du Plessis, I was a guest speaker at a Lutheran Charismatic Convention in the USA. During the Convention Dr Du Plessis came to me saying, "Dr Chant, your name is familiar to me. Were you a speaker at a Convention in Singapore and did you disagree with the way we were conducting the meetings?"

Of course, no such honour had ever been extended to me, I had only been one of the humble delegates. But I was the one who had written the letter of disagreement with the conduct of the meetings. In the interest of remaining in sweet fellowship in our present teaching together, and not wanting to exacerbate a potentially volatile conversation over a past matter, I must confess to dissembling.

Tongue in cheek I said, "I do have a brother Barry in Australia, perhaps he is the one you have in mind?" By this subterfuge I was able to persuade Dr Du Plessis that I was not a guest speaker at the Convention in Singapore, nor was I the one who had the cheek to challenge him and the members of the committee there. It was hardly my fault if he chose to assume the contrary!

On occasion it is sometimes better, in the words of Demosthenes (a Greek orator who fled from a difficult battle against Alexander the Great) to run away and live to fight another day! My wife tells me she warned Barry much later so he would know the story of my duplicity. Just in case he ever met and spent time with Dr Du Plessis and was accused of my perfidy.

We became well acquainted with David and his wife, who complained to Alison about all the travel she had to endure with her husband when she would much prefer to stay at home and play with her grandchildren. However, he was a great man who provided a splendid example to young Pentecostal pastors, especially through his adopted nick-name Mr Pentecost. He has written his exciting story, *A Man Called Mr Pentecost*, and he was invited to confer with Pope Paul VI, while he was one of the key members of the Roman Catholic-Pentecostal Dialogue, and he preached in many Roman Catholic churches during the Charismatic Renewal.

David's special reference when teaching Roman Catholics about the baptism in the Holy Spirit occurs in the story of the first miracle at the wedding in Cana in Galilee, where Mary, the mother of Jesus, says, "*Do whatever he tells you.*" From this he urged the Catholics to obey Mary, whom they revered deeply, to follow all the instructions given by Jesus, such as

> ... *wait for the gift my Father promised, which you have heard me speak about. For John baptized with water, but in a few days, you will be baptized with the Holy Spirit.* Acts 1:4b-5

1978 SYDNEY

I am with you and will watch over you wherever you go, and I will bring you back to this land. I will not leave you until I have done what I promised you. Genesis 28:15

This was the verse God quickened to us, among other signs, that we were doing the right thing in leaving Tasmania.

There was a large throng of people on the wharf in Devonport, Tasmania, holding a dazzling array of colourful streamers in their hands, many with tears in their eyes, waving goodbye to their loved ones on the ferry that would take them across Bass Strait to Melbourne. Among them was a group from my congregation in Launceston that I had cared for over the past fifteen years. Alison and I and our children were standing at the rear of the ship waving to our friends on the wharf. With deep emotion in our hearts and tears in our own eyes, we felt the ribbons gradually break the connection with the onlookers and fall to the ground.

Why were we there? Because a few months earlier on the way back from Singapore, Alan Langstaff, who was then the head of Temple Trust in Sydney, was seated next to me on the plane heading back to Australia. We had both attended the Convention in Singapore but were unknown to each other, so this was a divinely arranged and fortuitous circumstance. We talked about many things, including an invitation from Alan to use my newly fledged Correspondence Course as a foundation for a Bible college in Sydney.

I told him I would have to go home first and discuss the matter with Alison and my church council. The end result, after significant prayer, a reluctant agreement was reached by the council members, that this was indeed the will of God. So, we packed up some essentials into our car, and booked a passage on the ferry, sailing away from Tasmania with many tears. The streamers snapped one by one and soon the Tasmanian coast was out of sight. We found some seats in the main lounge room of the ship and reflected on our time in Launceston.

Arriving in Melbourne, we drove to Canberra where we stopped for the night. While there we visited the War Museum and also rented a catamaran to sail for an hour on Lake Burley Griffin. That was a lot of fun, until I discovered I was quite unable to turn the little boat around and get back to the wharf. Consequently, I found myself trapped in a luxury marina threatening any minute to bump into any number of vastly expensive yachts while the owners stood at the plate glass window of the club house waving frantically for us to get out of there! Somehow, by a miracle of divine grace, I managed to escape from the marina but still, for the life of me, I was unable to steer the catamaran back to its base. I had well exceeded my one-hour rental period before the exasperated owner of the boat came out in a motorboat and hauled us back to port. I presume I was not the only rank amateur he had had to rescue as he was cheerful and did not charge us any extra for the rental.

We enjoyed Canberra but eventually continued our journey and arrived in Sydney in time to attend the great 1979 Jesus Conference arranged by the Langstaff organisation, Temple Trust. Its opening rally was held on the steps of the Opera House in Sydney, attended by several thousand people. Another highlight of that conference was an evening rally at the Randwick Racecourse where more than ten thousand people worshipped God and listened to the Word preached.

The bulk of our belongings arrived in a moving truck, and we moved into Hebron House, owned by the Temple Trust. It was a large older home in Randwick that had enough space for our family and also space for my office, a lecture room, and a separate kitchen for students. In a short time, the college was quite well established, and we were comfortably housed. Temple Trust changed their name to Vision Ministries, and our department became Vision Bible College. It was not long before we outgrew this location, and we moved to a ten-storey building across the road from Sydney Central Station. We occupied two floors; I had a large office with a superb view over Sydney, and there were other offices for Alan and his staff; rooms devoted to lectures and other facilities; and room to print and publish their magazine, *New Day*. The cost was surprisingly reasonable, and the college flourished.

After many years ministering in Sydney, Alan decided to move to the USA. He wanted us to join him, but we demurred before finally agreeing, believing it was in harmony with the prophecy from Dick Mills that our college was eventually to be worldwide. Vision Ministries was handed over to Harry Westcott and Ian Jagelman. We disposed of our goods and chattels in various ways so we could travel sufficiently unburdened to the States. We took only the essentials, shipping the rest of our belongings to my brother Barry in Adelaide. We freighted important books to Alan's address, and they arrived some weeks after us.

I lift up my eyes to the mountains – where does my help come from? My help comes from the Lord, the Maker of heaven and earth. He will not let your foot slip – he who watches over you will not slumber; indeed, he who watches over Israel will neither slumber nor sleep. The Lord watches over you – the Lord is your shade at your right hand; the sun will not harm you by day, nor the moon by night, The Lord will keep you from all harm – he will watch over your life; the Lord will watch over your coming and going both now and evermore. Psalm 121:1-8

1981 MINNEAPOLIS

At various points you may wonder whether you are really in God's will, or have you mistaken a prophecy and taken an alternate path. However, be assured that -

In all things God works for the good of those who love him, and who have been called according to his purpose. Romans 8:28

Five days after our arrival in the States, Eric became violently ill. We had noticed that he was not his usual brisk and happy self but had thought this was a natural reaction to leaving his friends in Australia. Throughout the night his condition deteriorated until, in the early morning, we had no alternative but to contact a doctor. The verdict was immediate. Eric was not even permitted to return home for his toothbrush. Instead, he was rushed into emergency for an operation to remove his appendix! Vivid memories of my own experience when I was not much older than my son, came flashing into my mind. And then, piling poverty on misery we discovered that, for the first time in my frequent trips overseas, there was no traveller's insurance taken out on our behalf. This meant that we now owed $2,100 to the hospital. It doesn't seem like a lot now, but back then when we were living by faith, it was a fortune.

We had been in the States for less than a week and already we were facing worrying challenges. But I knew God had spoken to me, so we refused to be deterred. In fact, this incident inspired the fellow Christians in Minneapolis in an unexpected way. We were given the loan of a car, and finding a suitable house to rent, furniture arrived to install in our home. God moved on people's hearts and money was given to us to pay Eric's medical bill. The Lord had turned a potential tragedy into a triumph!

Just two months later, I had to fly to Singapore. I was fulfilling a previous arrangement to teach in their Bible school that I did not want to forgo. Sharon drove us to the airport in a second-hand Oldsmobile we had bought for a few hundred dollars. She had mastered driving on the right-hand side of the road and felt confident that she could find her way home. Later Alison shared their adventure with me –

"Only a mile down the road the dashboard red light had warned us the engine was running hot. We pulled into the nearest service station. In our ignorance we did not realise that this was just a gas (petrol) station with no competent mechanic. We asked for help and the attendant lifted the bonnet and began to unscrew the radiator cap. Even I knew that was not wise! The cap shot into the air and because of a slight tilt in my direction the contents hit me in the face. Hot water mixed with antifreeze is not the nicest combination! Soaking wet, my eyes filled with the solution, I staggered to the ladies' room and washed myself. Worse was to come!

The gas attendant filled up the car radiator with water and insisted that we should have no more trouble. We drove off obediently, but barely a mile down the road the red light blinked again, and we knew we would have to get help. Panic seized me as we drove off the freeway. This was unfamiliar territory. The streets seemed poor and unkempt. My memory began to stir with accounts of robberies and murders I had seen on the news and on television. The people all around us seemed unfriendly. We parked the car, and I made Sharon lock herself in while I attempted to find someone to rescue us. I walked nervously down the street; remember, I was an Australian in a strange country and I had read some lurid tales about America! I was convinced everyone carried a gun and would need little enough excuse to use it.

Finally, I reached a service station and asked to use the telephone. Imagine my horror when I opened the phone book and found not one of the people I knew listed there. We lived in the Minneapolis part of the Twin Cities, and we had driven into St Paul. The people I knew were all in Minneapolis, and the service station had no phone book for that city. Wet and cold from my dowsing, miserable and afraid, I cried out to God. Immediately he reminded me that only the Sunday before we had met a friendly couple from Texas, and they had given me their phone number which I had put in my purse. "If we can be of any help then let us know." Those were the words that rang in my ears. Of course, they now lived in St. Paul!

Quickly I pulled out my pocket diary and found the phone number, my voice a little wobbly by this time. Later at home, showered and warm, I thanked God for his thoughtful provision. Of course, I thanked my new friends as well. They were truly used by God to rescue us from our difficulty.

A week later, while Ken was still in Singapore, I became ill with a haemorrhage. We did not have medical insurance (in America there is no such thing as socialised medicine for the public). When the flow had not stopped after three weeks, Sharon finally telephoned the doctor. He advised her, if the bleeding continued, she must bring me into Emergency. Instead, Sharon decided to call a Christian friend, Dorothy Langstaff. God heard our prayers and half an hour later the haemorrhage miraculously ended!"

My return from Singapore was a time of great rejoicing! But there was a sharp chill in the air. We were about to experience the worst winter in 100 years. It snowed from November to April and for six months we were buried under a white blanket. This was our first experience of living in the harsh and dangerous environment of freezing cold weather. Driving on slippery roads where salt had been sprayed to lower the temperature and stop ice from forming (this also had the unfortunate effect of slowly rusting the floor of your car); frozen pipes in your house; clearing snow drifts from your driveway; and buying giant sacks of flour, sugar, pasta, and canned goods as big as a bucket, to ensure if you were snowed in you wouldn't starve to death!

It was a dangerous world for the naive and we had a great deal to learn about surviving in such an environment. Sharon had a life changing evening when she neglected to wear the correct clothing and on a return journey from dropping a friend off, she became lost on her way home. The fog was heavy, and she drove slowly but realised unless she found a service station she would run out of petrol and freeze to death. Never was a more earnest prayer issued from her lips that the one she said that night. To her relief lights loomed up on the side of the road and she welcomed the sight of a gas station. Filling up the petrol tank she vowed never to allow herself to get low again. Especially not in winter.

This was a case where we felt, as parents, how wise it is to teach your children to pray and trust God for themselves in whatever situation they may find themselves. And we learned to keep supplies inside the car, including matches and candles whose tiny flame could maintain life for a length of time until you were discovered. We were also told that carbon dioxide poisoning can be fatal when the windows are shut tight, and the fan is on recycle. This is especially risky for older vehicles that can have leaks from the exhaust that can enter the car's interior.

Alternatively, summer was a wonderful time of freedom but not to spend too much time outdoors where ferocious large mosquitoes (nicknamed the state bird) bred in the 10,000 lakes that dot the Minnesota landscape feast on fresh Australian blood; and the billions of gnats that follow you around in a cloud. They were by far worse than the Australian intrepid flies that stick to your body and make swatting a native sport.

We wondered after these adventures if we were really following God's leading, but we had faced many challenges before, and one cannot use difficulties and endangerment as a measure of God's will. After all, Paul suffered shipwrecks, snake bites, and imprisonment in chains. So, in comparison we had barely been inconvenienced! However, our troubles continued and once more I became ill.

Pain can be agonising and overwhelming and this was one of those events when I once more contacted a doctor for relief. He surmised it could be cancer, gall stones, or an aneurism. We did not have health insurance as taking private cover was beyond our means at the time. We sought prayer from Alan Langstaff and another pastor, Rod Lensch, who anointed me with oil and prayed the prayer of faith for total healing.

Perhaps my time had come? But then Alison, Sharon, and the boys would be left here in a strange country to fend for themselves. Alison said she also prayed earnestly in mental anguish but could get no peace as her mind was full of fear and thus was unable to hear the voice of God. Waking one morning a verse of Scripture came alive in her spirit –

With long life will I satisfy him and show him my salvation. Psalm 91:16

Faith rose in us, the faith that cannot be shaken, and we knew I was healed. Still, I attended the Xray appointment and the doctor, examining me again, would find nothing wrong in my body. He insisted on another Xray with the same results. God had healed this frail body once again!

Living in America was a superlative adventure, full of challenges, triumphs, and sorrows. Did we emerge heroes? Only God can tell. However, our trust in him deepened; our commitment to serve his people was expanded; and our faith heightened.

The Lord makes firm the steps of the one who delights in him; though he may stumble, he will not fall for the Lord upholds him with his hand. Psalm 37: 23-24

Taste and see that the Lord is good; blessed is the one who takes refuge in him. Psalm 34:8

1981 SNOW

Here are a few more stories on living in a morass of snow –

The car swerved. There was nothing I could do! One minute I was facing forward, the next the car had done a complete about face. This was my introduction to driving in the Minneapolis winter. Fortunately, the drivers around me were skilled and careful, used to snow country  and icy roads, so they managed to miss hitting me and there was no accident. We learned never to slam on the brakes when you are driving on icy roads but to pump them gently, so they don't lock and slide.

Another time we were on our way to a country church and didn't take a corner slowly enough, finishing up in a snowbank on the side of the road. We could see the lights of the church in the distance, so I decided to walk there to get help. I only just made it! We were told people die every winter thinking they can make it to a lighted building just a short distance away. But the cold is so severe in Minnesota that the body gradually freezes no matter how warmly you are dressed, as you must keep breathing the body slowly cools from the cold air entering the lungs. Many people lose their lives in this manner each winter.

Another time I was on a preaching trip and my car swerved on the icy road into a snow-covered ditch. When I opened the bonnet, I found the snow had come up to cover the engine and there was no way I could get the car going again. But God is good, and a carload of people stopped to see what I needed. They had heard me preach only the night before and were delighted to help. They took me to the nearest town where I could get a tractor truck driver to pull the car out of the ditch. God is so good to have helpers come along at just the right time.

Moving from Sydney and a mediterranean climate to Minnesota was an education. The temperature varied from 30F, or -1C, (with often a -30C windchill) to 100F, or 40C. Our favourite program on television was the weather forecast! We gathered each morning to hear what was to happen that day. Would it be snow, icy roads, bitter winds? Or sweltering gnat infested heat! We had to be ready for anything. We discovered that in winter we had to plug our car engine block into the house electricity each night or the car engine would not operate the next day. We had to clear our front path when it snowed but we ignored the backyard during winter, and this was always covered in snow. It never was warm enough to melt until Spring came. The only member of the family who used the backyard was our little dog. He would run around throwing the snow in the air with his nose and when he had finished his ablutions, he would scamper back inside with little snowballs attached to his belly hair. When the spring thaw came, we would find his little packages all over the yard, still frozen so easily tidied away.

One day I came in exhausted from shovelling the snow that had fallen that night from off our driveway so we could get the car out of the garage. Alison noticed my moustache, of which I was inordinately proud and waxed daily - it was frozen stiff! She reached up to feel it and not realising what would happen broke one half off! Ah well! Another victim to self-experience! I calmly broke off the other half and had a toothbrush moustache instead!

Our friends, the Langstaff's, who had arrived some months before us, took us to a local church basement where we could get some free winter clothing. Heavy coats, moon boots (knee high boots with lambswool lining), gloves and scarves. All were necessary and even when so clothed we had to wear the scarf over our mouth so as not to freeze by breathing in the frigid air. Gradually we learned to live with the cold and became quite adept at racing from the warm house to the warm car, and from the warm car to the warm shopping centre, or the warm church, without rugging up in the winter gear we needed to survive. It was amusing to see the women in the church wear their heavy boots to the church door and then pullout high heels from their purse to wear inside. We learned to keep survival supplies in the boot of the car in case of need should we have a breakdown at any time.

We also learned that snow is quite beautiful. On Christmas Eve, our first winter, the snowflakes landing on the cold double-glazed windows of the house, were perfect shapes, each one different from the last. However, on the streets the white snow becomes churned up and dirty from mud and soot from fires. Each day trucks with large scoops would patrol the streets to spray salt to melt the snow and then sweep it to the side of the road so the traffic could move. One winter the snowbanks that lined the streets built up to eight feet and it was difficult to see traffic coming from the left or right which slowed everyone down. Finally, the local council had to truck the snow away to make it possible to keep traffic flowing.

The snow wasn't the most dangerous part of the weather. If it rained and then froze, the roads would be like ice rinks, and no one could go anywhere that day. Everything closed down and no-one could go to work, or to school, or to church if it was a Sunday. And the winter could last for seven months, causing cabin fever, and depression from sun deprivation. One good thing about the winter was that all the houses were centrally heated, and we seldom caught colds or flu while we were there. No germs could live in the cold, and we did not have to go from a warm room to a cold room as in Tasmania where we had constant colds from the difference in temperature from our warm gas-fired lounge room to our freezing bedrooms.

After the long winter, the Spring with its beautiful new life, and Summer with its rising temperatures was a blessed relief. Everyone would work really hard to tend their once brown lawns into a verdant green, plough fields, and plant crops; and the 100 degree Fahrenheit heat, coupled with the rising damp from the 10,000 lakes would make the weather almost tropical and hasten the harvest. We were given permission to gather some corn cobs one year and that was fun. Alison learned how to preserve them and the abundant fruit to store for winter. It was a whole new way of living and hard for us Aussies to get used to, but we learned many things and managed to survive the five years we were there.

One of the things we found it hard to like were the swarms of mosquitoes and gnats that came from the lakes when they melted in the summer heat. If we were going anywhere, we had to run quickly to the car and slam the door in a hurry to keep out the cloud of insects which would follow us eagerly. Inevitably, we always shut a few in with us and we would be killing them for the first few miles of the trip. In the winter months we longed for the summer, but in the summer months we looked forward to the winter when any flu germs would die of the cold and the mozzies would disappear.

Another experience we had was a close shave with a tornado. The sky was a disturbing shade of grey-green, due to the large amount of water in the clouds. The air was eerily still. There was a basement in our house for just such occasions, but we were more fascinated by the inexplicable change in the weather to feel concern. Then the sirens went off. Loudspeakers were attached to the highest point on the telephone poles which dotted throughout the city. The siren was loud and long and brought back memories of the war years in Australia. There are on average 27 tornadoes a year in Minnesota, but this was the first to hit our area in Minneapolis. Dutifully we took some work down to the basement and waited for the sirens to end and tell us the tornado had passed. At the time, and even though we had descended to the nether regions of the house, it did not occur to us that our house could possibly be blown away as we had never experienced such a catastrophic event, our actions were the result of instructions for various events that would occasionally bring life in Minneapolis to a halt.

Sharon was even more nonchalant regarding the impending tornado and ignoring the protests from her colleagues walked outside the building to view the grey-green sky for herself. She said that while she was standing against the walls of the building a brisk wind sprang out of the stillness. The wind then pressed her against the building, which she found exhilarating, but as the strength of this increased felt it was time to do the smart thing and retreat indoors. It was a memorable event for us all! The tornado passed a few miles from us and so we were fortunate that we did not see any of the destruction that can accompany this type of weather.

After five years of living in this northern state, we had the opportunity to move to California, with its temperate climate and low rain fall. Here there were no flies and no mosquitoes because there was no standing water, but because of this dryness there were millions of fleas! Just like the Minnesotan giant mosquitoes they enjoyed my rich Australian blood and also thoroughly tormented our little dog, Paddington Bear, that we had brought with us. We may have had no snow or tornados but there were frequent earth tremors common to San Diego and California in general.

At first, we were very sensitive to any ground movement and wondered when God would design to allow the San Andreas Fault to collapse and slide us all into the Pacific Ocean. Each nighttime tremor would impel us out of our beds to stand in the doorway or bathroom, the two safest areas to protect you from a collapsing roof. But after a time, we would hear the windows rattle, feel the rocking motion of our bed, and recognise it was another tremor, roll over, and go back to sleep. As with the threat of a tsunami hitting the shores of Sydney or a deadly fire, the familiarity of daily living inures one to any future danger.

We were told to have a survival pack on hand: hiking boots, water bottles, backpacks, chocolate bars, and other canned groceries, to last us a few days or weeks if any catastrophe should befall our neighbourhood. However, I don't think we have ever done so, except for the winters in Minnesota where starving in winter was an immediate threat. In any event, if the San Andreeas earthquake should eventuate while we were living in California, and we survived, we were instructed to make our way to the desert outside the city and there we would be rescued by the United States army. It has been 30 years now and the earthquake has still not eventuated much to our relief as our grandson has made his home in Los Angeles.

As the rain and snow come down from heaven, and do not return to it without watering the earth and making it bud and flourish, so that it yields seed for the sower and bread for the eater, so is my Word that goes out from my mouth: it will not return to me empty, but will accomplish what I desire and achieve the purpose for which I sent it. Isaiah 55:10-11

1983 DUTY

"I am the slave of duty!" Thus, Frederic sings about himself in the comic opera by Gilbert and Sullivan, *The Pirates of Penzance.*

There have been several occasions over the years when I have been obliged to echo Frederic's sentiments. And I suppose if one must be a slave, it may as well be to duty as anything else. Somewhere around 1985, I was visiting Maryland, Baltimore, as a second keynote speaker for a charismatic Lutheran Church conference. At the end of one of the services, some people approached me and requested I go in person to a nearby hospital, lay hands and pray for a lady who was dying of cancer. I said I could not do so without obtaining permission from the dying woman. I thought this would be the end of the matter. Somewhat to my surprise the enquirer agreed with me. Accordingly, later that same day the sick lady's friend came back to me with an endorsement from the sufferer. So, reluctantly I told her to make an appointment for the next day, which she did. Why was I reluctant? We were all strangers to one another. And I could not see any connection between us upon which a prayer of faith could be built.

They all remained adamant that I should go to the hospital and that they were expecting a miracle even if I had no such hope. At the appointed time I walked from the church to the nearby hospital, took the elevator to the 8th floor and approached the lady's bed. When I looked at her my heart sank. Her complexion was sallow, her eyes deeply sunken, and her breath foul. I had not a shred of expectation that she would be healed. Nonetheless, succumbing to the demands of duty I anointed her head with oil in harmony with the instruction given by James in Chapter Five and prayed that God would grant her a miracle of healing. Would it happen? I did not know. I had very little faith to draw upon in that moment. And the lady was too ill to engage in conversation, so once the prayer was ended, I left the hospital.

You can imagine my astonishment when, the very next day, the people who had first requested me to go to the hospital came up to me with big smiles. Overnight their friend had shown a remarkable improvement! When I left Baltimore, a few days later, she was well on the way to a full recovery. I am confident that she was, by the grace of God, cured of her cancer and sent home to recuperate.

Assuming that she did receive a miracle of healing, can I legitimately claim any credit for it? Hardly! Except for whatever commendation may be due to me for doing my duty. However, the deed was entirely God's doing and I'm sure the faith of her friends played a big part in her miracle.

Like in the story of the centurion who believed Jesus could heal his servant. The centurion's faith made all the difference. (Luke 7:1-10)

Some years later I was back in Australia, preaching at a church in Victoria, and had just finished praying for all the people who had responded to my altar call. I was standing at the door of the church shaking hands with those who were departing and eager to get into my car and drive to a nearby restaurant for lunch. A couple suddenly presented their son to me and asked me to pray for a miracle of healing. I forget what was wrong with him except that he was ill enough that he was unable to attend school. I was rather exasperated because instead of joining the earlier prayer line, they had waited until everyone was going home, including myself and my family, and I was weary after preaching with all my heart, and working my way through a long prayer line.

I asked why they had not joined the prayer line and why they had waited until the service was over. I felt depleted and here they were bringing their child to me. I don't recall their response, but they insisted I should pray anyway. So, I did. But only as a matter of duty. Had you searched my soul at that moment you would not have found a skerrick of faith. I wish I could declare myself, "God's mighty man of faith and power!" (Samuel 10:1 & Judges 6:12) At times I have indeed lived up to this encomium and have indeed been able to wage warfare against the devil and all his forces with truly invincible courage, strength, and faith. Instead, in this instance I hung my head in some shame and regardless of my lack of any expectation of any miracle I did my duty, trusting in the mercy of God, laid hands on the boy, prayed, and left the matter in the hands of the Lord.

Does this always work? Unhappily, no. Nonetheless, in this case it did! I bade the parents and the boy farewell and drove away to the restaurant with my family without any real expectation that a miracle had occurred, or that the boy would be made whole. Imagine my astonishment when a few days later the parents reported that although there was a lack of any evidence of healing at the time, within a few days of that hollow prayer the boy had recovered sufficiently to go back to school. Later I learned that not only had he got well but had been promoted to being captain of his class. I was of course delighted but also chagrined because I knew that his recovery had nothing to do with me, or any great faith of mine.

On the contrary, it was purely an act of divine mercy. The parents were the ones who were believing for a miracle. I know only that, whether or not there was any evidence of God's presence, I had done my duty, which in this case resulted in a wonderful miracle of answered prayer!

These are the moments that are a mystery. But it certainly highlights the idea that whether you find success in your endeavours for Christ, or not, you must try, try, and try again!

Legend tells us that Robert the Bruce, in 1306, hid himself from the marauding English by hiding in a cave where he watched a spider many times try to anchor its web. But as often as it fell to the ground it climbed up the wall of the cave and tried again until it finally achieved success. Thus, giving rise to the saying, "If at first you don't succeed, try, try again." Or perhaps with more historical truth, let me quote a few lines from the poem by Alfred, Lord Tennyson, from *The Charge of the Light Brigade*. He wrote and published this epic encounter in 1854, recounting an incident in the battle of Balaklava. Here is a small excerpt -

> Forward, the Light Brigade!
> Was there a man dismayed?
> Not though the soldier knew
> Someone had blundered.
>   Theirs not to make reply,
>   Theirs not to reason why,
>   Theirs but to do and die.
>   Into the valley of Death
>   Rode the six hundred.

Thus is our relationship with our own Great Commander. If we know that he has spoken to us then the same proverb applies: *Ours is not to reason why, ours is but to do and die.* Why? Because we trust implicitly that he knows best. As the great Greek philosopher Socrates said, "Our prayers should be for blessings in general, for God knows best what is good for us."

Or to paraphrase Scripture - Those who put their hand to the plough, and then look back, are unfit for the kingdom of God. (Luke 9:62; see also 2 Peter 2:20-22).

And you could be even more a winner by heeding:

But the righteous will live by faith. And I take no pleasure in the one who shrinks back. But we do not belong to those who shrink back and are destroyed, but to those who have faith and are saved. Hebrews 10:38-39

1984 CRIMINAL

"Are you that notorious criminal," demanded the policeman, "whom we have been trying to apprehend for a long time? His name is the same as yours, Kenneth David Chant, and he is wanted for several serious crimes."

So said the officer of the law. This was my second potential arrest by the American police. I will come back to that, but first, I had been apprehended once before for exceeding the speed limit on a Minnesota Road but when the policeman heard my Australian accent, and heard I was on my way to preach at a church conference, he chuckled and gave me the signal to go on my way without penalty.

In the meantime, while we were living in Minneapolis, Dick Mills suggested that I should move to San Diego and become principal of a Bible college for Pastor Carl Austin of the Southwest Christian Centre. We were still working with Alan Langstaff, and enjoying our time in Minneapolis, when Alan's ministry began to take him in a different direction. It was obvious I was not needed anymore. So, the invitation from Carl seemed to come from God. Especially as the invitation included all the computers, and other assistance we would need to establish the College. I flew down for an interview and was accepted enthusiastically by the church, so flew home again to notify the family.

At this time, we had a secretary, Pat Eades, who had come to us from England because she felt it was God's will for her to help us with the

Correspondence Course. She had not completed the work we needed her to do so we talked about the opportunity together, prayed and agreed that this invitation to San Diego sounded like a wonderful opportunity to expand our College programme.

We rented a 28-foot Hertz moving van in which we stacked nearly everything we owned in the world, giving away what remained. Eric, our son who was then 18 years of age and a good driver, drove the truck, while myself and Alison followed in our car, with Pat and Baden in the back. We began the long 3,099 kilometre journey from Minneapolis to Los Angeles.

The second possible arrest occurred on our way to San Diego when we were bowling down the highway with Sharon's car in tow behind the truck. (At this time Sharon was back in Australia living in Adelaide). This policeman told Eric that an APB (All-Points Bulletin) had been issued for his arrest (as the driver of the truck) because we had missed a sign telling us to pull off the highway for a weighbridge test. This APB was a more serious matter than the first. Yet for some reason none of us can remember what happened afterwards except that we were able to continue our journey without hindrance and without penalty. Possibly our Australian accents, evident ignorance of American law, and God's favour, persuaded them to allow us to continue our journey.

On one of the three nights we spent on the road I had a very narrow brush with death. It was dark when we reached the hotel, and I was directing Eric to back the truck into its parking place. I was standing against a tree, in position behind the truck, when suddenly I saw this giant mudguard, which stood as high as my shoulder, coming towards me. It pressed me hard against the tree. I could feel my ribs beginning to creak, a stab of pain shot through me, and I knew in that split second that unless I could stop the truck my end was only a couple of breaths away. There was no air left in my lungs, and I could barely make a squeak. I was about to be crushed to death!

By an act of divine grace, Eric somehow heard my feeble cry and at once stopped the truck, realised what was wrong, and moved it forward enabling me to escape from the bark stabbing me in the back and the bumper crushing my chest. I carried a bruise that remained for several weeks, but I was alive! I will never cease being grateful to Eric and his sharp ears and prompt reflexes. It was not my time to meet God!

The next day we continued our drive to Los Angeles and the Anaheim Holiday Inn, near Disneyland, California. We had decided to stay in LA overnight so we could arrive in San Diego the next morning, giving us plenty of time to unload the truck and move into our new home. But when I went out in the morning to check on the truck, I couldn't find it. Quite bewildered I searched every part of the hotel parking lot and eventually had to accept that the truck was gone. That was when I called the local police and was close to being arrested for the third time. They asked me, "Are you the notorious criminal Kenneth David Chant?" I hastened to assure them that I was an Aussie from Minneapolis on the way to San Diego to start a Bible college.

After completing the logging of the report of our robbery I decided to stick to our original plan to stay in Anaheim an extra day so that I could take Eric and Baden to Disneyland. It did not want to rob them of this pleasure despite what had just happened. This I did while Alison and Pat stayed at the motel in case the police wanted to contact us. Banishing our troubles from my mind I set off with the boys and we had a delightful day at Disneyland arriving back at the motel early evening.

Before we left for San Diego the next morning the Los Angeles Police finally contacted us. They told us that had we let Eric sleep in the truck as he had requested to guard our possessions he would surely have been murdered before the thieves made off with our truck, silently reversing and driving away with barely a sound that disturbed us. However, fortunately I had insisted he sleep in a bed as he had driven all day and was very tired. These organised truck bandits were notorious in the area. We were dismayed by the loss of the Hertz removal van but grateful that God had guided me to save Eric's life. Feeling dispirited we drove from Anaheim to San Diego, arriving to an empty house that had been provided by the church.

We were greeted by the pastor of Southwest Christian Centre who had a congregation of several hundred people. This was the same pastor who had invited us to establish a Bible college for his people and other Christians in the area. He was not phased by the horror of our robbery, as the people of California are an interesting group, and drama is easily assimilated, perhaps because they live close to danger every day via the San Andreas fault, or perhaps because of the influence of Hollywood. However, there were mixed feelings amongst some 'spiritual' members of his congregation. Most were happy to see us, however, there were some with a kind of 'super faith', who protested that we must be unbelievers, or else such a disaster would not have befallen us. They plainly forgot that Jesus himself has warned us not to lay up treasures on earth where they can be stolen by thieves and robbers, but to store up treasure in heaven, for your heart will be where your treasure is. (Matthew 6:19-21)

We settled as well as we could into our empty new home. People who heard about our predicament began to bring over everything we would need to set up house. The church was very generous, and we ended up with more than enough goods to enjoy reasonable comfort. But, like a cook without a can opener, I was helpless to begin setting up the Bible college. Alison tells me that she remembers me sitting white-faced at our kitchen table, deeply chagrined by my lack of all that I needed to establish the new college. All my books, lecture notes, sermons, questionnaires, answer sheets were all gone along with our furniture, Pro Hart paintings, clothes, kitchen items, lamps, and other personal items belonging to the family.

A whole week of worry and some misery went by before I finally, if unhappily but nonetheless truthfully, told the Lord I accepted his divine providence and would trust him implicitly to work everything according to his gracious purpose. The very next day the Los Angeles Police Department called and told me they had found a Hertz truck hidden in bushland some one hundred miles north of San Diego, and the only stuff inside it was a pile of papers and books, everything else was gone. I urged them to leave the contents alone and I was on my way to meet them there.

Arriving a couple of hours later a policeman opened the truck and there, amazingly, were indeed all my books, papers, lecture notes, and other stuff I needed for the College. The robbers had taken everything else. We left the police to notify the Hertz Company about the location of their van, while I packed everything into my car using cardboard boxes. I was then driving a diesel Chevrolet station wagon which was large enough to hold all that was left in the truck.

So, all my needful college papers were there, but sadly everything else was gone. The police had verified that I was the person that had rented the removal van, and they allowed me to go on my way. Bidding the police farewell I drove somewhat joyfully back to San Diego, deeply grateful to God for his gracious providence. How good the Lord was, that even our valuable passports were still there, having been missed by the thieves. As well, we found a rolled up bundle of love letters, tied with a ribbon, that I had written to Alison over the years! Small blessings.

When I tried to lodge an insurance claim on the stolen goods, I was told by the company that the goods were not covered from one house to another, so they declined to make any payment. Happily, there was a lawyer in Pastor Austin's congregation who was able to write to the company telling them that I had brought with me from Minneapolis the policy which stated clearly that I was fully covered until the policy renewal date was passed. He insisted they make good on their promise, or I would take them to court. They promptly paid out the policy which was insufficient to cover all our stuff, but added to what the church had given us, it enabled us to establish adequately our home and the new Bible college.

We remained in San Diego for five years and then were invited back to Australia to take charge of a Bible college in Penrith, New South Wales. Without this promise of a home and a wage we would not have been able to return to Australia. God is good and guides us step by step for his purpose to be fulfilled.

Taste and see that the Lord is good; blessed is the one who takes refuge in him. Psalm 34:8

The Lord makes firm the steps of the one who delights in him; though he may stumble, he will not fall, for the Lord upholds him with his hand. Psalm 37:23

And to those two Scriptures let me shout, "Hallelujah!"

1985 VIU

This story is how Vision International University came into being by a set of unusual circumstances that could only have been directed by God who as I have experienced enjoys working everything – the good, the bad, and the ugly – for our good and his purposes. (Romans 8:28)

A large church in San Diego was deeply troubled. Its pastor had failed in multiple ways and the people, who loved their pastor, were deeply traumatized by what he had done. I was a member of the church and headed up the Bible college we had begun there over a year ago. Alison and the children had joined me in expectation of a wonderful worship experience. I had already visited the church and had gone back to Minneapolis with glowing reports but now my family looked at me with bewilderment. They felt instinctively that something was wrong, but they didn't know what it was. I had to agree with them. There did seem to be a remarkable change in the spiritual quality of the church since the time of my earlier visit. I had no choice but to confront the pastor and demand to know what had gone wrong. He promptly dismissed me from the church and the Bible college, and we were cast out with no job and no income.

A few days later some of the people from the congregation visited me. They had a tape recording of the pastor accusing me of all the crimes against God that he was committing! They wanted me to sue him for defamation of character. Whereupon I said, "Whatever he has done he has my total forgiveness, and I wish him well. If I am innocent then the Lord will defend me, if I am guilty may he do with me as he pleases." The church delegation was rather startled by this, but they graciously accepted my ruling, and we parted amicably after they had given me their tithes that they now declined to give to the church having now left themselves. I had based my opposition to a lawsuit on the words of Paul. So, I accepted the money in partial recompense of the salary I had lost due to my dismissal.

If any of you has a dispute with another, do you dare take it before the ungodly for judgment instead of before the Lord's people? Or do you not know that the Lord's people will judge the world? And if you are to judge the world, are you not competent to judge trivial cases? Do you not know that we will judge angels? How much more the things of this life! Therefore, if you have disputes about such matters, do you ask for a ruling from those whose way of life is scorned in the church? I say this to shame you. Is it possible that there is nobody among you wise enough to judge a dispute between believers? But instead, one brother takes another to court - and this in front of unbelievers. 1 Corinthians 6: 1-6

As it happens God did defend me as the lawyer who belonged to the church saw the pastor's car outside a pornographic store and entered to find him inside. He investigated further and found that all the Pastor had said about me was instead true of himself.

In the meantime, I had hired a school auditorium and set up a church with about one hundred people attending. But then the original church asked me to return so they could make a public apology to me. They then invited me to return to them as their pastor. My elders did not want me to go back. Alison did not want me to go back. But foolishly I felt it was my duty to return to care for the traumatized congregation and fulfil the terms of the leased building. (This was about the time I met Stan DeKoven as he had been called in as counsellor to many of the stricken people.) I didn't survive for long, maybe two years. I had a severe stomach haemorrhage due to extreme stress and had to resign from the church once again. I had cause to regret my stubborn refusal to listen to the counsel of my friends who told me to have nothing to do with the church anymore. Ah, well! It is easy to be wise after the disaster has happened, as they say in the classics. The church was taken over by several pastors but after all the trauma the church had gone through it did not survive.

But out of it all did come one great result: I met Dr Stan DeKoven.

Stan was a highly successful clinical psychologist who had established several clinics in Southern California. In the midst of his prosperity, even perhaps despite it, he felt a call of God to prepare himself for some kind of Christian ministry. So, he took himself back to school and earned himself a Doctorate in Christian Ministry, including Theology. Just about the time he had completed those studies we met in San Diego, and we had lunch together. We soon discovered we had common interests focussed on a local church-based Bible school. Stan and some of his associates had for some years endeavoured to begin this kind of ministry but they had no curriculum. It was a marriage made in heaven!

Here is a short excerpt taken from *Vision History* on the Vision International University website –

"Dr Stan has an interesting background which has provided him with unique skills in communication and has given him remarkable insight into the hearts of men and the workings of churches and institutions. He is able to go into a country and find a man who is trustworthy, with a deep desire to spread the Word of God and teach the deep things of God. Because of this he has been one of the reasons Vision has spread now to so many countries. His willingness to stay on track, travelling constantly to support and encourage the men and women he has discovered, has been one of the reasons why Vision is still growing and developing so wonderfully."

Stan embraced Vision Bible College, as it was then, and worked with me to develop a way to promote the course across the United States. By 1990, I was able to return to Australia and leave it in his hands.

Before the Covid pandemic Vision had well over 100,000 students in 150 countries. However, Covid hit us hard, greatly reducing our student numbers which have still not fully recovered. Currently (2024) according to our Ramona headquarters in California, we have -

- Ten Zone Leaders each of them responsible for building the Vision programme in their region, which requires courage, discipline, and unwavering faith in the providence of God.
- 5,000 satellite campuses each of which runs the Vision program under the oversight of its local regional director.
- 80,000 students worldwide and we are hoping this will steadily return to the pre-covid level and beyond.
- We are currently operating in 140 nations which again we are hoping to restore to the pre-covid level, or more.
- About 11 people work in our Ramona headquarters.
- In addition, Stan works in close liaison with two or three other organisations. There is Dr John Delgado, who once spoke at a CRC conference in Australia, and who has hundreds of Bible

students in Mexico, Cuba, and other Central American countries.
- Vision also has a part time Hispanic (Spanish) director who has helped plant Bible schools in Columbia, Dominican Republic and Honduras.
- We also partner with groups like Bethel, in Redding California, who have over 2,000 students in their African schools, and who use some of Bethel's courses combined with Vision material to provide theological balance to their experiential curriculum.
- Ken's books are found all over the world, in multiple languages, and more to come by God's grace.

And of course, there is our Australasian College which, since Alison and I retired some twenty-years ago, has been under the directorship of Denis Plant. (See 1999 VIC below)

Can I still proclaim our motto - *The whole Word to the whole World*? In a sense, I suppose it is true; but of course, it is far from literally true. We have a long way to go to turn that original boast into a fact. But because we now link up with other ministries who are teaching the Word of God around the world, this basic motto has far more chance of becoming a reality. This important link means that we have a reciprocal relationship where we use their books, and they use ours, which gives us all a far greater base for teaching.

Since we first met in 1985, Stan and I have remained excellent friends and partners in ministry, even though we seldom meet and live on opposite sides of the planet.

And I should have said this before, but will add it here, my brother Barry, is both my natural brother and my best friend! Our friendly sibling rivalry has spurred us both on to achieve far more than we could ever have imagined. He is also writing his biography, and I already know that it will far outstrip my efforts. I look forward to reading it!

There are many expressions attributed to the Bible but actually come from the hearts of his saints. This one is from the poet William Cowper, written in the 19th century -

God moves in a mysterious way,
His wonders to perform.
He plants his footsteps in the sea
And rides upon the storm.
Deep in the dark and hidden mines,
With never-failing skill,
He fashions all his bright designs
And works his sov'reign will.

As iron sharpens iron so one person sharpens another. Proverbs 27:17

First Board meeting of Vision Christian College from the left – Ken Chant, Stan DeKoven, Alison Chant, Ros Plant, Denis Plant, and Errol Stephenson.

1985 VCC

Wine bibbers versus abstainers!

I first met Denis Plant at a lunch for local pastors, before he left for Papua New Guinea as a missionary. He was introduced to me by Pastor Michael York. Denis and Michael both ordered sparkling water as they didn't want to expose themselves as alcohol drinkers in front of me. But when it came to my turn to order a drink, I ordered a Chardonnay much to their chagrin! After which, while I sipped my wine, they looked sourly upon their innocuous sparkling mineral water (which I found amusing)!

While in Papua New Guinea, Denis enrolled into and gained his Diploma of Theology through our College and then asked permission to introduce Vision to Papua New Guinea, which he did. So, when he returned to Australia, he was enthusiastic about Vision Christian College and knew how it was structured.

Around 1999, while on a CRC pastor's river cruise, he shared with me his vision from God to put a Bible college on the internet. He had a framework completed but was not happy with the studies available. "Why not use Vision," I suggested. This was a God moment and Denis was ready to do the work this would take. He converted the books I gave him from Word Star to Word and then to Word Perfect. Then he discovered Adobe which meant he could send out lessons over the internet without the risk of them being altered.

At this point Vision was the only one offering a Bible college course on-line as far as I know. Other colleges were advertising for students, but they were only asking for enrolments. So, Denis was one of the first to introduce the concept of an on-line Bible college and was involved in the birth of on-line learning.

It is wonderful how the Lord has brought different people at different times into the life of Vision Bible College to forward the work of taking *The whole Word to the whole World.* I feel this was one of those times. Meanwhile, after spending more than 50 years in ministry, I felt it was time to retire from the burden of office work, so I mentioned this to Denis, and he asked if he could take over the office duties. If I would allow this then he would be able to give his whole time to the College and give up his secular job. His only proviso was that I would remain as President. I agreed and a date was set for the transition on 1st July 2001.

Shortly after this Dr Stan DeKoven, president of the USA Vision International University, travelled to Australia, and we had our first World Director's meeting to give the transfer an official beginning. We took a historic photograph with myself and Alison; Denis and his wife,

Ros; Stan DeKoven, and Errol Stevenson, who has given his expertise to the College as its accountant for the last twenty-five years.

Denis has been able to take the College on to greater levels of recognition since he took over. He was successful in gaining recognition for the College as a Recognised Training Organisation (RTO), which enables us to offer accredited awards. With the help of Trish Hart, who took over the job of Registrar, and her husband Steve, who took over printing the books, Denis was able to expand the College to greater heights both within Australia and overseas. Denis has a missionary heart and has travelled widely promoting the College and establishing campuses. Our *Bible school in a Box* idea was modernised by putting the college material on a CD, and this helped with overseas colleges as we were able to add many extra helps, such as a Bible dictionary, to the programme.

Vision College has always been very flexible and because we work on the American system of building credits, we have been able to help as many as possible to do their studies over a period of years without losing credits. Now we have students from young to middle-aged to the elderly. Laymen and pastors, missionaries and deacons, men and women from all walks of life have done one or other of our courses as they seek to learn about the Word of God.

Our youngest student was a 14 year old pastor's son who was eagerly wanting to study the Word and prepare for ministry. Our oldest student was a 92 year old pastor from the USA who contacted Denis and said, "I have been a pastor for over 40 years, but I have never undertaken formal studies. I think it is time I gained some qualifications!"

In 2014, we celebrated Vision's 40th Anniversary. Denis worked incredibly hard getting people together and making it a great success. We had more than a hundred pastors, students and friends of Vision and special guests Bishop Harry Westcott and his wife Doreen. Harry looked after Vision while we were away in America for 10 years. Also, Dr Stan DeKoven, the president of Vision in the USA was another important guest. Some who could not attend sent video clips of congratulations so altogether it was a wonderful time of fellowship and rejoicing together.

Fight the good fight of the faith. Take hold of the eternal life to which you were called when you made your good confession in the presence of many witnesses. 1 Timothy 6:12

1988 JEWELLER

Jewellery has never been a high priority for us. Alison's engagement ring and her grandmother's engagement ring were lost in the theft we experienced in Los Angeles. This was really disappointing. Over the years we have lost, or had stolen, various watches and other items. However, neither of us has ever placed too much time or money into pursuing earthly gifts. So, it was delightful to have a friend who was not only a fellow pastor but also a skilled jeweller. Such a man was John Delgado.

Neither Alison nor I can remember just where we met John, but we soon became excellent friends. He heard that our golden wedding anniversary was approaching so he offered to make us two beautiful pieces of jewellery. One for me and one for Alison. We provided the money for the raw materials which he sourced and then used his expertise to craft the gifts to our specifications. Mine was a gold Cross on a gold chain with a tiny diamond fixed into the centre arm of the Cross. Later, Alison added another diamond at the apex of the cross as a gift for our 60th anniversary. For Alison, John made a gorgeous heart shaped necklace on a gold chain set with eleven small diamonds.

John is a New Yorker and speaks fluent Spanish, so he offered to take Vision to the Spanish speaking people of South America. When we heard that he had established several campuses in Cuba we were thrilled. The work there flourished as the Cubans were starved for good Bible teaching. Probably at my instigation, John came to Australia to be the guest speaker at one of our conferences. The pastors all enjoyed his ministry, except that when he finished, he probably made them wish we had invited someone else. He drew their attention to me and insisted that on top of whatever honorarium they were planning to give him, they should also remember me. He pointed out that Alison and I had a limited income and needed help. So, he urged the pastors at the conference to take up an offering for us. God stirred their hearts, and we received a remarkable $2,000 Australian! We were amazed at this gesture, but deeply grateful. As you will easily imagine, Alison and I look upon John as a friend forever!

Those who go out weeping, carrying seed to sow, will return with songs of joy, carrying sheaves with them. Psalm 126:6

1994 WISDOM

This is a subject I was asked to address at the Albury CRC Conference October in 1994. I thought I would include it in this book for young pastors who may need some wisdom from a father in the faith. My wife and I have now passed our 70th anniversary and have had a happy and fulfilling marriage. Here are the highlights from this sermon:

This year marked a milestone in my life with my wife, Alison. Forty years of marriage and forty years of ministry. Do you applaud? There was a time when neither would have seemed remarkable! But now among our pastors, both ministry and marriage fail with tragic frequency. It is heart breaking to trace back the list of pastors and observe how many are now missing from serving God.

You may ask me how I survived? Let me summarise the reasons in four key ideas. At another time I might choose a different set of reasons, but these will suffice for now.

First - I embraced the **Virtue of Christ**. Being a local pastor is an occupational hazard because of the constant close contact with all sorts of people. For instance, there are three kinds of women in the average church.

   1. The virtuous. These women are secure and contented.

2. The <u>disappointed</u>. These are good women, but women who are unhappy in marriage, or widowed and lonely. For them the pastor takes on an aura of perfection. They only ever see him when he is at his best, preaching the Word. They never see what he is like at home with his wife and family. Just an ordinary man who can be nice or nasty. They have a totally unrealistic view of their pastor and find themselves wishing they could have such a paragon! Then there are the most dangerous of all.

3. The <u>predatory</u>. Women on the prowl! Several times when I have been making home visits, I have been greeted by women in their underwear. But I have learned the principle, you can only be tempted and caught if you want to be caught! If you trust the Lord, he will keep you from danger. If you sense danger just turn and leave. The woman will see your disgust and either repent and change her ways or leave the church for easier prey.

Second - I conceived the **Word of Christ**. I hear many preachers who do not know their Bible. They learn doctrine but don't know their Bible intimately. They are hypocritical! Are we purveyors of doctrine or ministers of the Word? To minister the Word takes hard work, effort, and meditation to receive revelation. These take time and effort and so you must prioritise your time.

Third - I captured the **Dream of Christ**. There is no folly so great as trying to be someone else! You must learn who you really are, not who you think you are or who people say you are. When a young pastor, I was torn one way and then another by well-meaning people who wanted to change me to suit themselves. The trouble was each person had a different idea of who they wanted their pastor to be, and I learned you can't please everyone all the time.

I was enlightened by reading the book, *Twelve English Reformers* (mentioned in 1973 ORU.) It saved me from trying to live up to other people's expectations or from trying to emulate the life of another whom I admired. Each of the reformers had vastly different skills and abilities, personalities and character. One was gregarious, another aloof; one preached extemporaneously, another read his sermons; one preached with brief preparation, another studied and worked on his sermon for six days of the week; one was a bold extrovert, another was a shy introvert. They were all totally different from each other, but God used them all, just as they were.

Fourth - I learned **Who I am in Christ**. Pastors should be examined carefully before they are ordained. Their character must be fully formed, above reproach, honest, faithful, truthful, self- controlled, respectable, hospitable, and able to teach. (1 Tim 3:1-7) They must know the Word and what God says about them. (Ephesians 1) They must have a healthy fear of God and his judgment, because it is a fearful thing to fall into the hands of the living God.

If you take heed of these four principles, you have the best chance of never falling but instead, successfully completing the work for which Christ has redeemed you.

The Lord will judge his people. It is a dreadful thing to fall into the hands of the living God. Hebrews 10:30b-31

1990 PROMISES

The following are highlights from a sermon I preached in various forms in five different countries. If you can learn and live the truths contained in the following words you could become a walking revival!

No Christian can ever dispense with Bible reading. The reading and understanding of Scripture are more necessary to the health of our souls as regular meals are to the health of our bodies. Job tells us that he treasured the words spoken by God more than his daily bread. (Job 23:12b)

You should diligently read your Bible, the hard parts as well as the easy ones, as a matter of discipline and a balanced spiritual diet. Christ can be found in every book and the voice of God can speak to the reader's heart from any page.

This means that we must:

COME TO THE WORD

All connection with scripture must begin here. An open Bible and someone reading it. How can the Word of God get any entrance into your life unless you actually come to your Bible, day by day, open it, read it, and meditate upon it and get it off the page and into your mind and memory. Yet surveys show that less than 25% of Christians have read the Bible right through even once. The percentage that has read every part of it many times is infinitesimal. No wonder the church is weak. No wonder the saints fall defeated. No wonder the devil laughs at the average believer. Make no mistake. If you lack the Word, you will lack everything. But to be rich in the Word is to be rich in everything!

So, if you have not already done so, you should at once develop a program that will take you right through the Bible over and over again. There is simply no substitute for coming to the Bible regularly and consistently as the first step to a life of joyous victory.

Why should you read your Bible every day? To hear God's voice clearly in your life. It is bread for our souls, spiritual energy, liveliness of faith, toughness and resilience in dealing with the kingdom of darkness. These all depend upon a balanced and regular diet of the Word of God.

Then we must:

CONCEIVE THE WORD

To conceive the Word means to get an inner revelation of the Word. To get it from your mind and into your spirit. To have your 'spiritual eyes' opened. To know, deeply, personally, vitally the gospel riches and power that are available in Christ to the Spirit-filled believer.

We all experience a kind of 'credibility gap' when we read the promises of God. The promises seem so ephemeral. Our need so substantial. We sense a hiatus between where we are and where the promise is. That chasm must be bridged. The promise must catch fire in our hearts, blazing into light and truth, so that now the promise is the only thing that is true and all else is a lie.

Prayer is the main path to that transformation, as Paul shows by his own prayers. Answer this question. What was the main burden of Paul's prayer for the churches he founded? He did not pray that God would give them a mighty revival, nor that the Father would pour out his Spirit upon them, nor that great miracles would happen, nor that their financial needs might be met, and the like. In fact, he did not ask God to give the churches any of the things that are the constant burden of our prayer meetings. It is not wrong to pray for these things, but Paul had a better understanding. And what was that? He asked God to give them a **revelation** in his Word! (Ephesians 1:16-23 and Colossians 1:9-14)

Make Paul's prayer your own. Give heaven no rest until the promises of God explode into a glorious reality within your spirit. Then you will truly find yourself living in the dynamic of the 'immeasurable greatness of the power of God' he accomplished in Christ when he raised him from the dead and made him sit at his own right hand in the heavenlies.

The next step is to:

CONFESS THE WORD

God's exceedingly great and precious promises become effective only when they are boldly spoken in faith. In other words, you can come to the Word, and conceive the Word, and yet still fail to obtain the promise unless you go on to confess the Word. Having put the promise into your head, and then into your heart, you must now bring it into your mouth.

Scores of scriptures put before us the necessity of openly and vigorously speaking out whatever promise you want fulfilled in your life. Bold confession activates the promise. Why is this so? Why does God demand that we overcome reticence, shyness, timidity and vocalize his promise? Why does the fulfillment of his promise depend upon you speaking it aloud? I cannot say. I only know that scripture is unequivocal in its demand that the Word must be spoken by your mouth as well as believed in your heart. Even as when you believed for your salvation.

The promises of God are replete with the staggering resurrection power of Christ himself; but only one key can unlock that limitless strength: the sound of the voice of faith. That is the catalyst that unleashes the spiritual force of the promise.

In chemistry, a catalyst is a substance that activates a reaction between two or more substances but remains itself unchanged in the process. So, in the walk of faith, your believing confession of the promise of God brings the power of the promise into contact with your need and begins the process whereby the miracle you desire is made to happen. Again, just as some chemical reactions cannot begin until the right catalyst is added, so the promise of God lies dormant in relation to your need until you arouse it by the quickening sound of faith's bold affirmation of that promise.

For it is with your heart that you believe and are justified, and it is with your mouth that you profess your faith and are saved. Romans 10:9-10

Then last of all you must:

CONTEND FOR THE WORD

Sometimes, even after you have got the Word into your head by reading it, and into your heart by conceiving it, and into your mouth by confessing it the promise may still remain elusive and unfulfilled. How can that be? Because three strong enemies work against the realisation of the promise of God in your life. The world, the flesh and the devil. Those foes often oblige us to fight the fight of faith. To stand firm, confident that what God has spoken will surely be done.

O how marvellous are the rich things God has prepared for those who publicly declare that he will deliver them. Psalm 31:19

Psalm 31 shows this principle. Despite its eulogy of the 'abundant goodness' God has laid up for us, the Psalm still warns the warrior to be strong, to let your heart take courage, as you wait for the Lord (vs.24).

So then, never abandon that confidence in God, which alone can bring you his great reward. Having done the will of God, endure with boldness and steadfast trust, until you have received what has been promised. God finds no pleasure in those who shrink back from what he has called them to believe and receive. Determine rather to be among that adventurous company who refuse to be dismayed, who rise in Jesus' name and possess their spiritual possessions.

So, do not throw away your confidence; it will be richly rewarded. You need to persevere so that when you have done the will of God, you will receive what he has promised. Hebrews 10:35-36

My son, keep your father's command and do not forsake your mother's teaching. Bind them always on your heart; fasten them around your neck. When you walk, they will guide you; when you sleep, they will watch over you; when you awake, they will speak to you. For this command is a lamp, this teaching is a light, and correction and instruction are the way to life. Proverbs 6:20-23

1995 LIKING

We often look at ourselves from a human viewpoint. If I look at myself only from my own eye, or look at myself only through your eyes, then I would have to say what a worthless piece of tissue this ambulating corpse is. But Scripture challenges us not to see ourselves through our own eyes, or through the eyes of our neighbour, but only through the eyes of God.

"What does God think about me?" Let me listen. Do you know what I hear God saying? "I like you; you are a nice person to know." That, too, is what he says about you!

I can't remember the exact occasion, but it was about the time I first made this discovery. After spending years imagining that God could hardly stand the sight of me, that I was a spot upon his beautiful fabric, and that given half a chance he would take the roughest, most abrasive cleanser possible, and scour me right out of existence – after years of thinking that way about myself, I finally made this incredible discovery. God actually likes me! He wants to be my friend and wants me to be his friend. He is willing to trust me with some of the most priceless treasures heaven possesses. A mark of true friendship indeed!

The Lord says, "I have loved you (Ken) with an everlasting love." Do you know what happens when you find that God loves you ... even likes you? You find a few good reasons to like yourself. Then suddenly you think that everyone else likes you too.

I tell you honestly, it always surprises me to learn that someone doesn't like me. That's a shock to me. I can't believe it! How can anyone not like me? My astonishment does not stem from pride or conceit; it is simply an inescapable consequence of the discovery that God likes me. If you know that God likes you and is your friend, you gain a wonderful new identity. What a marvellous thing that is! Suddenly you begin to like yourself, you come to like everybody else and expect them to like you.

All of this is a product of what Christ has done for us. For, of course, the man God likes is not Ken Chant, son of James Oswald Chant and Vera Gwenneth Chant; no, the man God likes (and that I now like) is the new man in Christ – the new Ken Chant, who has been given a new identity as God's son, God's servant, God's friend in Jesus.

When I talk about this man, Ken Chant, I do not talk about a man born of human parents, but a man born supernaturally of his heavenly Father, by the Holy Spirit, through the name of Jesus Christ. That's who I am, and that's who you are too! A new creation! Thinking these thoughts reminded me of this song by David Ingles -

> Blessings and more blessings overtake me,
> All his commandments I observe
> While my soul doth prosper in the knowledge
> Of Jesus Christ, my Lord, the living Word.
> That's what I have, that's who I am
> I am a king come out of Abraham.
> Because of Christ, I reign in life with him
> That's what I have, that's who I am.
>
> *David Ingles Music, Tulsa, Oklahoma 1978*

God demonstrates his own love for us in this: While we were still sinners, Christ died for us. Romans 5:8

1995 HEALTH

This more measured ministry lifestyle continued successfully for several years. However, the schedule of travelling away from home most weekends, and spending long hours at my desk writing new textbooks for the College, eventually proved too much for my seventy plus years. I had developed an infection in one of my toes and my health began to fail culminating in a collapse in Albury while I was attending a national CRC church conference. I was carried off to hospital where I had a kind of surreal out of body experience. I felt that I was floating near the ceiling of the ward watching the doctors attending me and debating if they should amputate my right leg which was nearly black from my ankle to above my knee from the effects of virulent cellulitis. I remember thinking that I would like to express an opinion on this but was physically unconscious!

The doctors drew a red mark on my leg to monitor the progress of the infection. Every inch gained a new line. If this progressed to my thigh and my lymph glands it would have proved fatal so I was prepared by the doctor to accept that I would probably lose my leg. Meanwhile, the doctors were scouring the country for an antibiotic that would stop the infection. They finally found one in Melbourne and had it flown straight to the Albury hospital. It proved wholly effective in the rising infection, which was stopped, and my leg began to heal. Of course, the several hundred delegates at the conference had been praying for me and I have no doubt that their prayers were answered.

Why does God let such things happen? I was about to say, "I don't know!" but Alison has just chirped up telling me it was my own fault because, said she, "According to one of our counselling books, if you have more than 300 points of stress in your life you will become sick within three years." I suppose that is right and that often people blame God for things that are, in the end, their own fault.

However, I recovered fully and was discharged from hospital and went home to recuperate which Alison tells me I did in the backyard, seated in a deck chair placed under a gum tree, for several weeks. During this interlude I read through Georgette Heyer's collection of some thirty Regency Romances. You might think these books a strange choice, but I had neither strength, nor zeal for serious reading, and Heyer has inspired me with her ideas of chivalry and respect for women.

Some twelve months after these events, I drove to Broken Hill for a weekend of ministry. On Monday morning I started home again but this time I foolishly decided to drive all the way without any significant stop. It took me some fifteen hours and when I awoke the next morning the cellulitis had returned. The physician ordered me to bed at once, telling me to stay there until all trace of the inflammation had vanished, otherwise, said he, "You will die." So, for being such an unmitigated ass I felt another overwhelming rebuke from the Lord, adding his own warning to that of the medico, that if I did not take better care of myself, and slow down, I would deserve to die.

Heal me, Lord, and I will be healed; save me and I will be saved, for you are the one I praise. Jeremiah 17:14:

Praise the Lord, my soul, and forget not all his benefits— who forgives all your sins and heals all your diseases. Psalm 103:2-3

1998 OPERATION

I would like to say I had learned my lesson but the desire to minister, preach God's Word, pray for the sick was a driving force in my life. Writing is a lonely business, and preaching had always been a strong influence since I was saved all the way back in 1949. So, I was scheduled to preach in the town of Orange, a country town in New South Wales, around 5 hours from where we lived in Sydney. This was a church pastored by our friend Malcolm Taylor and we were looking forward to a time of blessing. However, during the night, I woke in excruciating pain and called to Alison to get help.

She woke the owners of the house where we were staying, and our friends drove us to the nearest hospital where I was told to wait my turn. The agony was unbearable by this time and when I was finally seen they drained 2 litres from my bladder. I'm surprised it didn't burst! Apologising the doctor quickly recognised my problem. It was my prostate. Since returning from the USA, I had already had a serious bout of cellulitis and here was another hurdle of growing older and working too hard. I had to stay in hospital for a time so there was no chance to preach for Malcolm. This was the first time in my life I had not been able to fulfil a promise to preach. The doctor recommended I be transferred to a new hospital in Lithgow where I was operated on and then went through a period of rest and rehabilitation. We thanked God heartily that we had come back to Australia before these two illnesses had hit me. Had we remained in the States we would have faced bankruptcy, as so many others in that fair land with its exorbitant medical costs have been.

Since then, I have had several other life-threatening illnesses, including pericarditis which my family thought would carry me off, and so was back in hospital once again for a period of time and another time of rehabilitation. There were only five people to go down with pericarditis in Penrith that year, and I was one of them. Clearly my workload was too great, and I needed to rethink my life and ministry efforts. I suppose we all reach this stage as we grow older. God has been extraordinarily good to me over the years, healing me and prolonging my life many times.

There were more illnesses to come, for as we grow older our bodies tire and age, however, my spirit has stayed alive and enthused. But more on that later. Here I am now, nudging 91, and hopeful of a few more years as God has not finished with me yet.

Surely his salvation is near all those who fear him, that his glory may dwell in our land. Love and faithfulness meet together; righteousness and peace kiss each other. Faithfulness springs forth from the earth and righteousness looks down from heaven. The Lord will indeed give what is good, and our land will yield its harvest. Righteousness goes before him and prepares the way for his steps. Psalm 85:9-13

2000 ETHICS

Several times over the years I have been amazed at the lack of ethical, and often unscriptural behaviour, in some pastors and church leaders.

On a trip to Singapore, I met a missionary whose only ministry was working his mailing list and collecting money from people who admired what they thought was his ministry in Asia.

Then there was a pastor I met while I was in Iloilo, Philippines, who lived in a fine house on the hill above the village where the people he was trying to reach for the gospel lived. He was lamenting his lack of success as a missionary. I told him if you want to reach them you will have to give up your luxuries and go down and live amongst the people. Isn't this what Jesus did for us!

A visiting speaker in Sydney told a story of taking a large sum out of church funds and donating it to an evangelist. He was praised by a group of pastors afterwards who failed to realise that what he had done was illegal! Money given for one purpose cannot be taken for another purpose. It is against the law!

A pastor friend of mine once sat under my teaching ministry and then proceeded to teach using the same material without any acknowledgement that I was the author. Normally this would not bother me but as it happened, I used this same material to teach in the same town as my friend a few months later. When I began teaching, a local pastor took me aside and rebuked me for using the same notes already taught to them by my friend! I was indignant, as you can imagine, and asked for an apology which was given. I then had to restart using different teaching material which I had fortunately brought with me. I will refrain from naming the perpetrator involved as he has gone to his reward, and I don't doubt it was sheer ignorance on his part. Young pastors had little training in ethics in those early days.

One day I picked up a book written by a Malaysian pastor. I thought, "This fellow writes well. In fact, this fellow's words are familiar … very familiar!" This was not the only time I saw my books with someone else's name on the cover! A pastor in America tore off my cover and put a new cover with his name on it. His explanation was that his people wouldn't read a book by me, so he had to put his name on the cover to make sure they read it!! In the interests of *The whole Word to the whole World* I forgave him. I have no interest in taking a Christian brother to court.

I was flummoxed when the pastor of a large church where I was conducting a Crusade asked me what story would I tell the congregation to raise money for my ministry. I said that I didn't have a story to tell, I'm just a teacher living by faith and the Lord provides. He was horrified and began rummaging through his files to find photos of children scrounging in a rubbish heap to show the people. Of course, I refused to participate in this deception!

A thriving church, with a large congregation and attendant Christian school had a problem with parents keeping up with student fees. The elders of the church wanted to sue the members of the congregation who were behind in their school payments. I suggested that a far better proposition would be to separate the school altogether from the church, establish a separate legal identity, and appoint a governing council.

In my view, Christians should not be suing their brothers and sisters in Christ, without first exhausting all other avenues. As Paul says, "Why not rather be wronged?" (1 Corinthians 6:1-6) However, these proposals were not acceptable to the Board members who were running the school for the church, and they chose to sue. This damaged the reputation of the school and the church.

A retired pastor in San Diego came to me angry because a young man, who had been brought up in his church, had gone out from it and planted a church which had grown to 8,000 members. That was fine but he had been told that the young man relaxed every Sunday by spending the whole night watching porn. I told the old man two things:

1. God is very patient but eventually this young man would be exposed.
2. Numerical growth has little to do with divine blessing, depending rather on natural skills. (Ecclesiastes 9:1-11)
3. To bring people to true spiritual maturity is impossible for us, it requires the work of the Holy Spirit.

There are many stories of well-meaning pastors who think they are doing the right Christian thing by concealing the shady past of a man who now wants to serve God with a fresh start. Several times we were sent a young man to work in our church without being told of his past misdemeanours. Had we been informed that he had previously been in trouble we could have shown more care for him and watched over him more diligently to prevent any repetition.

On at least one occasion I was sent a young man to be my assistant pastor only to discover sometime after he arrived that he had been guilty of a serious sin, which I then had to deal with. I understand that the pastor who sent the young man to me was trying to be gracious and not to prejudice my opinion against him, but it was unethical nonetheless to send me, in a spirit of Christian love, an assistant pastor whose character was blemished. I should have been told the true situation so that I could deal with it in the grace of God.

Accountability is essential for us all if we are to walk steadfastly in the truth of God's Word!

Another young pastor was sent to us because he tried to split a church on the mainland and the senior pastor wanted to send him away to begin again, thinking he had learned his lesson. Once again, I was not told what he had tried to do so was unprepared for his methods. Because I was not forewarned, he caused much trouble for me and finally left taking some of our people to start another church. This failed and he eventually moved back to the mainland.

After these experiences, I learned not to accept anyone else's recommendation to serve in a ministerial capacity without doing my own investigation into their character and spiritual maturity.

But solid food is for the mature, for those who have their powers of discernment trained by constant practice to distinguish good from evil. Hebrews 5:14

Who is wise and understanding among you? By his good conduct let him show his works in the meekness of wisdom. James 3:13

2003 PAINT

I have kept God busy protecting me over the years, however, confining myself to sitting at my desk writing has kept me out of trouble for the most part. But not this day. This time I was flying through the air! One moment I was on a ladder and the next I was spreadeagled between twenty large tins of paint. My head between two tins, my left arm between another two, and my right arm similarly grotesquely thrown out to save myself. My legs were also intertwined between paint tins but not touching them. Astonishingly, I'm sure with the Lord's help, my falling body missed every one of the paint tins which were scattered over the floor around the ladder.

I have no idea why I fell from the step ladder. My daughter says I should not have been there in the first place! When you still feel like a young man it is sometimes hard to remember one is in their 70s, and therefore no longer young. I got up gingerly to shout for help, staggered over to the door and called out to Shane Conlon, our local pastor, to help me. We were the only two at the church working bee on that day. By the time he reached me my pelvis was hurting, and I realised I had broken or cracked something inside me. Nonetheless both Shane and I thanked God that he had seen to it that I was mostly unhurt by what could have been a fatal fall.

The doctor sent me for an Xray which showed nothing wrong, but I knew something was seriously amiss as I could not lie down without pain and had to sleep in an armchair. I went back for an MRI and this showed a crack in the hip bone which the doctor told me was serious and I had to remain seated in my easy chair, except for toilet duties, until it mended. This could take up to six weeks. The doctor also told me that had the bone broken apart, then it could have pierced my bladder with catastrophic results.

This reminded me of a chorus -

> The steps of a good man are ordered by the Lord,
> And he delighteth in his way,
> Though he fall, though he fall, he shall not be cast down,
> For the Lord upholdeth him with his hand.

With his hand, with his hand,
For the Lord upholdeth him with his hand.
Though he fall, though he fall, he shall not be cast down.
For the Lord upholdeth him with his hand.

Inspired by Psalm 37:23-26

I was indeed not cast down, as I have gone on to have many other adventures despite my declining years. Life was meant to be lived to the full. As Jesus says -

The thief comes only to steal and kill and destroy; I have come that they may have life and have it to the full. John 10:10

2007 GREECE

Travelling from our home in Sydney to the Fenix Hotel in Athens took thirty-five hours, so Alison and I arrived exhausted, but we had to prop our eyes open, for we could not possibly miss the first session of the Vision World Zone Leaders Conference. A fine message was presented by Dr Stan Dekoven, the president of Vision International University. He spoke on the future of Vision and inspired us all. The next day (Tuesday) was wholly occupied with conference meetings, reports, strategy discussions, and the like. We were informed that currently the college had around 125,000 students in 143 countries. Also, that our African graduates had planted more than 1000 churches in West Africa over the past year, with an average size of 75 people.

The actual conference ended at noon on Wednesday, whereupon all those who had chosen to remain in Greece for the missionary tour, 'In the Steps of St Paul', boarded the 50-seat bus, filling every seat, and we set off for Thessaloniki, some 600 km north. This modern city (the second largest in Greece) has the same name and spelling (in Greek) as the biblical one. Once there I gave a 30-minute talk to the group, based on a passage from Paul's letter to the Thessalonians. We visited a museum, toured the city, then travelled about 100 kms to Kavala. This town is the port of ancient Philippi, and the place where the apostle Paul first set foot on European soil. Philippi itself is some distance inland, and extensive and impressive ruins of the city can be seen, including the probable place where Paul and Silas were imprisoned after they had been illegally flogged. They were released from their chains by an earthquake, and praising God for their miraculous deliverance, left Philippi, having established the first Christian church in Europe. We found it rather awe-inspiring to look at buildings and walk on pathways that the apostle himself once saw and trod. It was near Philippi at Lydia's Well, that Bishop Randy Gurley gave us a presentation (Lydia was the first convert at Philippi - Acts 16:11-15). Others also gave teachings at various New Testament sites as we travelled.

Greece, like Australia, was suffering from a severe drought, so the mountainous countryside was dry and brown, and the rivers low, with only an occasional patch of green in an otherwise parched landscape. But the drive from Athens to Thessaloniki, then to Kavala and Philippi was nonetheless spectacular, with every corner bringing a new vista of mountains and valleys, rivers and lakes, and the beautiful coastline. The bus was rather cramped, and not overly comfortable, but the things we saw along the way and at each stopping point made it all more than worthwhile.

On Friday, we returned to Athens, arriving at about 2200 hours for a very late dinner. On that return trip we finally saw Mount Olympus, which we had missed on the way north because night had fallen. However, we had no time to stop and had to content ourselves with a view from the highway, some kilometres distant from the mountain. On the way south we also detoured to Berea (now called Verria), where Paul found a welcome after he had been obliged to flee from Thessalonica by night. Standing in front of a monument to Paul, I gave a 15-minute talk on the mystery of the 'nobility' of the Berean Jews (in contrast with the attitude of the Jews in Thessalonica).

Saturday took us to the Peloponnese, the site of so much dramatic ancient history. We crossed the impressive Corinthian Canal (which has turned the Peloponnese into an island) and drove to the site of the ruins of ancient Corinth. These too are quite extensive, and very impressive, complete with a museum containing a fine array of ancient sculptures. We also visited briefly the mountain-top site of an old and massive Crusader fortress that stands high above the ruins.

In Corinth, among the ruins, I gave another 30-minute talk, based on Paul's statement to the Corinthians –

When I came to you brothers, I did not come to you with eloquence or superior wisdom as I proclaimed to you the testimony about God. For I resolved to know nothing while I was with you, except Jesus Christ and him crucified. I came to you in weakness and fear, and with much trembling. 1 Corinthians 2:1-3

After my talk, Brian Deventer, the Director of the European and Middle Eastern Mission, who hosted our trip through Greece, pointed out a stone at our feet with the name of a New Testament character clearly gouged into the stone. We could not believe it was just lying there exposed to the elements. Erastus is mentioned by Paul in Romans 16:23. The fact that Erastus was the director of public works explained why the sign was there. We also visited the Acropolis, but heavy rain forced us to abandon our tour half-way through. I took a few photos, but the grey day washed all colour out of them.

Alison and I greatly enjoyed our time in Greece, although I had a special advantage, for I could read Greek text fluently, even if I didn't always know fully what it meant. So, when we attended church and songs in Greek appeared on the screen I could sing them easily. It was also a great joy for us to see a Vision class in action in Athens, and I was invited to teach them for an hour. We had heard of these classes happening around the world, but this was the first time we had participated, or had the privilege of teaching the students, which happily I was able to do in English, since my ability for speaking Greek would have been rather inadequate for the task.

Alison and I had many reasons to thank God for such a high adventure - for getting us there and back again safely and for allowing us to visit a small class of the worldwide expansion of Vision College.

Erastus, who is the city's director of public works and our brother Quartus send you their greetings. Romans 16:23

And he said to them, "Go into all the world and proclaim the gospel to the whole of creation." Mark 16:15

2014 OAM

So now here is a 'wart' indeed. I am about to make a shameless boast. I am proud to announce that the Governor of New South Wales bestowed on me an OAM. That is, a Medal of the Order of Australia.

For the past ten or so years, I had finally slowed down somewhat and spent most of my time writing books, answering emails, occasionally preaching at our local CRC church, and attending CRC conferences and gatherings. *Warts and All* is most likely my last book, and I shall endeavour to get it published before my final journey to glory. It has been a far quieter existence than I ever thought probable. So, when I first received the letter, I thought it was a hoax. It said that I had been approved to receive the Medal and I thought some mischievous friend was trying to stir up trouble. However, when I read the letter more carefully, I began to think it might be serious. It required me to confirm that I was willing to receive the Medal before it could actually be awarded. I showed the letter to Alison and she laughed saying, "I have known about this for twelve months but was strictly enjoined to keep it secret!" which I can attest she did most admirably. I had been nominated by Pastor Dean Eaton, who initiated the process along with at least six other pastors who had to be included in the nomination.

On the appointed day I arrived at Government House along with Alison, and two guests we were allowed to bring with us - our daughter Sharon and one of our sons, Eric, who drove up from Canberra especially for the day, and who lived the closest to us. We all donned our finest clothes (shorts, or raggedy jeans were sternly forbidden) and drove proudly into the parking lot of Government House in Sydney. We flashed our invitation card for myself, and the other invited guests, to attend the event. We walked boldly into the magnificent stone building and took our seats among the one hundred or so of the other invitees.

In the meantime, I was instructed that when my name was called, I should walk sedately toward the then New South Wales State Governor, the Honourable Dame Marie Bashir, bow with dignity, allow her to pin the medal to my jacket, then step backward a couple of steps before turning and going back to my seat. The award was uniquely given to me for - *Services to religion and to theological education.* I was the only person at that ceremony to receive an award in the religious category. All the other recipients were given their award for serving the community in other ways. After everyone had received their medal, we were invited onto the lawns of Government House to receive a glass of champagne and enjoy an afternoon tea of finger food and other items offered, after which we returned to our car and drove home.

This was a very exciting year for us, as it was also the 40th anniversary of Vision College, which began in 1974. Dr Denis Plant had taken on the responsibility of recognising this milestone by arranging for as many of our students and friends of Vision to gather together to celebrate. Some who could not be there sent video greetings, so it was a wonderful occasion. Dr Stan DeKoven, President of Vision International University USA brought with him a citation of Special Congressional Recognition -

Presented to Dr Ken Chant in recognition of your leadership at Vision International University and in appreciation of your continued dedication, commitment, and mentorship to those serving in ministry throughout San Diego County.

> Signed by
> *Duncan Hunter*
> Member of Congress.
> Dated March 26th 2014

A book, *The History of Vision*, was available for purchase. My wife Alison had interviewed many of the regents of Vision and collected their stories.

This was also a significant year as Alison and I celebrated our 60th wedding anniversary. It was celebrated on Sydney Harbour on a dinner cruise, and our daughter-in-law put together a wonderful album of pictures and memorabilia to honour our love over so many years.

We also travelled to Adelaide to attend the CRC National Conference where Pastor Bill Vasilakis honoured us for 60 years of ministry. This meant a great deal to us especially as many of our fellow workers in the faith had already departed this earth and received their reward. Our journey still had a further 10 years.

We first met Bill around 1975 when he visited us in Launceston Tasmania. Bill had been impressed by my writing and used one of my lectures for a university subject and was interested to meet the author. We did not know it then, but in later years Bill was destined to become the chairman of the CRC Churches International. Bill has been a staunch friend over the years and delighted us recently by making a special trip to visit myself and Alison for my ninetieth birthday (June 6, 2024).

These celebrations were all truly memorable. After our many years of ministry, sacrifice, great triumphs and tragedies, hundreds of hours writing books, praying and believing, it was the culmination of a lifetime of service. So please forgive my overweening pride if I finish this anecdote with these Scriptures -

Well done good and faithful servant! You have been faithful with a few things; I will put you in charge of many things. Come and share in your master's happiness. Matthew 25:23

Now there is in store for me the crown of righteousness, which the Lord, the righteous Judge, will award to me on that day – and not only to me, but also to all who have longed for his appearing. 2 Timothy 4:8

2020 GENTLEMEN

I awoke one morning to realise I did not have any friends. At least, no-one I spent time with on a semi-regular basis apart from Alison. I no longer travelled for ministry, no longer spent time with fellow colleagues far and wide but had remained at my desk completing the last few books that I was inspired to write. My day consisted of rising around 6:30am, going into my office to eat my breakfast and watch or read the latest news; respond to any emails that had arrived; write and edit until lunchtime (although I often had my second coffee at around 10am); then I made my lunch and sat with Alison for a while and viewed something amusing or interesting on the television, or a musical performance on YouTube; then it was back to writing until about 6pm (or when inspiration failed); then I practiced choruses from memory on my Hawaiian guitar; and then dinner which had been prepared, relaxing, reading, watching, or listening to Audible.

On Sundays, if I felt up to the effort I would attend church, but more often than not it was live streaming the service from our local CRC church. This was the sum of the life of a man who was nearing the end of his years!

But then I discovered, what my wife likes to refer to as - *The League of Retired Gentlemen*. This was a group of Christian laymen from our church who gathered every Friday morning for two or three hours under a grove of gumtrees in Victoria Park, St Marys. If it rained they would take themselves off to the local restaurant. I joined this group when I was able and thoroughly enjoyed discussing, disseminating, and sometimes disparaging the troubles of the world and its leaders, until we solved all these problems to our satisfaction.

It was also a time where I felt the value that comes from experience and wisdom as they tossed around puzzling theological questions, shared amazing appliances they had bought their wives, like hot air fryers which both Alison and Sharon initially disparaged when I bought them one, but now use frequently! We also shared a time of prayer and unburdened our hearts in a deeper way than church meetings could allow. Then, of course, there were sausages on the BBQ and coffee and donuts.

When I was no longer able to attend, they came several times and set up in my driveway so I could sit with them and enjoy their fellowship. But gradually, any effort on my part diminished until I could no longer participate or even write at my desk.

These were fine gentlemen who enthusiastically made me feel welcome each time I showed up. They filled some of the lonely moments that come to us all when our lives shrink to the four walls of our homes. When I came to the point where I could no longer leave the house, one of the League, John Schild, came to our home every Wednesday morning for an hour or so, sharing a coffee, church and local news, and prayed for us.

Charles Wise brought a delicious curry several times which I always enjoyed, reminding me of my travels to Asia. (It was Charles who advised us about the army medals for which I found I was eligible.) And our pastors, Enoch Nagabyrava and Shane Conlon visited regularly despite their busy schedules. I thank them one and all for taking an interest in an old man!

Greater love has no one than this, that someone lay down his life (personal agenda) for his friends. John 15:13

Gracious words are a honeycomb, sweet to the soul and healing to the bones. Proverbs 16:24

2023 ANZAC

How frustrating! Across seven decades I could have participated in the Anzac Day marches. All I needed to do was apply for and receive my Army Service medals. I knew nothing about them until a friend, who was a member of the Retired Serviceman's League (RSL), suggested I should explore if I was eligible, especially as I still had my honourable discharge card from 1953. I was sceptical about whether the medals would still be available, Nonetheless Sharon wrote on my behalf to the relevant government authorities and enquired about the matter.

A couple of weeks later I was astonished to receive two finely crafted black boxes containing several medals, along with a letter from the Department of Defence which said -

> Dear Mr Chant,
>
> It is with pleasure I enclose the following awards which recognises your service in the Australian Defence Force -
> - Australian Defence Medal
> - Anniversary of National Service 1951-1972 Medal
>
> Please accept my congratulations on receiving these awards.
>
> Yours sincerely
>
> *Ian Heldon*
> Director of Honours and Awards

In one box was a large silver medal with a lapel bar from which it could be hung - *The Australian Defence Medal*. In the other box was a large bronze medal of the same size which could also be attached to a lapel bar - *The Anniversary of National Service Medal*. Both boxes contained two smaller medals, one to use as a tie clip, and the other as a lapel pin.

Both medals would have allowed me to march in any, and every, Anzac Day Parade across the more than sixty years since I became eligible for them. I doubt that I would have marched in all of them, but now I can't march in any! I suppose technically I could hire a wheelchair taxi to get me down to Sydney and be pushed in my wheelchair by an energetic person to be part of the parade. The Anzac Parade has always been a part of our lives as observers, and we have always honoured the greatest sacrifice of these noble men and women. But I will never do it now. Just the thought of so much effort is tiring! I will have to endure the loss for the rest of my life. However, any frustration that I feel is ameliorated by remembering that I loathed the regimented structure of army life!

There is a lesson to be learned here. I am not sure what it is, except that it certainly includes the aphorism, "Do it now!" and "Don't put off until tomorrow what you should do today!" Procrastination has been the bane of many an existence. At any rate Scripture says,

Look carefully then how you walk, not as unwise but as wise, making the best use of the time. Ephesians 5:15-16a

2024 TODAY

For the past couple of years, I have been confined to an electric armchair. It lies flat as a bed and stands me up so that I can reach for my walker. Its name is the Michelangelo and it is indeed a wonderfully comfortable and prestigious chair that God led my daughter to find second hand, but as good as new. Here I sit, praying daily for my family, friends in ministry, and the College programme worldwide.

My heart is full of gratitude to God for his blessing and guidance over the years of our retirement. I have been able to write the remainder of the books in the series of *Treasures from Paul. Thessalonians* was the last one completed, and I thought this was my last book. However, at the urging of my daughter, I have spent the last year dictating my anecdotes to Sharon, and with Alison, where we have had fun trying to remember all the memorable moments of our last seven decades of ministry together. If only we had kept a diary, or better yet a journal! But life felt too busy and exciting to engage in that discipline, but we do have some letters that were kept, and we have gained stories we had forgotten from our children.

My eyes have now deteriorated to a point that I can no longer read anything, not even large print, and can watch only TV programmes that are brightly lit. I am more than half deaf. My heart beats at only 40% and I cannot travel anywhere except in a wheelchair taxi, which I only employ if absolutely necessary. Getting old is the pits! And at 91, I cannot have much longer to live. But to quote my wife's description of me, "I am all packed up and ready to go when the Lord calls me."

Let me conclude with these Scriptures:

Remember your Creator in the days of your youth, before the days of trouble come and the years approach, when you will say, "I find no pleasure in them" – before the sun and the light and the moon and the stars grow dark, and the clouds return after the rain; when the keepers of the house tremble, and the strong men stoop, when the grinders cease because they are few, and those looking through the windows grow dim; when the doors to the street are closed and the sound of grinding fades; when people rise up at the sound of birds, but all their songs grow faint; when people are afraid of heights and of dangers in the streets; when the almond tree blossoms and the grasshopper drags himself along and desire is no longer stirred. Then people go to their eternal home and mourners go about the streets. Remember him - before the silver cord is severed, and the golden bowl is broken; before the pitcher is shattered at the spring, and the wheel broken at the well, and the dust returns to the ground it came from, and the spirit returns to God who gave it. Ecclesiastes 12:1-7

2024 FINALE

So, there it is! Warts and all! My final collection of anecdotes spanning my entire life including more than seventy years of ministry, which began when I was sixteen preaching in Finsbury Park Baptist Church on Simon of Cyrene carrying the cross for Jesus.

Unfortunately, that sermon was a fizzer!

I was so nervous and spoke so softly that I doubt anyone heard a word. Yet for all that, it was a miracle because it was the first time I had ever spoken in public without a trace of my usual speech impediment (my stammer). So, instead of resolving never to preach again, I girded up my loins and along with the Holy Spirit, I gained great confidence to continue preaching in scores of churches all around the world.

Over the years the speech impediment lessened until for many years now it has all but vanished. I still sense it hovering around somewhere in the back of my mind, but I can easily suppress it and today am untroubled.

It is very unlikely that I will ever preach again. The armchair in which I am sitting is a kind of prison in which I am both relaxing and dictating these memoirs to Alison. It is a remarkable chair with ten buttons that enable an almost infinite number of positions, but I do look upon it with mixed feelings of love and loathing. Love, because the number of variables allows me to stay comfortable day and night. Loathing, because it remains a pitiless prison holding me fast in its grip. However, there are far worse ways to spend the last season of one's life.

I hope you have been amused and amazed by these anecdotes. They represent a fairly comprehensive pastoral theology. I trust they will be appreciated by both pastors and a host of general readers. If nothing else they show that life is a mixed bag of both joy and sorrow, and that we are all fallible, making mistakes, heading in the wrong direction, and failing ourselves, our loved ones, and our Lord and Saviour. But it is those that refuse to be 'cast down' and lifting their faces rise up and continue the race that makes the difference on this earth. All of us will be held accountable and see him face to face one day. But as Scripture says, if I fear God and keep his commandments then I am satisfied.

Of making many books there is no end, and much study wearies the body. Now all has been heard; here is the conclusion of the matter: Fear God and keep his commandments, for this is the duty of all mankind. Ecclesiastes 12b-13

In the love, joy, grace, and peace of Christ,

K. D. Chant

Dr Ken Chant OAM, BMin, MRE, DMin, ThD, PhD

And yet my story is not entirely ended. My next adventure will be a step into eternity ...

2024 GOD

I called the preceding chapter *2024 Finale,* but there is always something even beyond the final ending and that is, **Eternity!**

I am going to bring this book to a conclusion with a presentation of why Christian faith is superior to atheism.

Over the years, my faith has not been as steadfast as some might imagine. I have had periods when I was under attack from the enemy and seriously doubted God's existence and wondered if there was any truth in the biblical promises. Each time one of these bouts of doubt has hit me, I have put myself through the exercise of asking what the consequences would be if there were no God. I did not want to be deluded! My arguments to myself would mostly follow the process suggested just below. Each time, of course I came to the triumphant conclusion that God was very real, and I would remember the countless times the Lord has intervened to save me from harm, to heal me and my family of a number of major illnesses and perform wonderful exploits throughout my life. As David remarked in the Psalms,

I remember the days of long ago. I meditate on all your works and consider what your hands have done. Psalm 143:5

Nonetheless, those periods of doubt and depression were very real and very painful. I would reason the matter out in the following manner - either God exists; or he does not exist.

At once we face a dilemma. The Christian cannot prove beyond all doubt that God does exist; but neither can the atheist prove beyond all doubt that God does not exist. So, both parties must rest upon the probability for which they can advance equal proofs. In other words, Christians can find plenty of evidence for their belief in God; yet atheists can also find many reasons for their claim that there is no God. In fact, both Christians and atheists must depend upon a faith affirmation for their respective viewpoints. That is, in the end, neither party can do more than say, "I *believe/don't believe* that God exists."

So then which affirmation makes the better sense? Consider the following arguments -

At death, if there is no God, then neither party will ever know if their choices were right or wrong for without God, death means total obliteration of every part of human existence. In the grave, all self-awareness, or indeed any awareness of anything at all, comes to an end. There is no thought, there is no perception, there is no knowledge. The person lying in the grave is as much annihilated as a crushed cockroach.

How dramatically things change if God does exist! At once, the Christian is aware of entering paradise to be with Christ in eternal joy, but the ungodly face the prospect of severe judgment (Hebrews 10:31). Why such harshness? Simply because, as Paul says, God's eternal glory and power are clearly visible to every intelligent observer in his lifetime; so, the unbeliever is left without excuse. (Romans 1:19-20) It is, as Scripture says, a fearful thing to fall into the hands of the living God!

Those who deny God must live without hope and be alone in the universe. Whereas the Christian, who is brimming with hope and more truly alive than any atheist can expect to be, faces a radiant future filled with abounding promise and endless delight. Once again, if in fact there is no God, the atheist will never know he was right whereas the Christian will die and never know he was wrong. But the Christian will have enjoyed a wonderful life, and the more truly God-saturated that life was, the more deeply satisfying and thrilling that life will have been.

I do not mean that Christian life is free from hurt or pain but that no tribulation or suffering can truly destroy the deep consolations and joys that Christ can give!

Many atheists base their arguments against the existence of God on the seeming silence of heaven and the apparent lack of divine intervention in the multitude of wars, famines, earthquakes and pestilence, floods and other catastrophes, that continually engulf nations, families, and individuals. Christians also face these disasters, but they face them holding the hand of Christ whom they know will never under any circumstance abandon them. And again, if that should prove to be a delusion, they will die never knowing this was not so.

In the meantime, they have found in their Christian life deep satisfaction, rich fulfillment, and a special kind of abounding happiness which no atheist can ever enjoy. I do not mean that atheists cannot be happy, but rather that there is a quality of life that every true Christian enjoys that no atheist can either comprehend or experience unless he comes into a knowledge of Christ.

Another issue is in the debate between theism (that is the belief in a divine being) and Christian belief. It is possible to be deeply theistic without being Christian. Or more explicitly to believe in a divine being but not the gospel message that Christ came as an act of divine intervention to live without sin and in the end to die for our sin, and to offer us salvation and an everlasting place in heaven with God. Why should anyone believe this? Because, as Paul says again, Christ was shown to be the Son of God with power by his resurrection from the dead. (Romans 1:4) Why should I believe that Jesus rose from the dead and not just a story made up by the disciples? Because Luke tells us that he was publicly shown to have risen from the dead by many infallible proofs. (Acts 1:3) Also, Paul asserts that five-hundred people saw Jesus alive again following his burial in the tomb. (1 Corinthians 15:6)

Since both atheism and theism ultimately depend on a declaration of faith rather than undeniable fact, or absolute proof, one has to then make a choice on the grounds of probability and desirability. The theistic view, especially when it leads on to the gospel with its rich hope and glorious promises, certainly seems more desirable than the bleak atheistic profession. It also seems to be more probable. Christians draw attention to the countless instances of deliberate design in the universe. In his book, *Is Atheism Dead?* published in 2021, Eric Metaxas describes the Grand Counter Narrative -

- Many things in our universe are calibrated so perfectly that they cannot have just happened but rather overwhelmingly point to some Designer.
- As well, scores of recent discoveries in physics, biology, and similar sciences, highlight the ever-increasing impossibility that these things all occur without design or intention. In other words, they point to some great all-powerful Designer, that is, God. Or, as one witty philosopher put it, "Something is, therefore, God is."

I prefer however, the words of the lovely song, *I Believe* -

> Every time I hear a new-born baby cry,
> or touch a leaf, or see the sky,
> then I know why, I believe.
> *Written by Drake, Abraham, Mendelsohn, and Stillman, 1953*

The above ideas were first expressed in a philosophical argument known as *Pascal's Wager*. Blaise Pascal was a 17th century French mathematician, philosopher and theologian. A description of the *Wager* is found in Pascal's book, *Pensées*.

The heavens declare the glory of God; the skies proclaim the work of his hands. Day after day they pour forth speech; night after night they reveal knowledge. Psalm 19:1-2.

*Ken passed away on September 25th 2024 in the early morning hours. He had returned to our local hospital as he was experiencing another bout of streptococcal mitis but this time, he was too frail to overcome, or you could say it was his time to travel heavenward having completed his last book - his Memoir. He is dearly missed!

ADDENDUM

BROTHERS – Barry Chant

In late 2024, I suffered a bout of serious ill-health. It was close to the time my brother Ken died. During those weeks, I lost ten kilograms in weight and found myself prone to unexpected tears. Sitting at lunch with friends one day I found myself choking up again. I apologised to my companions when one of them reached out his hand, laid it on mine, and said, "Barry, you have no need to apologise for anything. You've just lost your brother." It was only then that I realised it was not my ill-health that was to blame for my tears. It was my grief over Ken's dying. I had not realised how much it had affected me. Neither Ken nor I were wont to lay bare our feelings about anything much, but when I think about it, I realise how deeply we did love each other, even though we rarely expressed it.

My earliest memories of Ken are of our home in Woodville, South Australia in the 1930s. It was a modest weatherboard house but had some innovative features such as a walk-in pantry and an ironing board that folded down from the kitchen wall. Ken and I shared a small sleep-out at the back of the house. Woodville was a pretty good place to live. Ours was a quiet street with little traffic — neither we, nor any of our neighbours, had cars in those days. There was a large high school oval opposite, two sizeable paddocks just down the street and another abutting our back fence; they were all ideal as play areas. There were trees to climb, tunnels to dig, and games to play.

Ken and Coralie were several years older than I and sometimes conspired to get rid of me lest I spoil their fun. At least once, when I was about four years old, and we were tree-climbing in a nearby paddock, they told me that Mum had some sweets for me. I ran home to claim them, only to be disillusioned and disappointed!

During the War years, our father dug a deep air raid shelter in our backyard. We never needed it, but it later provided a wonderful place for us to play. This was also a time when we all learned a great deal about coping with difficulty. Food was rationed and items like butter had to be used sparingly. In our home, the problem was solved by each of us three children being given a small glass dish containing a week's supply of butter. I took the responsibility carefully and made sure I always had a little bit left for the last day. I don't remember what my sister Coralie did, but it was probably something similar. Ken? He said, "If I'm going to eat butter, I am going to enjoy eating it." And he would scoff the lot on the first two days. Interestingly, these practices were early indicators of our later lives. To his dying day, Ken treated life with relish and cheerfully embraced it with all his might.

Ken loved tinkering and building things. He was always busy, there were so many things he wanted to do and so much to explore. I remember sitting under a blanket with him in the 1940s, during the War years, as we beeped dots and dashes on a flashing Bakelite imitation Morse code set. Another of his hobbies was building a crystal set and then later a radio, listening with straining ears for the scratchy sound of voices or music as he twiddled the filament. He also enjoyed being sprawled out on the floor as we constructed Meccano models, joining the green and red steel strips and plates with child-finger-size nuts and bolts. Close friends of Ken will not be surprised at this. He was still building Meccano models in his eighties.

In his teenage years when Ken built his own radio and record player, he compiled a masterly set of vinyl LP boogie-woogie records. He and I used to lie in our beds at night listening to that mesmerising piano music as the pianist's fingers appeared to move faster than the mind could imagine. One album was entitled, *A Handful of Keys,* the name said it all. By that stage Ken was playing his own music and used to spend hours at night in the front room pounding out primal piano rhythms himself. He also took art classes, learned lettering, dabbled in weaving, and other crafts, and learned to play the banjo mandolin. He loved boogie-woogie music and taught himself to play it on the piano. He used to shut the dining room door and play for hours at night.

In the late 1940s, Ken had appendicitis surgery. Some days later he was writhing in agony. Doctors thought the pain would pass, but Dad insisted on them investigating further. There were, in fact, serious complications. Dad's insistence saved Ken's life. It was a sign of God's purpose for him.

One night Ken came home and sat on the side of my bed. I knew something significant had happened. The air was electric. I was sleepy and confused, but this made me sit up. Ken went on to tell me he had received the baptism in the Holy Spirit, he was so fired up by this experience he was like an Old Testament prophet! Sadly, the Baptist Union of the 1950s was not partial to such encounters. Ken was due to give his testimony at an open-air Baptist Youth Rally, I think at Waterfall Gully, in November 1952, and he did – all about his experience in the Spirit. It caused a reaction. His friend David White, who became a Baptist minister and was years later himself baptized in the Spirit, protested that it was 'not doctrinal'. Ken snorted with disgust – for him the Bible came before any doctrine.

At that time, Ken was planning to go into the Baptist College for training for ministry. He was preaching monthly at both Prospect and Seaton Baptist churches in South Australia. He preached one night at Prospect on being baptized in the Spirit. I understand that a day or so later, he received a phone call telling him his speaking services were no longer required. He was appalled that the Baptist authorities did not even call him in to speak with him. But rather than being discouraged, Ken began to contemplate hiring the Adelaide Town Hall and to preach there. Wiser heads told him it might be prudent to wait until he was more experienced before tackling such an enterprise. But that was Ken. Bold as a bullock.

It was Ken who encouraged me to be baptised in the Holy Spirit. In that same small sleep-out, on the eve of All Saints Day in 1952, we knelt at the foot of his bed, and I spoke in tongues for forty minutes as the Spirit flooded my being. It really was a hallowed night (it was Halloween). I've never recovered from it. Being empowered by the Spirit was one of many experiences in which Ken led the way for me. God had demonstrated his grace in such a marvellous way. To think that human beings could be temples for His Holy Spirit! We drank deeply of the living waters and our thirst was quenched. How could we ever go back? How could we ever be the same again?

Ironically, a handful of years later, I, too, was asked to leave the local congregation because of my experience in the Spirit. But fifteen years later again, the principal of the Baptist Theological College graciously and freely assisted me in my ministry studies and in 1980, Tabor College, of which I was Founding President, actually purchased the Baptist College property for our Bible school.

Ken was relatively disinterested in sport, although he enjoyed watching the international cricket matches and if he did go to a football match he would cheer and shout passionately with the best of them. This was illustrated in his preaching. Preaching with passion was the only way he knew. When I am speaking in public, I often just stand and chat with the people, especially in a home group or a classroom. Not Ken. Whether in a cottage or a cathedral, his style was the same. He would not waste time on pleasantries. Nor would he make any serious attempt to learn people's names. If he was going to preach God's Word, he would preach it as God's Word, with all his might. When I once suggested that in the classroom a more interactive style might be suitable, he looked at me with astonishment. "I am there," he said, "to tell them what I have to say, not to hear what they want to say."

Once as guest speaker at a church where Ken was pastoring, I was to preach straight after he gave the announcements. When he handed me the microphone, I remarked, "Thank you, Ken. That is the first time I have ever heard anyone preach the announcements." Even the notices had to be delivered with authority! On the other hand, I recall a pastors' gathering where Ken was called upon without notice to speak. He delivered an excellent presentation, complete with Scripture references, anecdotes and literary allusions as if he had been pondering it for weeks!

To some extent, Ken was a loner. Perhaps this was partly the result of a serious speech impediment that made it impossible for him to converse fluently. On the other hand, he did enjoy his own company. On one occasion, when he was in his early teens, we all went by train on a Sunday School picnic. Everyone was supposed to be in one allocated carriage, but Ken chose to sit by himself in another part of the train where he could read undisturbed. This was a pattern that he would often observe in his later life. When meals were served, a book was normally part of the menu. He would not have got away with this with a wife less patient than Alison. I suspect that her response sometimes was to join him with a book of her own. The only ones who could always safely interrupt him were his little granddaughters whom he loved even more than he loved his wartime butter. Even so, as much as Ken was relaxed and comfortable with his own company, he was a lively conversationalist and a genial host.

A pastor friend of mine who had worked with Ken for several years told me once how someone had accused Ken of not showing enough love to the people in his own congregation. My friend almost snorted with disgust as he related this to me. "That fellow had no idea of what love is," he said. "If anyone knew the true nature of love, and practised it, it was Ken!"

Ken's love was neither fickle nor sentimental. It was demonstrated in action and commitment. This was illustrated no better than by the way that he and Alison took our father into their home and cared for him faithfully for the last decade of his life.

Ken was a big help to me. It was through him praying for me that I was filled with the Holy Spirit, a story that is told in a couple of my books. Then he would advise me on the best books to read. I remember one night shortly after being baptized in the Holy Spirit I was going to the pictures with some young people from church. He just said that since being filled with the Holy Spirit, he couldn't do that anymore. So, I didn't go. (He developed a more balanced view as he matured).

At times when I was struggling with personal issues, I sought his wisdom. When he lived in Woomera for a time, I used to write to him. After he was married, and living in Ballarat, this continued from time to time. Later, in 1963, it was Ken who persuaded me to leave Murray Bridge and join the staff at Sturt Street Christian Revival Crusade. "What if I take your advice and it proves to be wrong?" I asked. "That's your stupid fault for taking my advice," he answered, with his usual care and compassion! As it happens, I did act on it, and he was right. Since then, to our mutual benefit, we have sparked each other more than once in discussion and debate.

Back to the days of youth. Ken, Coralie and I were all active in our local church. Ken's zeal prompted him to be an activist for growth but generally his proposals were, to use a biblical phrase, 'of the flesh'. Why not organise dances in the church hall to attract young people? Then through the friendship of a couple of Methodist friends, he was baptised in the Holy Spirit. He now became an advocate for more prayer meetings! When the Spirit came, Ken found a new passion—an empowered zeal for the kingdom, for the church, for Jesus. It never left him. Interestingly, he also found a new voice — he could now speak confidently and ironically was to become known for his eloquence and fluency of expression.

When Ken and Alison married, I was around 16 years old. I had seen Ally in a prayer meeting, pouring out her heart to God and I remember thinking to myself, "I want to marry a girl like that." And I did. Well, actually not exactly alike, but my choice was someone equally spiritual and absolutely right for me.

Three or four years later, I chatted with Ken and Alison about a young man who seemed to be destined for a remarkable ministry. Ken said simply: "Not enough tears yet." I said something foolish like, "What do you know about tears?" I had never seen him cry. Alison told me later of a heart-breaking experience of betrayal and disappointment Ken had previously endured in his first pastorate. And I was to learn at a later date that their second baby son had died a few days after birth. They both knew what it was to suffer hardship for Christ. Sadly, it was not the only time. In years to come they were to experience even more trials and weep more tears. But tears are often what is needed to water the seed of the Word. Ken knew experientially the truth of 1 Peter 2:21: that Christ called us to follow him through the footsteps of suffering.

When he was around 27 years old, Ken was invited to take over the leadership of the Adelaide Crusade Centre while the senior pastor was overseas. Before he undertook this prodigious responsibility, he spent a few days in the country seeking the Lord. He visited Vanessa and me on his return. I still have a vivid recollection of him entering our home like a prophet from the wilderness, his clothing unkempt and fire in his eyes. A Bible college student later wrote:

> *Pastor Ken with eyes like coals*
> *Burns the Word into our souls!*

Typically, Ken followed his own distinctive path whereas I pursued more traditional avenues. Ken left school because he simply couldn't see any relevance for him in the subjects he was required to study, whereas I never asked whether the subjects were relevant or not. If that was the curriculum, I would follow it. I just enjoyed the study. Then when I graduated with a degree in theology, Ken wrote and congratulated me on my 'erudition'. This was, I assumed, a compliment, but I didn't know what the word 'erudition' meant — which basically negated the very thing he was saying!

Ken was involved in many other ministries as well. He planted churches in Tasmania, pastored churches in New South Wales, South Australia, Victoria and the United States, wrote numerous books and hundreds of articles, participated in a number of boards and councils, and spoke at conferences and seminars. And he was an avid reader. He loved words and embraced them with joy; no philatelist could have collected his stamps more zealously. And he did eventually undertake formal studies ultimately to doctoral level.

Even so, through it all he remained an individual thinker. While his writings are peppered with quotations from the classics there are relatively few quotations from theologians. He liked to read and reflect and form his own conclusions. His works offer stimulating and challenging insights. The fact that students from many countries in the world have undertaken Vision College courses is a testimony to the power of his writing.

Ken's views represented his deep convictions and his absolute confidence in God's Word. Sometimes, however, he just enjoyed arguing for the sake of it. I recall once debating with him something to do with Shakespeare. I had completed an honours degree in English literature but that did not deter him. Eventually, although I knew I was right and he knew I was right, he won the argument. He wore me down and I just couldn't be bothered prolonging the debate any further!

Ken was always frustrated by the fact that there seemed to be no reason why some churches grew, and others did not. He used to denounce those preachers who gave lectures or sermons on topics like, *Seven Ways to Build a Growing Church* or *Five Secrets of Successful Ministry,* as being misleading. There was more to it than that. He usually preached like an Arminian, but I think at heart he was a Calvinist — God was Sovereign and that was that. Ken had little tolerance for folly or sham. He believed fervently that love for God was a matter of heart, strength, soul and mind.

It was in Tasmania, in 1974, that the Launceston College of Theology was born. It was small —just a handful of students studying by correspondence. But its mission statement was, *The whole Word to the whole World.* I remember reading that for the first time and thinking, "Come on, Ken. You are in Launceston, Tasmania. What are you talking about?" Well, today I have to eat my words. Fifty years later, Vision College is continuing to function in many nations of the world. And Ken is rightly honoured for his pioneering faith, vision and endurance.

It has been fascinating to look back and observe how God led us both through similar but not identical paths. We both love teaching; we are both authors; we both have moderate musical skills; we both lament the shallowness of some contemporary Christian music. Ken's founding and developing of Vision College was his best-known achievement; the establishment of Tabor College was probably mine. But there were also differences. For example, I love playing sport, but Ken was not an enthusiast, although he did try his hand at archery for a time and if he did find himself at a sporting event he would cheer and shout with the best of them. I enjoy camping, bushwalking and rock-climbing; Ken preferred dinner at a five-star hotel!

Of all his accomplishments, the one for which he may be most widely known is one that may also be thought to be of small importance. I speak of the composition of his song, *Fill my Eyes*. It is a prayer in which, surprisingly, he expressed his love for Christ in a more personal manner than he usually did when he preached. Poetry and music seemed to liberate the deep and meaningful passion that he too often kept close-hidden in his heart.

Over the decades, Vanessa and I came to love and esteem Ken and Alison very much. We were often separated by huge distances for long periods, but our mutual love has continued unabated. And Ken has countless admirers and supporters around the world. He is honoured far and wide. All his fans are to be commended for their acclaim.

However, I have unique insights into his life and ministry. For I have one blessing that not one of them has ever had or will ever have. He was my brother. And for that, with all my heart, I never cease to thank God.

A friend loves at all times, and a brother is born for a time of adversity.
Proverbs 17:17

BILL VASILAKIS

On behalf of CRC Churches International, I honour Pastor Ken Chant as one of our spiritual Fathers and a genuine hero of the CRC. Ken was deeply loved and highly respected by all of his CRC family. He was a living legend amongst us.

What an extraordinary journey Ken embarked on when he was ordained as a CRC Pastor in 1954, the year I was born. Ken was Leo Harris's key associate pastor for several years in the 1950's. In 1959 he led the Adelaide Assembly (our first CRC Church) while Pastor Harris was away overseas for nearly 12 months and Ken was only 25 years old. He was totally loyal to Leo as he was a man of great integrity. Leo's own family were not loyal to him and tried to usurp his leadership of our Adelaide founding church.

Along with his brother Barry, Ken influenced generations of pastors and leaders not just in the CRC, but across the entire body of Christ.

Ken's life and incisive teaching ministry through his prophetic preaching and 50 plus books touched the lives of hundreds of thousands of people across the globe. What an audacious vision he had when he commenced his Bible correspondence course with a handful of students in the early 1970's from Launceston Tasmania.

What a vision! To take *the whole Word to the whole World.*

My first meeting with Ken was as a 19 year old student at Crusade Bible College. I was awed by him then and I still am. I remember vividly his lectures as they were deeply impacting and greatly helped form me as a new follower of Jesus. I devoured every new book Ken produced, and they helped me during my university years. His writings about Science and Faith being complementary and not contradictory enabled me to get a high distinction in a paper I wrote.

Though Ken was so intelligent and widely read in so many disciplines, he remained humble and had no pretences about him. I had many discussions with Ken over the decades, and though I felt I was a dumb-cluck in his presence, he never made me feel this way but was genuinely interested in my opinions on a host of spiritual matters.

I especially remember the nights in Bible College when Ken was discussing a deep concept and provoking us to think critically and question everything. He would throw in red herrings left and right. Some students were snowflakes and got up and walked out, unable to grasp the intellectual concepts he was imparting, enraged by his audacity to make us question everything we knew. Then he would turn the discussion on its head, and we would leave challenged and imprinted with another gem of truth or revelation like a sharp arrow into our hearts. Life changing concepts that are with me to this day.

Ken loved Jesus till the end, adored his wife Alison and was so proud of his children and grandchildren. He is in heaven now with Jesus, but he will continue to live and minister here on earth through his prolific writings. I am zealous to ensure his key books are read by generations of future CRC Pastors and Leaders. I have no doubts that Pastor Ken Chant will continue to be one of our most influential CRC Ministers.

My condolences to dear Alison, his helpmate of over 70 years who strongly supported her man in all his ministry endeavours. Ken mentioned to me he could not have achieved what Jesus called him to do without Alison being by his side. Thank you, Alison, for allowing me to visit Ken a couple of times in his final months. It was a privilege to share with both of you and to pray together.

Ken is having a wow of a time in heaven, and no doubt was thrilled to receive Jesus's welcome and embrace; and to hear the words 'Well done my good and faithful servant, enter into the joyous realm of your Lord and Master.'

CHORUSES – Alison Chant

Since Barry, Ken's brother, told me that Ken's chorus was being sung without any acknowledgement, I thought I would set the record straight by including it in the Addendum. My husband loved music! I used to tease him by saying music was the only thing that brought tears to his eyes. But over the years this changed as his capacity for expressing emotion changed and grew.

During our years before the establishment of Vision Colleges, Ken had time to sit at the piano and create tunes and worship the Lord in song. He wrote many choruses which were sung by our congregation with enthusiasm but only two of them made their way into the *Resource* chorus books begun by Denis and Nolene Prince. The first was a worship chorus -

> Fill my eyes Oh my God with a vision of the cross
> Fill my heart with love for Jesus the Nazarene
> Fill my mouth with thy praise,
> Let me sing through endless days
> Take my will let my life be wholly thine.

There is a story attached to this chorus. Ken had been teaching on the Doctrine of God in the Adelaide CRC Bible College (circa 1960) and he was driving home still feeling the anointing from giving the lectures. This song came into his mind, and he sang it all the way home. As soon as he arrived, he rushed inside and wrote it down - words and music, so he wouldn't forget it. Later Nolene Prince took Ken's music outline and expanded the tune into a music score from which she could lead a choir of Bible students to sing it with beautiful harmonies.

The other chorus was more of a praise chorus, very lively, with a catchy tune –

> Be glad O sons of Zion
> All ye sons of Zion
> And rejoice in the Lord your God
> All ye daughters
> Daughters of the Lord
> Ever be glad and rejoice
> For the Lord hath done great things
> Ha ha! (with emphasis)
> Lai lai lai, lai lai lai
> For He hath done great things
> Ha ha! (with emphasis)

In our Launceston church we had quite an orchestra from an organ to a trombone and half a dozen other instruments in between. We reached heights of worship we have seldom been able to achieve since then. Probably in hindsight because we were seeking God so earnestly at that time to see what the future held for us. God did give us direction and the Launceston College of Theology was born and in time became Vision Colleges.

Now my beloved husband has gone to be with the Lord in the early hours of September 25th, 2024, but even though I feel half of me is missing I cannot wish him back to go on suffering the indignities of old age and the frustrations of his failing sight and hearing. I praise God that on the last day his mind was still clear, and his voice was still strong, he was joking with the doctor, now a familiar figure, who expected him to recover from this recent illness and return home in a few days. Ken's only thought, from his hospital bed, was for me to go home and rest as I was very tired. During that night he went to sleep and woke up in heaven!

He was a wonderful husband and helped me to grow and develop and learn and he never held me back. I had the wonderful privilege of being his wife for 70+ years. I was amazed at the patience and sweetness he showed me in the last few months of his life despite his circumstances. He was a gentleman to the end, and I rejoice he is now with Jesus, no doubt having some theological questions answered!

After streptococcal mitis attacked his back in October 2023, and he came close to death in the hospital at Box Hill, Melbourne, God gave Ken enough time to dictate this story, *Warts and All*. God's timing is perfect! I recall the prophetic words of Dick Mills back in the 80s when he told Ken that he would not die until he had written his last book. And this is it! (Although Ken would joke that he had to keep writing to keep living, which is why he wrote so many books! But really it was the inspiration from heaven and Ken's deep desire to educate believers that he dedicated his time and effort into unpacking God's Word for them.)

I would like to end with the last words he wrote in his last theological book, *Thessalonians* (pages 376-377). This was so apropos it reminded me that Pastor Leo Harris preached some little time before he died a sermon with this theme, "What would I preach today if this was my last sermon?" Perhaps he too was getting a nudge from the Holy Spirit.

Here then are Ken's last words in his last textbook for his students, *Thessalonians*. Ken did not know how soon after writing these words he would be called home, but God knew, and his timing is always perfect -

> Seize the day! Put no trust in tomorrow. That is, make the most of this day because who knows what tomorrow will bring? For us, that idea requires us to stir up our faith, because no promise of God can be fulfilled until we make it happen. That is, we have to take hold of the promise and
>
> - Affirm it, and
> - Expect it to be fulfilled, and
> - Look for its fulfillment.

Thus, Paul goes on to say that the promise about all things turning to our good belong only to those who love God. One cannot truly love without wholly trusting.

And to those who serve God. But serving God, too, is an act of faith, which alone can link us to the will of God. And we serve the Lord, because we believe that only in his service can we find perfect happiness and prosperity. So, away with laziness, away with timidity, away with unbelief, away with excuses! We are Christians, God is on our side. How can we lose?

Let us rather believe boldly, serve bravely, expect greatly, and see God do wonderful things!

WRITING – Alison Chant

Ken's experience with the Word of God was profound. He had such a hunger for the Word that he read through the whole Bible each year, trying out different translations each time. Some he liked and used again and again, others he only read once and that was enough. He searched for the face of God and was not disappointed. The Almighty was continually giving him ideas for sermons and when his eyes gave way at the age of eighty-nine he had at least two hundred ideas he had not used.

When Ken was writing his books, he would feel the anointing of God come upon him as it did when he was preaching. He would begin to write and then the anointing would come, and the writing flowed easily. I have quotes from one of his first books, *Faith Dynamics,* and they are quite lyrical!

> God is able, he is concerned about you! He is interested in your welfare! He is merciful and kind! He is Saviour and Healer. He is not tomorrow but today! He is the same yesterday, today, and forever! He is willing to answer your prayer and bring you your heart's desires.
>
> Above all faith encounters the Holy Spirit. Faith perceives his presence in the world, recognises his activity, unites itself to him,

draws on his resources, is nourished by his influence, enriched by his wisdom, invigorated by his touch, directed by his will, emboldened by his example and inspired by his love.

One thing about his writing annoyed me and this was his use of obscure words that were hardly ever used by others. I would say, "Why don't you use five or six smaller words to describe what you want to express?" His rebuttal was always based on the premise of why he should use words that did not convey his meaning when he could use just one word that described exactly what he meant! Evidently theology needs certain words which are not normally used by the average person to explain the deep truths of God.

Ken's instructions to his students would include having both an English dictionary AND a Bible dictionary at hand when they were trying to read, understand, and answer the questions for each lesson. Australian students would often groan over his use of sophisticated language (including his daughter) and because of this we did not think his books would be accepted in third world countries. Unaccountably this was not the case, the books were accepted, and with great joy. Perhaps a contributing factor was the difficulties these students had to overcome in learning to read and speak English as a second language, it is a rigorous and challenging activity. Whatever the reason, the fact that his books were well received in other countries gave Ken much satisfaction as he felt vindicated on his precise choice of words.

For truly I tell you, until heaven and earth disappear, not the smallest letter, not the least stroke of a pen, will by any means disappear from the Law until everything shall be accomplished. Matthew 5:18 NIV

STUDENT – Sidney Martin

My name is Sidney Martin, and I have been a student at Vision Bible College for a couple of years. I have had the privilege of studying many of the courses written by Ken Chant, covering a wide range of topics - from the letters by Paul, to the work of the Holy Spirit in the lives of believers. But my connection to Dr Ken Chant's writings goes back a bit further. I came across his books for the first time as a teenager, since my

Dad, now with the Lord, had been a student at Vision College back in the 1980s. So much have I learned from his books.

I am sure that many of you would agree that he had a remarkable ability to unpack many difficult theological concepts in a way that they were easy to grasp. He didn't just explain doctrine; he showed us how to live it out in our daily lives, drawing from his own experiences. A great teacher. Always biblically grounded. No 'tickling the ear' in his writings. I can assure you of that.

One of the things I would appreciate most about his writings, as a philologist, was his seamless blending of theology and literature. He would weave literary quotes into the text to introduce or further explain an idea, reflecting his love for theology and his deep appreciation for the arts. He was what we Aussies would call an 'all-rounder' - like a cricket player who can both bat and bowl well. It is also like these footy players who pull an offload out of nowhere and they even make it look easy. This is Ken Chant.

Sadly, I haven't had the chance to meet him personally, but I can tell you that after reading many of his books I feel I have come to know the person behind the words. Patient. Brave. Wise. Humble. Well-educated. And deeply sincere.

That's the Ken Chant I've come to know through his writings. He wouldn't shy away from admitting his own struggles and shortcomings and that he had sometimes missed the mark in life - haven't we all - but he would always point us back to the author and finisher of our faith (Heb 12: 2), encouraging us to persevere and be overcomers.

As I write these words, a line from *The Witness* comes to mind, one of my Dad's favourite lines, too: "Come to the Light giver, Jesus, the Light giver, and let Him pour His life on you." I believe this is what Ken Chant would have said, too. So let us then come to the Light giver and let Him touch our lives.

There's so much more I could say but I think his life and legacy speak louder than any words. Thank you, Ken, for sharing the gospel like you did! I am looking forward to seeing you in heaven!

STUDENT - Merilyn Teague

Ken Chant, a dear brother in Christ and one of my three best lecturers in Bible College 1961+1962 that I enjoyed here in Adelaide at CBS. For three months nightly throughout the week he taught we 28 Aussie students of the Doctrine of the Holy Spirit. He always had us sitting on the edge of our chairs listening to his exposition of the Word. I remember well Ken tried to find an unusual, rare word for each of his lectures, also sermons! He was known to 'compose' the word that suited his teaching point, often bringing humour or a smile on our faces.

Ken was most emphatic when teaching. He was most enthusiastic and often expressed his excitement of that which he had learned in his personal Bible study. He loved the Lord passionately. To his final breath of his wonderful life on earth Ken was a gift to the Church, from the Lord.

Having Dr Ken Chant as a Lecturer at our Bible College was an unforgettable, enriching time for me and I'm sure all other BS students, too. 8 students from 28 went to PNG as missionaries. Myself being one of the first called by the Lord of the Harvest. We all answered the call.

We six girls all lived and served Jesus together in PNG, differing gifts from the Lord and academic training. Also, from that same class about three to four pastors faithfully served Jesus in their local Church till they graduated with high honours to go to meet their Lord and Master. One

remains aged 92 here in South Australia. All we girls are still here in Adelaide, loving Jesus, serving Him where He has planted us.

Anyway, this is all about Ken Chant. Pastor Ken was one of the pastors of my Church here in Adelaide, CRC. He served alongside the founder, Pastor Leo Harris, for several years. My early teenage years as a new Christian, with all my family: we all feasted on the Word, learning much more about Jesus from Ken and Barry Chant, brothers as Pastors in CRC, Adelaide. Alison became a dear sister to my mother, and I had the privilege of teaching Dale Chant as a small boy in our Sunday School classes, back in 1958-60. We were all 'hungry' to know more about Jesus through the teaching of the Word, by Pastors Leo Harris, Ken and Barry Chant. Unforgettable days!

Ken remained friends of mine and my parents, also my first brother, Baden Teague. The last few times Ken and Alison visited Adelaide, I was happy to have afternoon tea with them, reminiscing on the happy, blessed days we shared with my parents and Pastor Leo Harris, altogether in CRC, Adelaide ...

Also, Baden enjoyed fellowship with Ken, two brothers in Christ, loving Jesus and both keen theologians of the Word. Ken and Alison also happily joined Baden in worship at St Peter's Cathedral, where my brother + his wife Kathy are regular members. Baden is one of their Lay Preachers at their Evensong!

Keeping dear Alison in my prayers that our Heavenly Father will comfort her, rest her, keep her in His Peace as she holds on to the HOPE of Jesus and His imminent Return!

THOUGHTS – Sharon Chant Jones

As the only daughter and a 'rainbow baby' (born following the death of a sibling) I was adored by my parents, however, they also watched over me with a determined vigilance which had its down sides growing up! However, I have many happy memories but here are a few which show my father's view on several subjects ....

In the event of a catastrophic event, my father did not believe in hoarding food and other necessary items. I remember encouraging him at the end of 1999, when the worldwide threat of Y2K was consuming the news, to make sure he had plenty of canned and dry food stored away. He smiled with a lift of his brow, "Are you prepared to shoot your neighbours when they come to take your food?" I was dismayed. My neighbours wouldn't do that and how would they know? But upon reflection I realised you could only hide the fact you weren't starving for so long before the community would be suspicious that you were thriving, and they were dying.

And then, during Covid, I became a total believer at the possible perfidy of my neighbours, when the empty grocery shelves at my local grocery store were depleted within days of toilet paper, pasta, rice, and other necessary items to sustain life. It was disturbing to see grocery carts full of toilet paper leaving the store and initially nobody stopping this hoarding tendency of terrified people. I mean, toilet paper! No one could ever have predicted that the first item to disappear would be this staple of human existence. My brother speculates that we have three days of food stored in the local shops and then its anarchy. I pray it never comes to that in my lifetime because I would not shoot people to protect my food source, I would rather trust God. And, like my father, live the words of Paul when he states in Philippians 1:21, 'For to me to live is Christ, to die is gain.'

My father adored steam trains and rode them whenever he had an opportunity. He would often send me emails about the latest days and times to attend the Steam Festival and ride an 'old choofer', asking if I was interested in going. I wasn't. I had been on several train rides with him over the years, but it wasn't a particular love of mine. Looking back, I can see now that they were hints for me to take him. I wish he had just come out and asked me, but he wasn't like that. He didn't want me to go unless I wanted to go.

Now it is too late, so of course I feel regret that I didn't make the time. I encourage you, be vigilant, and if someone is suggesting something to you, recognise that it is their wish that you participate in some way. Make time for the people you love before it is too late to do so.

My father dreamed of owning a yacht, but it never fit into his financial means, nor could he take time to care for a yacht as many readers of this book would be aware - ministry is a 24/7 business. He was never bitter about this, and I learned that although you may have dreams that you long to come to fruition, you are blessed if only one or two of them ever eventuates. And that's okay. Our journey on earth is one of Christian growth, and then we have our journey in heaven to look forward to where the impossible becomes probable. I hope that in heaven my father is now enjoying a brisk sail across the heavenly seas with Peter and the other fishermen; or driving a yellow jaguar on the streets of gold.

My father had the 'bounce back' Chant gene, as did his father, and probably his ancestors before them. He almost died several times in the last two years of his life. It became a running joke for him that God didn't want him and kept sending him back! But if it had not been for that prolonged departure this book would never have been written. I asked him many times over the last decade to put his experiences on paper, but he could never bring himself to spend time doing that when he had another book expounding Scripture burning in his spirit. And then, after *Thessalonians*, he was done, tired out after several bouts of septicaemia. Now confined to his armchair, I could finally get him started. Wherever we were – in hospital, or in his comfortable chair that he enjoyed so much, we worked daily to draw stories from his memories. Between my mother and myself we typed diligently. He would say that's enough now, having run out of stories and preparing for the book to end, but then the next day he would think of something else and so off we would go again.

Sometimes he would disclaim, "No-one is going to read this stuff!" but we ignored this, instead telling him, "Everyone should write a history of their life to encourage others that God is just a prayer away during the worst and best of times, guiding and comforting on this rocky road of living." And as you have read, my father tripped over plenty of rocks and made plenty of mistakes, as have I, but this is how we grow and learn to trust in God. Like a child learning to walk, we must take every step clinging to God's hand like cling wrap, never letting go lest we slip into despair.

When I think of all the decisions my father made that had difficult and sometimes heart wrenching repercussions you wonder where God was in all of that. But somehow our heavenly Father was able to bring good out of it all. I don't know why we expect the Christian walk to be free from suffering for it is certainly not what happened to Jesus. My father rarely interfered in my life, and sometimes I wish he had spoken up more when he could see I was heading toward a dangerous precipice with blinders on. But for better or worse he kept his counsel to himself unless I specifically asked him a question. So, I encourage you to get advice. Ask questions. After all, you don't have to take the advice, but at least you will be informed. Don't wait for people to send up warning flares, trying to get your attention, as by then it is often too late as you suffer the repercussions of your actions.

Get Scripture into your mind and heart so when the Holy Spirit speaks to you through God's Word you are positioned to hear His voice! That is the best thing, and the most important thing my father taught me!

Now it really is the end of the book!

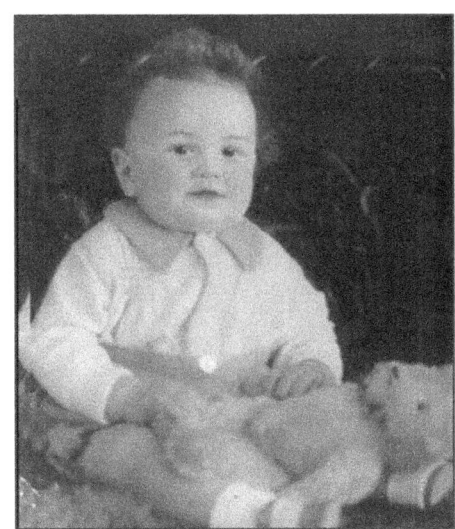

www.ingramcontent.com/pod-product-compliance
Lightning Source LLC
Chambersburg PA
CBHW042318090526
44583CB00024BA/3025